The Job Search Solution

The Job Search Solution

THE ULTIMATE SYSTEM FOR FINDING A GREAT JOB NOW!

Tony Beshara

AMACOM

American Management Association

New York • Atlanta • Brussels • Chicago • Mexico City • San Francisco
Shanghai • Tokyo • Toronto • Washington, D.C.

Special discounts on bulk quantities of AMACOM books are available to corporations, professional associations, and other organizations. For details, contact Special Sales Department, AMACOM, a division of American Management Association, 1601 Broadway, New York, NY 10019.
Tel.: 212-903-8316. Fax: 212-903-8083.
Website: www.amacombooks.org

This publication is designed to provide accurate and authoritative information in regard to the subject matter covered. It is sold with the understanding that the publisher is not engaged in rendering legal, accounting, or other professional service. If legal advice or other expert assistance is required, the services of a competent professional person should be sought.

Library of Congress Cataloging-in-Publication Data

Beshara, Tony, 1948-
    The job search solution : the ultimate system for finding a great job now! / Tony Beshara.
        p.   cm.
    Includes bibliographical references and index.
    ISBN 0-8144-7332-6 (pbk.)
    1. Job hunting.   2. Job hunting—Psychological aspects.
3. Interviewing.   4. Self-presentation.   I. Title.

HF5382.7.B472   2006
650.14—dc22

2005023660

Printing number

10   9   8   7   6   5   4   3   2   1

Dedicated to:
Chrissy, my wife and soul mate,

to
Christianne, our Angel in Heaven,

and to
her four awesome brothers (her description),
Adam, Brian, Michael, and James

• • • Contents

The Job Search Solution

· · · **Prologue**

"If you can't explain it simply, you don't know your subject."
—ALBERT EINSTEIN, SCIENTIST

This book is about a simple process that can be outlined as follows:

- Find a job or change jobs.

- Find employers with "pain"—that is, an actual current need to hire someone (as many as you can).

- Get interviews with employers with "pain" (as many as you can).

- Sell yourself hard in initial interviews (as many times as you can).

- Sell yourself in follow-up interviews (as many times as you can).

- Get offers (as many as you can).

- Negotiate offers (as many as you can).

- Accept an offer.

- Go to work!

As you can see, the steps in finding a job seem simple. However, although these steps appear to be simple, the process can be complicated and difficult. Above all, the process is an emotional strain. No matter how often a person changes jobs or looks for a job, the process is never easy. The *Job Search Solution* "system" allows you to personally *manage* your own job search process.

I am Tony Beshara. I've been in the business of finding jobs for just about every kind of professional for thirty-one years. I have personally found more than six thousand individuals jobs. Every day, I sit behind a desk making close to two hundred calls. I have personally interviewed more than twenty-four thousand people on all professional levels and have worked with more than twenty-one thousand hiring authorities. Our firm has used the process I have perfected to place more than one hundred thousand people. I am one of the most successful placement and recruitment professionals in the United States.

In this book, I will provide you with a day-to-day, detailed system that I have developed over the years to ensure your personal success at finding a job. If you work the *Job Search Solution* system, it will work for you. And, just as Einstein suggested, I can explain very simply what to do. But the proven, perfected formula of the way to do it is not simple. It has taken thirty-one years to discover and perfect the formula for the system. It is all here in this book!

What This Book Is Not

This book is not a research book. It is not a book loaded with economic data, employment statistics, or academic, theoretical stuff. It does not cite all kinds of websites that might be of value to a job seeker. In fact, I have specifically avoided including things like that simply because there are hundreds of them and they change on a daily basis.

I am not trying to say that researching websites or other materials for things that will help you find a job is without value. In fact, it is a good idea to find as many websites, written materials, or anything else that might help you to find a job as you can. As you will quickly learn from reading this book, I recommend any activity—short of illegal or immoral ones—that will help you to find a job. I had to do a lot of research in graduate school and my dissertation mostly involved research. But research isn't the foundation of finding a job. *Massive action* is!

What This Book Is

This book is the quickest way to find a job in any economy. It is a complete, self-managed job search process that has helped more than one hundred thousand people find jobs or career opportunities. It is that simple!

Acknowledgments

Our firm was started by Mildred Babich in 1952. Women who founded businesses then were very rare. We still use the process developed by Ms. Babich. I have revised and improved it as needed. Her dedication to professionalism and service set the foundation for the reputation that our firm still enjoys today.

I would like to thank Brian Wallace, for doing the initial editing of this manuscript, as well as Jan Miller and her organization, especially Jennifer Holder who persisted in finding a publisher. AMACOM Books, especially Ellen Kadin, has been a pleasure to work with

I am grateful to Jeff and Amy Mills, whose real-life experiences are referenced in this book. Acknowledgement goes to the *Dr. Phil* show, Shannon O'Conner, and the entire team that produced the "Jeff and Amy Mills" segment.

A special thanks to Phil McGraw himself. He is as congruent with integrity and character offstage as he appears to the millions of people he touches over the airwaves. His personal encouragement in writing this book was appreciated.

Also, thank you to the thousands of people I have worked with in their personal job searches who have taught me what I will now pass along to you.

And a special note of gratitude to my wife and best friend of thirty-eight years, Chrissy. She has been the finest mental, emotional, and spiritual support that God could ever bless a person with.

· · · **Introduction**

While traveling with Chrissy—my wife and best friend for more than thirty-eight years—to appear on our first *Dr. Phil* show, she mentioned, as a fan of Dr. Phil, she had noticed that he often shared the books his guests had written. She said that because one of the themes of the show would be about finding a job, it would have been ideal for me to have written a book about all the things I had learned in my thirty-one years of finding people jobs. You are now holding that book.

When I first received the call to appear on the *Dr. Phil* show, the producers were preparing an episode called "Going for Broke." The major theme of this episode related to how easily two-income families in America can go broke. The show featured four middle-class couples that, for various reasons, were in or getting close to bankruptcy. Sudden job loss and/or mismanagement of money had sent some of them from combined incomes of $60,000 to $80,000 a year to the brink of bankruptcy.

One of the four couples appearing on the show was Amy and Jeff Mills, who had moved from Denver, Colorado, to Austin, Texas, after Jeff struggled for eighteen months to regain employment in his industry. Amy and Jeff, along with their four young children, moved in with Amy's sister, her husband, and two children who lived in a 1,600-square-foot house in Austin. Although Austin's economy had been hit hard after the high-tech bust of the 1990s, supportive family members were there and Jeff was optimistic that he could find gainful employment. Austin's economy happens to be one of the toughest in Texas by virtue of its primary dependence on high-tech manufacturing. When high tech slows down in Austin, so does Austin's entire economy.

You cannot say Jeff didn't try. He gets high marks on creativity for one of his unique tactics: renting a flatbed truck, filling its bed with a portable home office (desk, computer, and phone included), and parking and sitting with it in various parts of Austin. He showcased a large sign advertising his website, www.dudeonthecorner.com, with the idea of generating enough publicity to land a good, high-paying job. Unfortunately, despite his entrepreneurial, creative edge, he did not get very far in the job hunt.

I was glad to be considered an "expert." Dr. Phil kindly touted my abilities as a recruiter with over thirty successful years in the business. The goal was to help Jeff Mills find a job. My role was to comment on Jeff's past and current job-seeking efforts and offer myself and my firm's resources to help him find a job.

I discovered that Jeff was a thirty-five-year-old MBA with a membership in Mensa, the group whose members consist of only people with an I.Q. in the top 1 percent of the population. He had ten years of experience as an accountant and three years as a programmer. Jeff had been making $60,000 a year. When he was laid off in June 2002, Jeff began to look for a job in Denver. His specific and recent experience focused on valuation software—a very narrow application of software that proved to be not relevant to the work needed at other firms. Jeff had become overspecialized. Additionally, most of his accounting experience was three years old, which put him at a disadvantage compared to the other candidates whose accounting experience was more up to date.

The economic climate certainly did not help Jeff. Most of those people laid off in recent years have been shocked to discover how hard it is to find a job in a recessionary economy. The strategies that worked previously simply do not work anymore. When Jeff was laid off, he had no idea how hard it was going to be to find a job. He tried the usual approaches: calling friends, answering help-wanted advertisements, and e-mailing résumés. He thought, "I'm a good employee; I'm smart. Someone will hire me." Nothing happened.

After a painstaking and unsuccessful search for a new job in Denver, Jeff and his family sold most of their belongings and moved to Austin with high expectations. And again, nothing happened.

On the show, I made a two-minute observation about how Jeff's strategy for finding a job was well intentioned, but mostly wrong. I agreed that on behalf of Babich & Associates, I would take Jeff on as a candidate to help him find quality work in Texas.

What This Book Will Do for You

This book is an experiential journey that will take you through the steps that got Jeff Mills and many people like him the jobs they wanted.

Most of the employment books on the market are riddled with vacuous advice, long-winded sections on how to build the perfect résumé and other equally useless pages of information. Those books talk about so-called dream jobs and unrealistic goals.

Some may ask: "What does Tony's book do that the others don't?" I keep things simple and real. For example, I do not waste your time going on and on about how to write a résumé! Many of the other books will drag you through tedious, long-winded sections on how to write the perfect résumé. I cannot figure out why these books waste so much paper on a topic that is so specific. There is *one* simple format for résumés that works 95 percent of the time. I will discuss it in Chapter 5. The others are a waste of time.

Another example of how my book is different concerns the highly important interviews. I'll teach you how to master, and then surpass the first interview. I cannot find another book on the market that addresses how a job candidate should confidently structure his or her interview, and then, hopefully, successfully progress through the inevitable multiple interviews. *Structuring an interview* is crucial and I will clearly show you the steps.

I was unable to find a single title that addresses this crucial fact: *most of the business hiring done in the United States is not done by professional interviewers or professional "hirers."* It is carried out by people who may know what they do professionally—great accountants, lawyers, engineers, manufacturing people, and so forth—but when it comes to screening, interviewing, and hiring, they are lost!

Consider that 97 percent of the 12 million businesses in the United States have fewer than one hundred employees; 85 percent of those businesses have fewer than twenty people. The reality is that companies are guilty of being unfocused, grossly unorganized, illogical, ignorant about most things, ambitious beyond their own abilities, fearful, without clear goals or common sense, wrapped up in their own corporate egos, and without many passionate employees. Essentially, the companies are reflections of the people who run them. The particular nature of each employer determines the individual approach you should take in getting the job. You are going to develop a strategy for getting the job despite the employer's flaws! Get ready to be surprised, enlightened, comforted, and instructed by the ultimate system for finding a great job now!

My Experience Is in the Real World

This proven job search plan is delivered by a guy who is on the front lines and in the trenches on a daily basis. Most of the books written about how to get a job are written by theorists who have not actually helped get people jobs. My day-to-day responsibilities are solely concerned with finding people jobs.

I have been successfully finding people real jobs for more than thirty-one years. After receiving a Ph.D. in higher education from St. Louis University, I began to forge a career working outside academia—in the real employment world.

I have personally placed more than six thousand people, and I am adding to that list every day. Just to name a few, I have placed everything from accountants, attorneys, CFOs, managers, and mechanics to mathematicians, programmers, and physicists. I have successfully found lucrative placement for more than one hundred occupation types. I have met and interviewed more than twenty-four thousand people of all professions and services. I have worked with more than twenty-one thousand different companies; many of which have hired candidates from me.

The firm that I now own, Babich & Associates, has been in the placement and recruitment business since 1952. I joined the organization in 1973 and bought it from the founder, Mildred Babich, in 1989. We are the oldest placement firm in Texas and the Southwest. Since its founding, the firm has helped more than one hundred thousand people find jobs. We have developed surefire techniques that help people find new jobs and new careers. We implement a highly personalized approach—which means working with one candidate and one employer at a time. *One candidate and one job opportunity at a time!*

I started in this business in 1973 during the beginning of a recession. Employment recessions seem to follow economic recessions, but not always.

How we define the term *recession* is determined by many factors. Employment recessions can be national, regional, statewide, or community based. If the furniture plant where you and 450 other employees work closes in your town of 2,000 people in rural Arkansas, and you are laid off, it may not be a recession throughout the country, but it certainly is in your town! This book will explore in detail the impact that recessions have on employment.

How to Avoid the Ka-Ka

There is a story about the magistrate who was sent in the late 1800s to address the tribes in one of the African countries that his country was colonizing. Through an interpreter, he made a speech in front of the first group of tribesmen. Every time he would tell them what his country was going to do for the tribe, they would yell "ka-ka." Excitedly, he told them they would have a better diet; they yelled "ka-ka." Encouraged by their response, he told them their children would be better educated; they yelled "ka-ka." Gratified that what he was saying was being so well received, he told them how they would be healthier; they yelled "ka-ka."

Proud of himself and the enthusiastic reception he had been given, he ventured out to the next community and tribe. As he was walking through the jungle, his interpreter warned him that the local elephants had a tendency to defecate on the trail and it was important for them, while on the trail, to watch out and not step in the "ka-ka."

Well, there is a lot of ka-ka out there about how to find a job or change careers. Throughout this book, when we come to a topic that generates many so-called expert opinions that don't work, I will identify the "ka-ka."

One example, which will be elaborated upon later in the book, is the purported success of finding a job over the Internet, especially through job boards. This is mostly ka-ka. The probability is so remote that the effort is hardly worth it. The last statistic I read stated that 2 percent of the people who posted résumés on the Internet got results. First, 2 out of 100 are not very good odds. Secondly, what are "results"? Does that mean they got a job, an interview, or a call from a recruiter? There is no way of documenting the success of job boards. Now there are very good ways of using the Internet to help you find a job, but posting one's résumé on the job boards doesn't seem to be one of them. The problem is that candidates have no idea how many résumés are posted and how few of them ever really get into a hiring manager's hands. Worse, they believe it should be one of the *primary* ways of finding a job. Unfortunately, there is a lot of this kind of ka-ka concerning how to look for and find a job.

What This All Means to You

The underlying techniques in this book work on most every level of business in which you will try to find a job. They will work in any kind of economy and job market. These strategies have been proven repeatedly in real experience. If you follow the recommendations and techniques I provide here, the probability of you getting the job you want will increase by 85 percent. That, quite simply, is what you will gain from *The Job Search Solution.*

1 : The Emotional and Psychological Dimensions of Finding a Job

"Any device whatever by which one frees himself from fear is a natural good."

—EPICURES, GREEK PHILOSOPHER

"You can't expect to prevent negative feelings altogether. And you can't expect to experience positive feelings all the time. The Law of Emotional Choice directs us to acknowledge our feelings but also to refuse to get stuck in the negative ones."

—GREG ANDERSEN, QUOTE MASTER

Next to the death of a spouse, child, or parent, the fourth most emotional thing we do (tied with divorce) is look for a job. No matter what anybody tells you, changing jobs (and the difficulties in doing so) can be an emotionally debilitating experience for anyone; and certainly difficult for any of the other important people in your life: spouses, relatives, friends, and any significant people who touch your life.

Between 15 and 20 million Americans will find themselves changing jobs this year! That is a lot of emotion!

Among other benefits, our jobs give us a sense of belonging, a sense of contributing to a group or a society, and, mostly, a great sense of personal growth. Our jobs make us feel productive and useful. We describe ourselves in terms of work, and what we do, and we identify with it. A large part of our identities and self-respect are dependent on our jobs. The sudden loss of employment or dissatisfaction with the job that we may have causes a great disruption in our lives. These types of issues reorder our priorities and have a tendency to damage our self-esteem.

Acknowledge Your Emotions

Just about every negative emotion that a person can experience usually accompanies the loss of a job. That is why, on the emotional severity scale, losing a job ranks right behind the experience of death. In fact, the death of a spouse and loss of a job are the two life events that are emotionally devastating for the longest period of time. The issue is not to deny that you're going to experience these emotions, but how you're going to minimize them so they have the least effect on you, your psyche, and your ability to go out and find a new job.

I recently talked to a job candidate who, for a number of years, was a hiring manager with whom I placed people. He hadn't had to look for a job in twelve years. All of a sudden, he became unemployed. That was six months ago. One of the rules that he used to have for hiring people was that they be currently employed. He shared with me that, since he has been unemployed for so long, he has much more empathy for all the unemployed people whom he would have never considered hiring in the past. He had no idea how emotionally and psychologically difficult it was to look for a job, especially in the high-tech arena in which he had been employed.

He realized that—in many cases—losing a job had absolutely nothing to do with performance, tenure, attitude, level of position, or experience. It was the so-called luck of the draw that caused him to be unemployed. His company had been sold and there was a replication of his position in the firm that bought his company. The company simply no longer needed two regional managers, so he was laid off. For the company, it was a simple business decision, but the decision was devastating to him.

Understand That the Process Itself Will Be Emotional

"Every one who got where he is had to begin where he was."
—ROBERT LOUIS STEVENSON, AUTHOR OF *TREASURE ISLAND*

As you get over the fear and emotions of *having* to look for a job, you are now going to go through the same emotions while *actually looking* for one. Most of the emotions that we have discussed will carry over into the interviewing and job-finding process. Hopes will be dashed. Your ego will be assaulted.

You will be lied to and strung out; encouraged, then deflated. We will address the causes of these frustrations in a subsequent chapter. Just be ready for the emotional strain.

If you think having a job while you're looking for one is emotionally or psychologically easy, you should think again. Being employed while looking for a job is slightly more comforting than being out of work and looking for a job. However, the stress of trying to find a job (which is a job in itself) while you are currently trying to perform your best at the job you have (which you don't like or you know isn't going to last) is often more difficult than simply devoting all your efforts and focus on finding a job.

An erratic economy can make this experience even more emotionally challenging. When the employment picture is rough and uncertain, thousands of people are out of work, looking for jobs. Not only are you going through emotionally difficult times, but so are many others. Quick and unexpected downsizing, layoffs, and firings occur on a regular basis. I know of many candidates (whose companies are downsizing) who get assurances on a Friday that their job is not in jeopardy, but then on Monday, they are told they are being laid off! You can't do much about the economy. You can, however, control how you react to it.

Get Over It—Life Isn't Fair

"If you let conditions stop you from working, they'll always stop you."

—James T. Farrell, Novelist

The sooner you get over all these emotions and put them in perspective, the better off you are going to be.

People who can process emotions by analyzing them deal more constructively with the grief that goes along with them. People who express their grief get over it faster. The faster and more quickly you deal with all your negative emotions and analyze them deeply, the faster you will be able to put them in perspective and move on to other issues that are more important—such as finding a new job.

Express Your Feelings in Detail

Please, please, please, don't overlook this exercise. Write down the feelings and thoughts you have about each one of these emotions. It is only going to take a few minutes. Along with some of the other suggestions that follow, you'll be empowered to put these emotions in their proper perspective and be able to move on faster. You're not going to ignore these feelings or try to deny them. Again, you're going to delve into them so deeply that you understand them, and therefore you'll be able to release them from being distracting in your mind. Try to answer the following questions:

- How were you *frustrated* in your previous or current employment?

- What were the *disappointments* you had with the job or company you left or are now experiencing in your current employment?

- Did you lose or are you losing *self-esteem*? How?

- Were you *shocked* at being laid off, fired, or forced to look for a new job?

- Who is to *blame* for your having to look for new job? Describe the situation in detail.

- Describe your *disillusionment* with the entire situation. How did it come about?

- Describe the *shame* you feel in needing to look for a new job. Describe what other people will think and say about you, about your having to find a new job, about your being fired or laid off, and so forth.

- Do you feel *isolated* by having to look for a new job? Can other people really understand?

- Are you *denying* any of the things or situations that happened? Can you describe them clearly, even if emotionally?

- Whom do you feel *hostile* toward, if anyone? Why do they deserve your hostility?

- Complete this sentence: I am *angry* because: _____
  (Really go into an in-depth explanation as to why you're angry. Be as angry as you want to be; write as long as you would like.)

- Do you feel *guilty* about what happened in losing your job or the reason that you need to look for a new one? Is there anything you could have done to prevent the situation?

- Describe the *depressed feelings* you might have about the situation. Do you feel sad, empty, or fatigued about it? How does "poor you" feel about this whole thing? How do you describe "poor you"? Describe in detail.

- Describe, if it applies, how *unfair* the entire situation is. Describe it in detail.

- Write down all the things that make you *fearful* about this situation. Be as detailed as you need to describe exactly what you are afraid of—even ridiculous fears.

After you have written out your explanations in detail, read them at least three times, preferably out loud. I want you to really feel every one of the emotions that you're experiencing. It is important to focus on and deeply appreciate every feeling you have had, even if this isn't a pleasant experience. Read the answer to each one of the questions, and when you come to the end of the question, ask yourself aloud: "Can I let this feeling go?" Then ask yourself aloud: "Do I want to let this feeling go?" Do not be surprised if the answer to each one of these questions is no.

It is not uncommon to want to hold on to these feelings during the grieving period. The important thing is to feel these emotions repeatedly, until you genuinely, sincerely feel like you have let them go.

Realize that you may never let all of the emotions go, and you may never eliminate them completely from your emotional memory. The objective is not to eliminate them altogether, but to minimize their impact on you, so that you can move forward toward a positive emotional state to interview well and attain a new job. It is advisable to use this technique three or four times at one sitting and to do two or three sittings a day—until the emotions are neutralized.

There are two other variations of this exercise. The first is to use a tape recorder and record an audio version of your emotions, instead of writing them down. Then listen to the tape to recapture the emotions before you release them. The other variation is to discuss them, after you have written them, with a loving spouse, empathetic friend, or coach. Ask that person to just listen to you non-judgmentally, thereby helping you to clarify your feelings—no matter what the feelings are.

Visualize Your Feelings

Another way to deal with the same feelings in order to minimize their impact on your current situation is to deal with them in a visual and auditory manner. The technique is to close your eyes and visualize each of the previous questions. This means playing a movie of—or picturing in your mind—each instance of frustration, disappointment, loss of self-esteem, shock, and so forth. You should put yourself in each picture or movie. Have it up close and in color in your mind. Try to make the picture as detailed as you possibly can. And as you run the "movie" in your mind, at a certain point make it turn black-and-white and project it as far out in front of you as you possibly can, until it becomes merely a speck far out in front of you. When the picture changes and gets sent far away, so do the emotions that are associated with it.

> There are other kinds of ways to deal with these feelings and fears. I read about one Native American shaman who recommended that a person go out (preferably in a forest for privacy, or wherever a person feels comfortable in nature) and dig a hole into the ground. The person lies on his stomach, flat on the ground with his head over the hole, and screams his feelings, crying and speaking whatever emotions need to be expressed in the hole. The final step is to take a seed, place it in the hole, and cover it with dirt; thereby symbolically "composting" negative feelings and helping plant something new and positive that can grow.

Doing this kind of exercise, over and over, neutralizes the emotion that is associated with being up close, in color, and involved in the picture itself.

Of all the things you can do to put your emotions in perspective, writing your feelings down in detail and visualizing them are the most efficient. Dealing with anger and fear in an honest, forthright, and detailed manner helps to relieve the acidity of the emotions.

Jeff and Amy's Emotional Roller Coaster

Amy told me that she and Jeff identified with everything I wrote in this chapter. Jeff wasn't fired; he was laid off because of the economic conditions of the company. Although it was a division of a large publishing company, it was still a small company with thirty people and a family atmosphere. "I was just plain sad about it," Jeff said. "I totally didn't expect it because the company had never had a layoff before. They treated me so well and none of us ever thought it would happen."

At first Jeff was confident that he'd find a new job quickly. After all, the last time he looked for a job, he found one right away. In 1999, a software developer with an accounting background had no trouble getting offers. But this time he really got nowhere. He had no idea it would take eighteen months and a move to Texas to find employment.

Jeff had a few telephone interviews while in Colorado. However, not one face-to-face interview materialized. "I would get my hopes up so high about each opportunity, only to go really into the dumps when nothing panned out," he said. "And I'm the kind of guy who gets real high and when I got disappointed, I'd get real low; it really got scary."

"This had never happened to us before," Amy said, "and it was terrible. We began to vent at each other. It got really tense. We had a real sense of grief, just like a death in the family. We mourned the job loss. We played the blame game with each other often. We'd be up, then down and we had never been at each other like that before. Then, after being at each other's throat, Jeff would retreat to the basement for days at a time. We just weren't ready for this . . . it was awful . . . it was a tremendous strain on the marriage."

Some family members had little empathy for Jeff and Amy's situation. They assumed that he just wasn't looking for a job hard enough or that he really didn't want to work all that much. This kind of reaction by family and friends is not uncommon. People have a hard time understanding what someone else is going through. Even Jeff and Amy had never been through anything like this before, so they, too, had no idea what to expect. In a form of despair, they spiraled down. They stopped going to church, where they had been fairly active. Jeff retreated into himself. Amy tried to encourage him, but he often perceived it as nagging. They just weren't prepared for this life-changing experience. It was an emotional roller coaster.

Thankfully, Jeff and Amy's marriage was strong enough to survive the situation. Four little children and their love for one another endured—not easily—but it did. As Amy says, "Had we known how emotionally and psychologically difficult this was going to be, we might have prepared for it. If we had had the information in this chapter, it might have been a lot easier."

Jeff and Amy are openly sharing their experience in order to help others. The emotional ordeal they went through happens to thousands, even millions of people.

2 · Start Taking Massive Action Now!

"The journey of a hundred miles begins with the first step."
—Lao Tzu, Chinese Philosopher

The first step toward being successful at any endeavor must be to take action. Action is power! But when looking for a job, especially in a difficult job market, only *massive action* will get you the results that you need. What do I mean by massive action? It's simple: Be prepared to interview more times than you ever imagined. You need to perform better in interviews than you ever imagined. You need to sell yourself harder than you ever thought you would. And it is going to take longer than you ever imagined.

This is a numbers game, pure and simple. The ability to find a job today depends on the number of interviews that you can get. The way you are going to go about getting these interviews is complicated—and the majority of this book is devoted to this process. *Numbers, numbers, numbers!* Numbers of contacts; numbers of friends; numbers of phone calls; numbers of face-to-face interviews with people who may or may not have a job opportunity; numbers of first, second, third, fourth, and fifth interviews with anyone able to hire you. These are all necessary for you to find even a reasonable job opportunity in today's economy.

You are going to be depressed, dejected, rejected, refused, denied, forgotten, ignored, lied to, storied to, insulted, emotionally stomped on, messed with, postponed, forgotten on hold, eliminated, jilted, and conspired against. And after all that abuse, you are going to have to get up and run the risk of it happening again.

The reality is that there are hordes of well-qualified candidates who are every bit as good as you—some even better—who are competing for the same job you want. The difference between you and them will be your determination to take massive amounts of action: You are going to interview at more places, you are going to sell yourself better than your competition, and you are going to have more job offers than anyone else.

Ways to Control the Process

> *"Do what you do best and the score takes care of itself."*
> —JOHN WOODEN, FAMOUS UCLA BASKETBALL COACH

Now that you have designed a plan for managing your emotions, you need to become aware of one of the most important tenets of this book: You can't control getting a job as much as you can control the *process* of getting a job. The essence of this book is to make you aware of the process that it takes to find a job. If you manage the *process,* the *result* (landing a great job) will take care of itself. I cannot emphasize this enough. Most of the job-finding books out there do a reasonably decent job of describing things like résumés, surface interviewing, and negotiating. What they neglect is an intense, detailed analysis of the process that is required to find a job.

If you manage the process of finding a job and do it in all the correct ways, finding an excellent opportunity will just be a matter of course. It is that simple—not easy, but simple.

Passion, Intensity, and Enthusiasm

> *"Live with passion."*
> —TONY ROBBINS, MOTIVATIONAL SPEAKER/WRITER

> *"To be a great champion you must believe that you are the best. If you're not, pretend that you are."*
> —MUHAMMAD ALI, HEAVYWEIGHT CHAMPION BOXER

Most individuals lose out in the job-seeking game because they don't develop a passionate intensity and enthusiastic approach to the process of looking for a job. Passion, intensity, and enthusiasm for the process of finding a job are conditioned emotions. When most people look for a job, they are scared to death. They don't like looking for a job because they run the risk of rejection. No one likes to be rejected.

Interviewing from a defensive, scared emotional position will never get you a job. You may have to "fake it until you make it" throughout the entire ordeal. You must learn to act like you enjoy this process. You can take six months to muddle through trying to find a job—during which time you become depressed, dejected, sad, and pissed off—and then realize that you need to approach finding a job in a psychologically motivated and enthusiastic way. Or, you can get rid of all those garbage emotions now, even it if it's a matter of pretending you like what you have to do, and then doing it to the best of your ability.

What matters is your ability to organize and institute an effective job search that is going to get you employed in a new job as quickly as possible. The people you might think are being fake or false by acting passionate, enthusiastic, and "loving every moment of it," are the ones getting the jobs. They are not necessarily the most qualified candidates, but they are the ones selling themselves the best. Being passionate, intense, enthusiastic, and committed when you do not feel that way takes a lot of practice. So, start acting enthusiastic about finding a job!

Being passionate about finding a job means that you don't postpone the start of your job search in any way. You approach your job search like it is a job itself. You approach it like it is a life-and-death matter. This is a 24-hours-a-day, 7-days-a-week, 365-days-a-year committed endeavor to finding a new job. You need to eat it, sleep it, drink it, and live it until you find a job.

Assessment of Your Personality Style Relative to Others

Another crucial tenet of this book is that *we all see the world through our own eyes.* We don't see the world as it is; we see the world as we are! You need to realize that the people you interview with are seeing the world through their own eyes. They are not seeing the world the way it really is—or, most likely, in the way that you see the world.

Therefore, it is in your best interest to discern to the best of your ability how the interviewer sees the world and then communicate with that person within his or her viewpoint.

Since looking for a job is an emotionally stressful experience, there is a tendency for candidates who are interviewing to want to present the world only in the way that they see it. When we are emotionally stressed, we have a tendency to focus more on our own security and ourselves, rather than on the security and well-being of other people.

There is a paradigm in sales that states: *If you see the world through John's eyes, you know how John buys.* In other words, if you understand and communicate with John in the way John understands and communicates with himself (and others), John is going to understand you better and be more likely to buy from you—or, in the case of a job candidate, hire you.

It is therefore important for you to take a moment and analyze the style in which you communicate the way that you see the world.

The following diagram presents four basic personality styles. Modern psychology might disagree with these in certain specifics and there might be six instead of four, or maybe even eight, but it really doesn't matter. What is important is that you think about the personality styles that you are going to encounter in interviewing situations and, at the same time, identify the personality style you possess so that you can better "sell" them. The four basic personality styles are *analytical, driver, amiable,* and *expressive.*

Analytical: Like the name denotes, this type of professional has a tendency to see things in a very analytical way. They like facts, details, numbers, and are oriented to the bottom line. They have a tendency to be well organized and stick to specific schedules. They are sticklers for detail, and are not risk-takers. Their personality traits tend to be trusting, patient, not assertive, somewhat passive, easygoing, even paced, motivated by their own internal recognition, and calculating. Professionally, they have a tendency to be engineers, mathematicians, accountants, scientists, chemists, and technically oriented people who work in positions that require high degrees of exactness and patience.

ANALYTICAL

TYPES OF PROFESSIONALS:
Engineers, Mathematicians, Accountants, Scientists, Chemists, Technical Professionals

LIKES:
Facts, details, numbers, wants to know the bottom line, neatness, organization, stickler for timeliness, not a risk taker

DRIVER

TYPES OF PROFESSIONALS:
Plant Managers, Ex-Military Officers, Leaders who push, Technical Managers

LIKES:
To get right to the point, limited on time, always being busy, immediate results, choices, power, independence, forceful, positive

HOW THEY SEE THE WORLD

Logic, reason, numbers, facts, prestige, previous experiences, absolutes, position, title, how fast they can progress, external trappings, what they think about the product or company

PERSONALITY TRAITS:
Trusting, patient, nonassertive, passive, easygoing, even-paced, internal recognition, motivated, calculating

PERSONALITY TRAITS:
Distrusting, assertive, impatient, energetic, active, external recognition, motivated, impulsive, fast-paced

AMIABLE

TYPES OF PROFESSIONALS:
Some Sales, Tangible Sales Support, Customer Service, Secretaries, Office Personnel, Politicians, Training

LIKES:
Relationships, friends, to be liked, traditional values, not a risk taker, support of others, careful decisions, somewhat "wishy-washy"

EXPRESSIVE

TYPES OF PROFESSIONALS
Aggressive Sales, Actors, Comedians, Intangible Sales, Creative Professionals, Service Sales

LIKES:
Being a dreamer, uses hunches to make decisions, to be with people, makes quick decisions, to plan, takes risks, to focus on generalities, not time-oriented

HOW THEY SEE THE WORLD

Emotions, gut feelings, what others think, future opportunities, who they work for and with, whom they sell to, how they *feel* about the product or company

PERSONALITY TRAITS:
Feeling, relationship-oriented, agreeable, genuine, compliant, sociable, intuitive, sensitive, kinesthetic

PERSONALITY TRAITS:
Very outgoing, engaging, creative, expresses ideas well, articulate

Driver: The driver-type professional likes to be blunt, direct, and to the point. Usually limited on time, the driver is always busy, looks for immediate results, makes decisions quickly, likes to be in the power position, is independent and forceful, and, for the most part, is a real "can do" person. Drivers have a tendency to be assertive, distrusting, impatient, energetic, high energy, motivated mostly by external recognition, impulsive, and fast paced. They are plant managers, CEOs, CFOs, and managers in general. Driver types of personalities combined with an analytical style would more likely be engineering managers, CFOs, controllers, accounting managers, and so forth. Drivers coupled with an expressive personality would more likely be presidents, vice presidents of sales, sales managers, and so forth.

Amiable: The amiable-type professional likes relationships and to be liked. This type is easygoing, looks for the support of others, is not a big risk taker, makes careful decisions, and can appear to be wishy-washy. They also, as with analyticals, have a tendency to be trusting, patient, somewhat passive, easygoing, even-keeled, and are motivated by their own internal recognition. They have a tendency to be involved in low-pressure sales, sales support, customer support, customer service, and so forth. If they are amiable along with being expressive, they can be great ombudsmen types of people who understand everyone in the organization and have a tendency to create a bridge between people and departments.

Expressive: The expressive-type professional has a tendency to be a dreamer, use hunches to make decisions, is gregarious and outgoing, follows his or her gut, makes quick decisions based on feelings, takes risks regularly, focuses on the big picture, and has a tendency to be relationship-oriented. If an expressive is also somewhat of a driver, this person probably likes sales, sales management, leadership in the sales type of organization, and leadership positions that require a lot of interaction with other people. If an expressive also has amiable traits, then this person would have a tendency to excel in customer service management, sales support management, and human-resources director types of positions.

I don't want to imply that each one of these personality types is exclusive of the others. It is not overly important, for example, that the vice president of sales you were interviewing with is 98 percent driver and 2 percent expressive. The point is that you need to recognize that if you are interviewing with a vice president of sales, he or she is likely going to have a tendency to be more of a driver than an amiable.

Opposites Do *Not* Attract

So why is all of this important? Well, I'll tell you. If you are an amiable-type personality and you go to interview with a hard-charging, driving, take-no-prisoners, pushy, forceful, my-way-or-the-highway vice president of sales, you better be ready to "morph" your personality, at least for the duration of an interview, to be a hundred times more aggressive, assertive, and downright pushy than you normally are. If, as an amiable, you go to interview with a driver-type personality and decide to just be yourself, you won't get to first base. If you are an expressive type of person—fun-loving, free-wheeling, and outgoing, with a bubbly personality—and you interview with an analytical vice president of finance, you should morph your style to be more analytical and exacting. If an expressive personality is just being himself or herself in an over-the-top, jovial way with an analytical driver who wants to get to the bottom line and do it right now, this person isn't going to get hired. The expression "opposites attract" doesn't apply in job interviews.

Look back at the diagram of the personality traits and take a moment to analyze it. On the following exercise page, describe at least the primary and secondary personality traits that represent you. Write down in detail the reasons that you think these personality traits describe you. It's important for you to get a really good idea of the kind of personality you are as it relates to these four personality traits. If you think that you are primarily an analytical personality and secondarily an amiable personality, write out in detail why you would describe yourself in those ways. Doing this in a wild-guess manner will not get you the results you need.

Once you have figured out the personality traits that best fit you, do the exercises that follow. Then practice with your spouse, coach, family member, or friend the ways in which you would communicate with people who are different from the kind of personality that you are. This takes some practice. You need to be prepared to communicate with people in the manner in which they see the world. This exercise can help to eliminate a pronounced personality mismatch that would result in failure.

EXERCISE #1

Based on what you have learned so far, how would you describe your personality? Are you primarily an analytical, driver, amiable, or expressive type? Are you secondarily an analytical, driver, amiable, or expressive type?

Describe your *primary* personality style:

_____

How do you know?

_____

Describe your *secondary* personality style:

_____

How do you know?

_____

Now, answer the following questions as though you were addressing a person with the designated personality style taking into account your own primary and secondary personality styles.

What are your strongest assets?
(Analytical)

_____

_____

(Driver)

_____

_____

(Expressive)

_____

_____

(Amiable)

_____

_____

What was the biggest challenge you had in your last job?

(Analytical)

_____

_____

(Driver)

_____

_____

(Expressive)

_____

_____

(Amiable)

_____

_____

What are you looking for in an opportunity with our company or any other?

(Driver)

_____

_____

(Analytical)

_____

_____

(Expressive)

_____

_____

(Amiable)

_____

_____

EXERCISE #2

You are an accountant. You are being interviewed by the controller of a $50 million company. He asks you what your strongest assets are. He asks you what was the biggest challenge you had in your last job. He asks you what you are looking for in an opportunity with his or anybody else's company. How might you answer his questions?

What are your strongest assets?

_____

_____

Your answer might be: "I am very careful about producing exact, definite accounting reports that have no mistakes. In all my previous positions, I have always received accolades about the near-perfect reports that I provided."

What was the biggest challenge you had in your last job?

_____

_____

Your answer might be: "The biggest challenge I had was to get the reports out not only accurately but on time. Because we had several subsidiaries, the information that I needed for my reports came from many different sources. It was very difficult to get all the people who provided this information to me to provide it in a timely manner. I was constantly getting the information barely on time. I then had to incorporate all that information into my reports. I had to do it very quickly and accurately. It was not easy, but I was still able to produce accurate and reliable reports."

What are you looking for in an opportunity either with our company or any other?

_____

_____

Your answer might be: "I'd like to find a solid, stable organization where the people trust me and I trust them. I would like to be appreciated for my ability to work independently and I _don't_ need a lot of external recognition. I just want a solid, stable, dependable company that sets clear expectations because I can and will deliver more than is expected."

EXERCISE #3

Now, for the sake of example, let's say that you, the accountant, have become one of the finalists for the job. You're told that you're going be interviewed by the president of the company. You find out that the president of the company has been with the business for twenty years. He came out of the sales ranks to reach the presidency; and he is very aggressive and expects everybody to be part of the team. The president of this company is going to ask you exactly the same questions. How are you going to respond?

What are your strongest assets?

_____

_____

Your answer might be: "I pride myself in providing accurate reports promptly. My reports get right to the point and highlight the essential information that people need to make decisions. I realize that busy managers need to make quick decisions. When they need information, they need it immediately and accurately. I realize that everybody's time is limited, so I'm excellent at presenting the bottom-line facts. I have always been recognized by upper management as being able to produce accurate reports that result in competent decisions."

What was the biggest challenge you had in your last job?

_____

_____

Your answer might be: "The upper management in my last company was very demanding. They were powerful, assertive individuals who required immediate and accurate results. The kinds of reports that I had to produce involved getting input from several sources at the last minute. Although it was difficult, and I had to move quickly, I was always able to produce these reports so that the upper management was confident in the decisions they made based on the correct information that I provided."

What are you looking for in an opportunity with our company or any other?

_____

_____

Your answer might be: "I am extremely impressed with your company and the opportunity that it might provide me. I understand that you have been with the company for twenty years and, from what everybody tells me, you are an excellent leader. I am looking for that kind of leadership. I would like a high degree of stability with trust for the management. I see that in this organization. I do best in organizations with independent, energetic, and powerful leaders. I see that in this organization and that's why I would like to work here."

Same Answers, Different Words

In this example, the accounting candidate is answering the same questions with basically the same answers but with different terminology, depending on the interviewer. The accountant's answers are really the same in each of the interviews. However, the things he emphasized and the terminology he used to emphasize his answers took into account the kind of personality with whom he was interviewing. This is a simple process if you understand exactly what you need to do.

When the accountant was interviewing with the controller, most likely he was interviewing with a person who saw the world in about the same way that he did. However, when he talked to the president of the company, he answered the questions with more forcefulness, more power, and emphasized the importance of the *driver* leader. If he had answered the questions of the president in the same way that he answered the questions of the controller, he would not have addressed the kinds of things that a driver type wants to hear.

Notice that the accountant really didn't change the answers to the questions. He barely changed the terminology used to give the same answer. In the first case, the terminology and style fit the analytical type of person—that is, the controller—and in the second case, the terminology and style fit the driver-type personality of the president.

This technique simply requires that you learn and think about the kind of person with whom you are going to interview, and then you just practice. Once you get the method down, it can become a consciously automatic thing.

Ways to Develop a Positive Attitude

> *"Attitude is more important than the past, than education, than money, than circumstances, than what people do or say. It is more important than appearance, giftedness, or skill. We cannot change our past. We cannot change the fact that people act in a certain way. We cannot change the inevitable. The only thing we can do is play on the one string we have, and that is our attitude."*
> —CHARLES SWINDOLL, MINISTER/AUTHOR

Yes, you knew you would hear that attitude is everything! After thirty-one years in my field of work, if you were to ask me the one most important thing that makes a difference between the people who change jobs successfully and those who don't, it would be attitude.

You have a choice in your attitude. You can adopt a positive mental attitude regarding your searching for a job or a depressive, negative one. You can learn to love the situation or you can curse every moment of the experience. Either you can develop a positive attitude about having to find a new job or you can settle for the normal, almost natural negative curse of it.

Key point: *You will find a better job more quickly and have less anxiety about the process the sooner you get a positive attitude.*

One of the most profound books on the human psychology that has ever been written was authored by Dr. Viktor Frankl. The book, *Man's Search for Meaning,* chronicles the lessons Frankl learned as a Jewish psychiatrist imprisoned in the Nazi death camps of Auschwitz and Dachau. He gives a moving account of his life amid the horrors of these camps. His experiences in the camps led to his theory of the psychology that stresses man's freedom to transcend suffering and find a meaning to his life regardless of the circumstances. Frankl's conclusion is that the highest value man has is his ability to choose his attitude over things that he cannot control. The people who survived the concentration camps chose a meaning in their life and used that meaning as a reason to survive.

I recommend that you work on your attitude. You absolutely need to develop a superpositive mental attitude. The first step toward developing a positive attitude is not only to accept the present circumstance but also to appreciate and actually be grateful for your present circumstance, exactly as it is. The first step means that you must embrace and begin to cherish the current circumstance because you know that you are going to grow from it. The sooner you start looking at the positive aspects of looking for a new job, the better off you are going to be.

It is not as though you won't have some negative feelings or negative thoughts. When you are turned down for an interview, rejected on a job offer, or get told you're going to get an offer and you don't, you're going to feel negative, dejected, or depressed. What a well-developed, positive mental attitude will do is help you to rebound more quickly, respond with an acknowledgement of your feelings, and move on to the next situation. A positive attitude does not mean that people deny negative or sad feelings. Instead, they put those feelings in perspective and get over them quickly enough to be able to respond in a positive way to the next situation.

The Need to Set Goals/Intentions

> *"Give me a stock clerk with a goal and I'll give you a man who will make history. Give me a man with no goals, and I'll give you a stock clerk."*
>
> —J. C. PENNEY, DEPARTMENT STORE FOUNDER

Success in any endeavor is pure chance if you don't have goals. You need to be thinking about changing jobs or getting a new job *all the time*. In fact, it may almost wind up being an obsession. The adage "Where the mind goes, energy flows" applies in the job-seeking effort. Just about every waking moment should have you mentally focused on changing or getting a new job. It has to be a passionate, personal mission that doesn't end until you are successful.

Key point: *The universe wants to give you what you want, but you need to make every effort possible to ask.*

Over the years, in researching and working with goals for others and myself, I have concluded that there should be an *intention* side of goals, so I have combined these concepts as one. Intentions have a softer side to them than strictly being goals. The challenge with goals is that by definition they need to be finite—that is, time sensitive. That can be relatively harsh. People often become very disappointed when they don't reach a goal. Intentions, on the other hand, have a tendency to be more subtle. They are spiritually deeper and more permanent.

Goals/intentions need to be **S.M.A.R.T.,** (an acronym used by Ken Blanchard in his book *Leadership and the One-Minute Manager*.) This means they must be:

S . . . Specific and Simple. Stated in the present with sensory-based language

M . . . Manageable, Measurable, and Motivational. I can, I do, and I feel

A . . . Attainable and Achievable. What I can control

R . . . Relevant, Risk-oriented, challenge/skill balanced. Meaningful, a stretch, hard but doable

T . . . Trackable and Timed. Measure the process and set dates of accomplishment

Specific and Simple. Goals/intentions should not be broad generalities. A statement such as "to get a better job and be happy" is not a specific goal/ intention. Goals/intentions need to be stated in the present tense and be sensory based. You need to state them as though they were already accomplished. Also, it is best to state them in sensory—that is, seeing, feeling, hearing, and even smelling and tasting—based language. An example of a specific and simple goal/intention in a job search situation is: "I see myself getting five face-to-face interviews a week. I can hear the sound of a hiring manager making an appointment to interview me. I feel the rush of success and anticipation for the opportunity to sell myself."

Manageable, Measurable, and Motivational. Having manageable, measurable, and motivational goals/intentions leads to reasonable outcomes. Manageable goals are ones that you can personally manage. Having a goal/intention to grow wings and fly is not manageable. Having a goal/intention to become a better person is not measurable. A motivational goal/intention must be the kind of goal that you personally can get excited about, that moves you to action and that truly inspires you. Many people make the mistake of developing a goal that really belongs to someone else. The goal of finding a new job has to be your goal/intention. It must motivate you.

Attainable and Achievable. You need to develop goals/intentions that, even though they might be a stretch, can be attained, are achievable, and are within the realm of possibility relative to what you are capable of. You can control the activities necessary to get a new job; you may not be able to control getting a job offer.

Relevant and Risk-Oriented. Your goal/intention must be meaningful and there needs to be a possibility that the goal/intention will not be attained. The goal that inherently does not have some risk to it is not a goal. Many people, for the sake of writing a goal/intention, often write something that is easily within the realm of what they already do and the chance of them not succeeding is very, very slim. The challenge of a goal must be balanced. For a goal to be valid, it must imply that there is reasonable risk and that there is challenge. In addition, the goal/intention must presuppose that the person has the ability, even if it is in pressing the person to his or her limits to attain the goal.

Trackable and Timed. Your goals/intentions need to be trackable and timed. "Trackable" necessitates numbers being associated with it. You must be able to measure goals by hard numbers. A goal for interviews would stipulate a certain number of interviews during a week. A timed goal/intention is a necessity. This may seem rather elementary, but many people design goals/intentions that don't have time limits. They let themselves off the hook at the beginning. The trackable, timed aspect of goals/intentions must be proportionate and relative to the size of the goal/intention.

An example of a **S.M.A.R.T.** goal/intention would be "It is December 21, 2—. I am going to experience my first Christmas with my new company and my new job. I feel so grateful for my new opportunity. Most people are happy about Christmas—well, I am doubly happy. I feel so fulfilled with my new job. I see the new paycheck that is $_____ a month. My spouse sees the paycheck too and is joyous. I am challenged every day. I am growing on a daily basis. I hear my family experiencing the shared happiness of my new job. I love my new job!"

The previous goal/intention encompasses all of the **S.M.A.R.T.** attributes, but especially note that it is specific and stated in sensory-based language. It is also simple, measurable, certainly motivational, achievable, relevant, challenge/skill balanced, and timed.

Make Goals/Intentions Part of the Process

There are *process* goals/intentions and *outcome* goals/intentions. Outcome goals/intentions involve outperforming other people or focusing on a specific set of outcomes; process goals/intentions focus on the specific challenges of a situation. In my experience, when it comes to looking for a job, process goals are much more important and reasonable than outcome goals. The reason is simple. With regard to being offered a job, the outcome is nowhere near as controllable for an individual as are the events in the process of finding a job. For example, setting goals/intentions of making a certain number of calls to employers to set interviews, or attaining a qualified number of interviews every week, is a lot more specific, manageable, measurable, attainable, trackable, and timed than the general goal of "accepting a job offer." The timing in accepting a job offer, even though you are actively looking for one, is often too unpredictable to be an effective goal/intention. So, the idea is to set goals around the process of finding a job and let the result take care of itself.

Don't Keep Your Goals/Intentions Secret

Research reveals that *public* goals/intentions are more effective than *private* goals/intentions. This simply means that a person needs to write out his or her goals/intentions and put them in a place where other people are aware of them. Psychologically you are more apt to achieve your goals/intention if you know that other people are "watching."

Make Goals/Intentions Positive, Not Negative

Research also reveals that goals/intentions need to be stated with a positive connotation. The mind and the emotions really don't know the difference between a positive statement and a negative statement. Many studies have been done to prove this fact, but goals/intentions stated in a "I don't want to . . ." manner, simply reinforce whatever the person doesn't want to do.

Sample Goals/Intentions

Goals/intentions regarding a job search might appear something like this:

1. "Today it is the first day of my job search. I see myself waking up excited about the opportunity of finding a new job. As I smell the fresh coffee that I pour, I feel confident knowing that I'm going to manage the process of finding a new job. As I sit, relaxing and drinking my coffee, I begin to think of how I am going to execute the plan that I made the evening before. I know that this is a little scary and I feel the trepidation of not knowing what is going to happen. I begin my plan for the day. This is an exciting day."

2. "After I've prepared myself for the day, I see my family smiling and giving me the encouragement to manage the process of finding a new job. By noon of every day, I will have accomplished at least thirty phone calls to prospective employers to try to arrange interviews. I hear myself speaking to prospective employers and I hear them granting me an interview time. I feel the rush of success in knowing that now that I have interviews, I am going to successfully sell myself."

3. "I see myself getting ten face-to-face interviews a week. That is an average of two interviews a day. I hear myself practicing the interviewing techniques that I am going to use in each individual interview. I feel well prepared for every interview I will have. I am confident. I feel great. I know that with this preparation, I will perform extremely well in each one of these interviews."

Since you should recite these aloud every day, they will also function as *affirmations*. Affirmations are assertions of belief. They are positive statements that reinforce an activity or a state of being. In this case, you are affirming with every sense you have the successful finding of a new job. The more you positively reinforce the emotional and spiritual parts of your psyche, the more likely the physical side will follow. Suffice it to say, affirmations, like goals/intentions, work if they are reasonable. They must be recited repeatedly to create the effect necessary.

Your Specific Job-Search Goals

> *"One step—choosing a goal and sticking to it—changes everything."*
> —BEN STEIN, AUTHOR, ACTOR, INVESTOR

On the following form, write out ten goals related to your job search based on what you learned about goals/intentions. Research also reveals a person cannot reasonably deal with more than ten goals in any one focused endeavor.

Name _____ Date _____

Job Search Goals:

1. _____
   _____

2. _____
   _____

3. _____
   _____

4. _____
   _____

5. _____
   _____

6. _____
   _____

7. _____
   _____

8. _____
   _____

9. _____
   _____

10. _____
    _____

A Daily Plan

Next to writing down and setting goals, the most essential part of trying to find a job is to write both a weekly and daily plan. When you are dealing with event-oriented situations like finding a new job, making it longer than a weekly plan is not advisable. Planning is merely the activity side of goals. Planning is organizing the activities that are necessary to reach a goal. When the goal is clear, the planning should be very clear. Most people look for a job with no plan other than to "find a job." Well-designed and executed plans ensure a successful job search. Without executing a reasonable plan, a job seeker is going to have the process work him or her, rather than the individual working the process.

Your attitude toward the plan needs to be as passionate, intense, and enthusiastic as your attitude toward the whole idea of finding or changing jobs. You must adopt an unwavering commitment to working the plan every single day until you find a job. I caution you, no matter what happens, you must stick to the plan. There are going to be tons of setbacks in the process of finding a job. For every positive event, like an initial interview and follow-up second and third interviews, there are going be twenty-five to thirty negative events. You are going to become discouraged, disheartened, frustrated, mad, dejected, depressed, and forlorn. Well-written goals and a plan that you stick to, no matter what happens, will ensure your success.

Just as companies develop a system of conducting their business, you are going to develop a system of finding a job. This system emanates from the goals that you wrote. It is activated by making a plan and sticking to it. Finding a job is a numbers game—the numbers of cold calls you make; résumés you send; initial interviews you get; and subsequent second, third, and fourth interviews you get, which all go into creating a system. If you work the system, the system will work for you.

Here is what a daily plan should look like if you are looking for a job on a full-time basis:

5:30 A.M. Awake and drink that first cup of coffee. Find a relatively dark place where you can quietly contemplate your feelings and emotions. Express thoughts of gratitude! No matter how difficult things are, express only gratitude. Objectively acknowledge all your feelings and thoughts.

5:45 A.M. Enthusiastically read aloud the goals/intentions/affirmations that you have written. Do this three times.

6:00 A.M. to 6:30 A.M. Briefly reflect on the upcoming day's events—meetings, interviews, follow-ups, people you will be contacting, business meals—and visualize your success. Also, take a quick look at the business section of your local paper to see if there is any development that could have an impact on your job search.

6:30 A.M. to 7:15 A.M. Physical exercise. Run, ride a bike, take a brisk walk, anything aerobic to break a sweat. In order to perform well in the job-finding process, a person must be in good physical condition. If you are overweight, you need to start a diet. Your physical appearance in interviewing situations is crucial. The way you look and feel physically will be part of the interview evaluation; when you are in good physical shape, you perform better mentally and emotionally.

7:15 A.M. to 7:45 A.M. Shower and dress for the day. Dress in your business "uniform." If you dress like a top-notch businessperson, you will think like a top-notch businessperson. If you approach your day of job seeking in your pajamas and house slippers, unshaven and needing a bath, you just plain won't feel good about yourself. So dress every morning like you are preparing to go to your job, since your current "job" is to find one.

7:45 A.M. to 8:15 A.M. You are at your desk or your job search "office" and sitting with your second cup of coffee and reading or listening to a motivational book, a tape, or CD. Just one half hour, every day, of positive, motivational concepts will carry you.

8:15 A.M. to 8:30 A.M. Review your plan for the day. These are written-out calls, follow-ups, interviews, research, and any physical action that you planned the evening before.

8:30 A.M. to 11:30 A.M. In the beginning of your job search, you're going to spend most of this time cold calling companies to get interviews, as well as calling any kind of consultant, recruiter, counselor, friend, enemy, relative, previous and present business acquaintances, previous employers, in-laws, outlaws—anyone who can get you an interview. As you go along in the process, the activities that you designate for this time period can be altered depending on the situation. For example, if you have an interview one morning at 9:00, you won't plan to make any calls at 9 A.M. In general, this period of time during the day will be devoted to cold calling, "warm" calling, interviewing, following up over the telephone on interviews that you had, and taking *immediate* action that is going to result in an interview. It is important to recognize that you should spend this time of the day doing *immediate* activities that are going to get you an interview. Do not spend this time tinkering around on the Internet by visiting job boards or interesting websites;

e-mailing résumés to prospective companies without knowing if they have an opening; and, in general, confusing activity with productivity.

Key point: *The further removed the activity you engage in is from getting you an interview, the less valuable it is. Interviews are most important.*

11:30 A.M. to 12:15 P.M. Take a thirty-minute lunch break if you don't have a business luncheon planned. Try to eat lunch in a quiet environment where you can slow down from the intense pressure of the morning and relax. A fifteen-minute walk outside, if possible, is good to do during this time. A walk clears the mind and is a good way to help relieve the stress of the morning. Don't try to go to the gym for an hour workout in the middle of the day. You will get out of the flow. If you have to go to the gym for a real workout, do it in the evening.

12:15 P.M. to 12:30 P.M. Review e-mails, respond to them, and review your plans for the afternoon.

12:30 P.M. to 4:45 P.M. In the beginning of your job search, you are going to spend this time just like you did in the morning. You are going to spend it cold calling and performing *immediate* activities that are going to get you face-to-face interviews. This involves contacting all the previously mentioned types of people. As you get into the process, you will have interviews in the afternoon and, again, nothing is more important than those interviews. Again, stay flexible, but don't confuse activity with progress. Between 12:30 P.M. and 1:15 P.M. is often a great time to catch hiring managers when their administrative personnel—that is, the "gatekeepers"—are at lunch. Often, managers will answer their own phones then. You're going to stop at nothing, short of something illegal or immoral, to get yourself in front of a hiring manager.

5:00 P.M. to 5:30 P.M. This time should be used to make follow-up phone calls to people whom you might have interviewed with that same day, or to follow-up with e-mails that you might have gotten during the day that require a phone call. Between 5:00 P.M. and 6:00 P.M. is also a great time to try to talk with hiring managers whose administrative gatekeepers have gone for the day. Rarely do hiring managers, these days, walk out of their office right at 5:00 P.M.

5:30 P.M. to 10:00 P.M. This is the time to do all the paperwork, the secondary activities that are important but may not directly get you an interview. Things like mailing your résumé to a prospective employer, responding to job ads, writing the introductory letters and e-mails attached to your résumé, doing research on the Internet about companies that you might contact, deciding on a sector of business that you will cold call the next day and researching those companies, finding names of their hiring managers, phone calls to friends, mentors, and supporters who might help you get interviews, and so forth.

It is also important to devote this time to your family or loved ones. Depending on the age of your children or your family commitments, you should spend time in family endeavors. You need to support the people who support you, and this is a good time to do it. It may also be the time that you do some kind of spiritual giving one or two days a week. Volunteering, teaching, community service, or any kind of going out of your way for nothing in return can be done during this time. You can also spend this time reading motivational material, such as stories, books, and articles about people who have overcome difficult times. Feeding the mind and spirit is an essential aspect of successfully finding a new job. I can't emphasize enough how this type of study is vital to counterbalancing all the negatives that you will experience. Some planning for the next day might also be done at this time, depending on your personal commitments.

10:00 P.M. to 10:30 P.M. As you prepare for bed, review the events of the day. Acknowledge gratitude for all the happenings of the day, preferably with your family. Even if the results of the day were negative or uneventful, an "attitude of gratitude" must be offered up.

A Daily Plan If You Are Employed

Normally, the process of finding a job when you have one takes longer, primarily because you can't devote 100 percent of your time to your job search. The process itself is more difficult and the activities of finding a job must be juggled with keeping the one you've got. Here is what a daily schedule might look like if you are currently employed:

5:30 A.M. Awake and do exactly the same activities as the previous schedule. Quietly contemplate your feelings and emotions, and acknowledge them.

5:40 A.M. Enthusiastically read aloud the goals/affirmations that you have written. Do this three times.

6:00 A.M. to 6:30 A.M. Same as above. Reflect on the day ahead and visualize your success. (Don't forget to include your current job in these thoughts.)

6:30 A.M. to 7:00 A.M. Physical exercise. The same as the previous schedule.

7:00 A.M. to 7:15 A.M. Review the plan you wrote the night before regarding all the things you'll do to find a new job. As you progress in your job search, since you are working, you may be able to talk to hiring managers about interviewing you early in the morning at 7:00 A.M. or 7:15 A.M. Next to getting a job, the interview is the most important thing you can do, so if you get a chance to have an interview this early in the morning, take it.

7:15 A.M. to 8:00 A.M. Do all things necessary to prepare and get to work.

8:00 A.M. to 12 noon. Function in your job. Depending on the job you have, you may be able to peek at your personal e-mails during the day or make one or two phone calls to recruiters, agencies, or contacts that might be able to get you interviews. In general, it is *not* a good idea to schedule job-finding activities during your actual work hours.

12:00 P.M. to 1:00 P.M. When having your lunch break, spend only ten to fifteen minutes actually eating. Find a place where you can make telephone calls, check personal e-mails, send résumés, cold call, schedule interviews, follow-up on interviews, talk to recruiters, agencies, and so forth. Obviously, doing this for only forty-five minutes during a busy day is going to be a difficult task, so you must use your time efficiently.

1:00 P.M. to 5:00 P.M. Do your job! Maybe a phone call or two in an effort to change jobs might be possible. If you are in outside sales, it is much easier to execute job-finding activities while you are still working. Try to focus on doing a good job at the one you have. When you're looking to leave a current job, you are usually unhappy about the job, the environment, the situation, and so forth. That is why you are leaving. But you don't know how long it is going to take to find a job, so to keep the one you have, you'd better do it well.

5:00 P.M. to 6:30 P.M. Get to the place where you work on your job search. Making calls, following up on résumés, sending résumés, responding to e-mails, following up on interviews that have already taken place can all be done at this time. Calling prospective employers from now until 6:00 P.M. is reasonable to do because most are still in their offices. It is not the best scenario, but it's all you can do. As you progress in your process of finding a new job, you will often use this 5:00 P.M. to 6:00 P.M. time frame to conduct interviews. Employers, for the most part, are willing to do this for a really good candidate.

6:30 P.M. to 8:00 P.M. This should be just like the previous schedule. Take care of some secondary job-search activities, but mainly this is a time for family. If your family is as supportive as they should be in helping you find a new job, they should recognize the difficulties of finding a job while you are employed. As a result, they'll give you a chance to take care of some of the things you just can't do during a busy workday.

8:00 P.M. to 8:30 P.M. Exercise. Some type of aerobic exercise is best.

8:30 P.M. to 10:00 P.M. You may still have some family activities. Again, if the family is supporting your job-changing efforts, they may give you a chance to do research on organizations that you plan to call the next day. Write down the names and phone numbers of companies you're going to call either at lunch or at 5:00 P.M. Research the companies, review their websites, and identify the people to call. E-mail résumés and leave voice mails for hiring managers at this time. It is not always easy, but you have to do what you have to do.

Saturday

Begin your Saturday the way you begin every other workday of the week. You might want to wake up a little later; but when you do, it is still important to create a routine that you can rely on during the emotional distress of finding a job. So, spend some time when you wake up on a Saturday morning exactly the same way that you do every other morning.

Don't think you can take Saturdays off completely. These days, many company mangers are willing to interview on Saturday mornings. If you are currently employed and have a hard time getting away from work to interview during the week, this is a great time to suggest an interview. It has its challenges. For example, Saturday morning interviews have a tendency to be too casual and not sufficiently businesslike. The attitude and atmosphere are normally not as crisp and professional as a normal weekday. There is a tendency for employers to want to interview at a Starbucks, or a restaurant. However, an interview at a Starbucks is better than no interview at all. Since the hiring authority is more casual, you need to be more intense and sell yourself harder.

Saturday Afternoon

Saturday afternoon is a great time to do volunteer work.

Sunday

Sunday is supposed to be a day of devotion, rest, and relaxation. Formal devotions on Saturday or Sunday are traditional in our country. It is also good to take time out to rest and relax on a Sunday. But frankly, if you are out of work for any length of time, it's very hard to tell your mortgage company or the company that financed your car that you need to rest and relax. So, if you really need a new job, you should spend at least an hour or two researching companies and planning your job search for the following week. The Sunday classified ads are excellent to review. Responding to classified ads for specific positions is not the main reason I recommend reading the ads. The probability of you finding a job by responding to a classified ad is about 1 in 350. However, the classified ads are going to tell you what companies or industries or professions might be hiring. So reviewing the Sunday classified ads is going to provide a wealth of opportunities for you to call about during the next week.

Jeff and Amy's Reaction

As Amy and Jeff read this chapter, Jeff commented that keeping up his motivation, enthusiasm, and passion for finding a job was the most difficult thing that he encountered. When it came to planning, goal/intention setting—even the execution of the plans—he was excellent. What he discovered was that a person must be able to do it all: set goals, plan, and execute while keeping the mental toughness in place. Some things come more naturally to different people than do others.

Anyone, especially Jeff, would have a hard time maintaining a positive attitude because it was so hard to even land interviews. On the other hand, he was very good in the interviewing process. He was outgoing, positive, upbeat, and sold himself extremely well when he got into the interviewing process. The problem was that he didn't create enough of those opportunities for himself. His attitude was, "Where are the rewards?" It was just very difficult for him.

The numbers were not working for Jeff because there weren't enough interviews and it was hard for him to maintain a positive attitude. Focusing on the process of finding a job and not worrying about results as much as just managing the process don't come naturally—especially if nobody instructs you on how to do it. Jeff admitted that this sounds simple enough, but that it's actually very hard to do. He had no problem with passion and intensity when he got an interview. When the rejection of not getting additional interviews sunk in, he would revert back to a minor depression and begin to hate the process of finding a job.

There is no doubt that Amy was trying to help and, objectively, Jeff knew that. However, it was hard for them to practice his interviewing techniques together, because when she felt like she was offering constructive criticism, he took it as personal criticism. This is a common scenario for spouses in the job search situation. People can become so self-conscious about everything going on in their lives regarding finding a job, especially if they've been out of work for a while, that even constructive criticism can be misconstrued and taken personally. Amy mentioned that she almost wished that Jeff had an independent person or somewhat removed friend who could objectively hold him accountable for his job search activities.

When it came to planning, setting goals/intentions, and following those goals, Jeff was also excellent in this category. Jeff has always had near-term, intermediate, and long-term goals. He was excellent at making a plan and sticking to it. Jeff planned his time and his activities on a daily, weekly, and monthly basis.

None of the aspects of looking for a job discussed in this chapter are difficult to understand. However, *understanding* them and *doing* them are often two different things. The things that come naturally to us are always easy to do. Setting goals/intentions, planning, working the plan, interviewing well, and genuinely getting people to like him are things that came easy for Jeff. He really didn't need much instruction in these areas. Being able to counterbalance the mental and emotional strain of this kind of job search did not come naturally to Jeff. The lesson here is that a person needs to work harder at aspects of this process that don't come naturally to him or her and still maintain and perfect the aspects that do come easier.

3   The Key to the Whole Process: Getting Face-to-Face Interviews

> *"Those who say some people are just lucky because they are in the right place at the right time don't realize that the lucky ones show up at a lot of places a lot of times."*
>
> —TONY BESHARA

The most important thing you can do to get a job is to interview. Nothing else matters unless you can get a face-to-face interview with the hiring manager—a hiring manager with authority and pain (an urgent need to hire someone).

No matter how well you might interview, in spite of what you might think, you can't really control getting a job offer. You can influence a hiring manager to offer a job by interviewing well and proving to the employer that, based on the interviews, you are the best person for the job. However, when it comes down to the event of offering someone a job, the real control is in the hands of the employer.

Key point: *While you cannot control job offers, you can control interviews, the number of them, and how they are conducted.*

Getting interviews is hard work. It requires tenacity, persistence, determination, and the courage to thrust yourself upon people even though it doesn't come naturally for you to do so. Most people are not comfortable with selling other people on interviewing them with the possibility of being hired. It can be daunting, burdensome, and an excruciating task.

No one likes being rejected. The risk of being rejected goes with the interview. The sooner you face that reality and prepare for possible rejection, the sooner you're going to be able to find a job. Pristine résumés, brilliant re-

46

search, great contacts, even superior previous job performance, do not help you to find a job to anywhere near the extent that getting numerous interviews and performing well in each interview does.

Exploring All Sources for Interviews

The initial interviews, if they're successful, will lead to subsequent second, third, or fourth interviews that will eventually land you a job. The most effective vehicle is going to be you picking up the phone and calling anyone and everyone you can, whether you know them or not, to find people who might be able to grant you time for an interview.

Studies have shown that most job seekers consider several different ways of getting interviews, especially in the beginning of their job search. And after a month, or so, they abandon many of the ways that they might approach getting interviews and stick with one or two methods. This is a mistake. The key is to use every one of the methods until you find a job. You need to be relentless about this.

It has been estimated that 60 percent of the people who find jobs find them through networking. I guess that depends on how you define the word *networking*. If you define networking as calling people whom you know, this estimate of 60 percent is probably an exaggeration. If you consider networking calling anybody and talking to them regarding a job with which you're somewhat familiar, then this statistic may not be too far off. I personally think that you should get an interview with anybody who will listen! Call and try to meet with as many people as you possibly can.

Previous Employers, Peers, and Subordinates

People you have worked with who have gone to other companies are great sources of opportunity leads. This group of people should be the very first to approach when you need to find a new job. Sit down and brainstorm the names of all the people you have worked with, or for, or have worked for you, in every company that has ever employed you.

Don't hesitate to call previous employers, even if the individual people you worked for or with are gone. Just because you did not like working at a place five or ten years ago, doesn't mean the same group of people, ownership, or culture is still there. Over a period of fifteen years or so, I placed the same packaging engineer with the same company three times. The company had changed hands four times during that time.

Caution: I do not recommend going back to work for an organization you have left unless the culture has completely changed. All the reasons you left an organization the first time are usually still present. Even if you were laid off or downsized, the truth is that the organization thought more highly of its own self-survival than it did of you. They really don't change that much. The principle should be to never go back to work for an organization that either you left or one that left you, unless there is a complete change in management, ownership, or culture.

Family

The bigger your extended family, the better off you are. During the first few days that you begin looking for a job, you should call every member of your family—brothers, sisters, parents, uncles, aunts, first cousins, second cousins, third cousins, any cousin, in-laws, and their cousins—to let them know you're actively looking for a job and you would like to talk to anybody whom they might suggest.

Some people are embarrassed about calling people in their family and letting them know that they are either out of work and looking for a new job or looking for a job change. Get over it! Would you rather be embarrassed by not being able to pay the mortgage or by letting your family know that you need a job? Call them, tell them that you're actively looking for a job, and ask them if they know of anybody who might be interested in your type of background. Offer to send one of your résumés. Keep a record of everyone you call and their responses. Tell them that you would like their help, and that you would like to call them back in a week or so.

Friends

Talk to your friends just as you would talk to your relatives. Call them and let them know that you're looking for a job and ask them if they would know of anybody who might need someone with your kind of background. Offer to send a copy of your résumé. Make a note about when you called them and ask if you can follow up with them in a week or so to see if they might have thought of anybody with whom you can interview. Even ask your friends for their friends who might be of help in your job search and ask them if you can use your friend's name in calling them.

Acquaintances

Acquaintances are different from friends. They are people you know, but not that well. They're people whom you occasionally, or even rarely, run into or contact from time to time. A study back in the 1970s found that people looking for jobs were more likely to find opportunities through acquaintances than through friends. The study concluded that often people make friends with people they work with or who occupy the same world. So when a large organization has a layoff, it's likely that a person's friends will be laid off too. But acquaintances may operate within a completely different work world.

> I have known many people over the years who, when looking for a job, had cards printed so that when they were folded they were the size of a business card. They had their name and address, e-mail address, and telephone number on one side and a very short version of their résumé as a person opened up the card. Every time they ran into somebody during their job search, they would give the person a "business card." As they handed someone a card, they would mention that they were actively looking for a job and that if the person knew anybody who needed an excellent employee, they would love the opportunity to interview. Excellent idea!

People in your church, athletic club, neighborhood, social club, golf or tennis club, volunteer organizations, and parents of children who are friends with your children are all people you should make aware that you're looking for a new job. Even acquaintances of your spouse are people who might be able to help you.

Competitors

Most of us know who our business competitors are. After talking to previous employers, it is a logical idea to call and solicit all of your company's competitors for a job. Capitalize on your familiarity with them. Candidates often tell me that they know a lot about their competitors but they just would not want to go work for one of them. This usually stems from an organization painting their competitors as people with horns and tails. The truth is that most of us don't really know much about our competitors except in relation to competitive situations with them. We don't intrinsically understand them. No matter what the party line has been about your competitors, you need a job and it is in your best interest to call them and see if they have an opportunity for you.

Caution: If you are in most forms of sales, and/or some tactical development types of positions, you may have signed a non-compete agreement with your current employer that, at least theoretically, prohibits you from working for your competitor. If you signed a non-compete agreement when you went to work at your current organization, pull it out, read it, and be aware of what you can and cannot do and the risk you might run.

Suppliers and Distributors

Write down all the people to whom you currently supply goods and services, as well as all the people who might distribute your goods or services to end users. The knowledge you have is probably applicable to the people who supply you goods and services or to the people to whom you distribute your goods and services. A software developer, for instance, develops software that may be sold through distributors. If you worked for the software vendor and you know how the software works, you were of value to the distributor. If your company manufactures parts that are sold to and by another manufacturer, you may have a great deal of knowledge that is of value to that other company.

Customers

In some situations, customers might be great people to approach for a new job. If you have sold to them or had reason to have contact with them and built a good relationship with them, customers may have a great opportunity for you.

Caution: If you are presently employed, *do not*, I repeat, *do not* call and solicit your competitors, suppliers, distributors, or customers about a new job. No matter how trustworthy you think they are, you cannot afford to lose your job. No matter what you think, the probability of it getting back to your current employer that you're looking for a job from one of these sources is almost 100 percent. I cannot tell you the number of times that I've encountered candidates who have lost their jobs because they told a competitor, supplier, distributor, or customer that they were thinking about changing jobs and got fired when it got back to their employer. The value of talking about a new job to a competitor, supplier, distributor, or customer is limited only to people who are unemployed and looking for a job full-time.

Trade and Professional Associations

Some professions and trades have more active associations than others. Some businesses are heavily involved in professional and trade organizations and some are not. *The Encyclopedia of Associations* lists twenty-three thousand national and international groups for just about every occupation you can imagine. So if you haven't been active in an association, you can at least find the ones you ought to become involved with or at least become a member of. The most important aspect of being an active member in an association is that you receive a membership directory, which can be used for contacting potential employers. Some associations publish job opportunities for their members.

Trade shows for trade and professional associations not only give you great personal exposure, but you can often find out which companies are expanding and which are contracting. Often trade shows have placement committees that organize publications of job opportunities. If you are out of work, these trade shows are a great place to interview many organizations in a short period of time. If you are presently employed, it may not be advisable to be that obvious; but as you introduce yourself, collecting business cards and information about other people, this information can be helpful for contacting them later on a more confidential basis.

Alumni Associations, Fraternity and Sorority Members

Don't hesitate to take advantage of any contacts in these kinds of organizations that you might have. This is an excellent source of many potential employers outside your normal sphere of influence. Alumni directories will give you the list of names and addresses and business affiliations of all members. Call fellow alumni and speak to them about their careers, companies, and industries. They may have job openings in their organization or know of openings somewhere else.

College and University Placement Offices

If you are out of undergraduate school more than a year or two, it's not likely that the undergraduate placement office at your college or university could help you that much. But you never know. Often, organizations that are expanding will list their current openings with the college or university placement office. You may be overqualified or too experienced for the positions that they might list, but as we will see and discuss in a future topic, knowing which organizations are expanding, no matter how much or little, provides great prospects for you to call.

It also doesn't hurt to list your name and experience with graduate school placement offices or at least call them and find out the listings that they may have. I have known of organizations that listed short-term project assignments in the graduate school offices of some MBA programs. It is amazing how often these short-term projects become long-term permanent positions. Take advantage of every resource that might be available to you. You're only limited by your own imagination.

Job-Search and Career Counseling Programs

The only difficulty I have with these kinds of organizations is that they can often be sophisticated pity parties. Sitting around with a group of people who are all bitching and moaning about the difficult employment market isn't going to find you a job. Make your own judgment! Go to these kinds of organizations and meetings if they indeed help you with your attitude. It's even possible that one of the other people in such a program will come across a job in your field that they are not qualified for and pass the information along to you. Just don't expect much in the way of actual job-search results.

Job Fairs

Job fairs were more popular when the employment market was much easier than it is now. These fairs are designed to have several employers come together and interview many people in one day. In recent years, job fairs have attracted thousands of people who are exposed to very few hiring organizations. If you are presently employed, do not go to a job fair. I have known of a few employed candidates who, since they were looking for a job, attended a job fair—only to discover their own organization was there. They were promptly terminated.

Religious, Community, and Social Organizations

It is important to tell people you know in these organizations that you are looking for a job. Common values are one major criterion that most people use in hiring others. This factor may not be obvious or even conscious to most people, but as I've mentioned before, we all have a tendency to hire people we like. And we have a tendency to like people whose values and beliefs are very much like our own.

Bankers, Loan Officers, Venture-Capital Firms, Lawyers, CPAs

These groups of people will be surprising sources of many opportunities that might lead to the job you need. Bank and loan officers, especially in small communities, know a lot of the businesses that are expanding or looking for people simply because they lend money to these organizations and often know who is on the rise. Small businesses, which make up 97 percent of the employers in this country, often establish great relationships with bankers, so the bankers can help them expand when they need to. These relationships are usually personal between the banker and the owner or owners of the companies. So it certainly doesn't hurt to ask the bankers and loan officers you know if they are aware of any organizations that might be expanding.

Venture-capital firms are organizations that provide money, typically, for start-up companies. These companies have a tendency to fund many homogeneous types of organizations. It is not uncommon for these companies to impose one of their own members on a company that they have funded to see to it that their investment is protected. Whether they are just providing money or also have someone on the inside, these firms can be excellent sources of information on available jobs.

Attorneys who specialize in medium to small businesses, labor law, or certain other kinds of legal specialties often know organizations that are expanding because they represent them or give them advice. I personally know an attorney who specializes in legal advice to high-tech firms. He knows just about every high-tech company in the region. He may not necessarily know of their expansion plans, but he certainly knows who they are. He helps the smaller ones incorporate and helps the larger ones with their legal issues. It is not uncommon for a company's external legal counsel to know their growth plans.

Recording All the Names to Contact

"Everyone knows at least 200 people."
> —JOE GIRARD, AUTHOR OF
> *HOW TO SELL ANYTHING TO ANYBODY*

Here are simple forms to help you brainstorm and recall the names and telephone numbers of the previous employers, peers, subordinates, family, friends, and acquaintances you need to call.

PREVIOUS EMPLOYERS

(Think back on every supervisor/boss you've ever had. Where are they now?)

Name _____ Company _____
Phone _____

Name _____ Company _____
Phone _____

Name _____ Company _____
Phone _____

PREVIOUS PEERS

(Force yourself to think of at least four for every job you have had.)

Name _____ Company _____
Phone _____

Name _____ Company _____
Phone _____

Name _____ Company _____
Phone _____

PREVIOUS SUBORDINATES

(Force yourself to think of at least four for every job you have had, if you have had subordinates.)

Name _____ Company _____
Phone _____

Name _____ Company _____
Phone _____

Name _____ Company _____
Phone _____

FAMILY MEMBERS (no matter how distant)

Name _____ Phone _____

Name _____ Phone _____

Name _____ Phone _____

ACQUAINTANCES

(Pull out that church directory, PTA directory, Neighborhood Association directory, and so forth)

Think about this long and hard, you know more people than you think!

Name _____ Phone _____

Name _____ Phone _____

Name _____ Phone _____

COMPETITORS

Name _____ Company _____
Phone _____

Name _____ Company _____
Phone _____

Name _____ Company _____
Phone _____

SUPPLIERS AND DISTRIBUTORS

Name _____ Company _____
Phone _____

Name _____ Company _____
Phone _____

Name _____ Company _____
Phone _____

Name _____ Company _____
Phone _____

CUSTOMERS

Name _____ Company _____
Phone _____

Name _____ Company _____
Phone _____

Name _____ Company _____
Phone _____

Name _____ Company _____
Phone _____

Posting Your Résumé on the Internet

You can post your résumé on Internet job boards, but don't expect much in the way of interviews. Only 2 percent to 5 percent of the résumés on the Internet ever get any response. And 40 percent to 50 percent of the résumés e-mailed unsolicited to companies end up in spam folders.

The biggest concern about posting your résumé is security. You have lost control of your résumé. It will float around in cyberspace indefinitely, even if you remove it from the job boards. Long after you find a job, your résumé will still be out there. (We placed one candidate who, six months after she was on the job, was called on the carpet because her résumé had been accidentally found on the Internet. It was a vestige of her earlier job search that had migrated to several job boards without her knowledge.)

On top of that, all kinds of crazies have access to your personal information. You can expect to be contacted by people who will try to sell you something other than a job, knowing that you are in a vulnerable position. Private investigators and lawyers looking for people to subpoena use the job boards.

Thieves will ask you for your social security number or driver's license number in the guise of doing an employment background check before you are interviewed.

So, post your résumé if you must, but be careful!

Finding Crazy Ways of Making Contacts

As long as we're talking about making contacts, it might be good to mention here some of the more zany ways that I have seen people either look for a job or get interviews. We're going to talk about the more traditional ways of getting interviews in the rest of this chapter, but I might as well bring up here some of the more crazy ideas that I have seen work.

Cold Call a Building

Start at the very top of a building and walk into every office on every floor of the building, introduce yourself and ask for an audience or appointment with the highest-ranking manager in the office. If you don't get an appointment, leave a résumé with the receptionist.

Stand on a Street Corner

This is not all that crazy of an idea. Most of us have seen people do it. This is not too far off from what Jeff Mills did, except he got more elaborate by setting up an office on a flatbed truck. If you were going to stand on a corner or a busy intersection, the most effective way to do it is to dress in a nice business suit and either carry or wear a great big sign that states what you're trying to do. Not too long ago, less than a mile from our office at one of the busiest intersections in Dallas, Texas, a new MBA grad stood at an intersection in his suit with a briefcase and a stylish sign that said, "New MBA needs work." He took his station at 7:45 A.M. and by noon he was hired.

Have a Party for Yourself

Throw a party and invite everyone you know, and have them invite everyone they know. One of my crazy rugby buddies did this. (We were younger then.) He rented a warehouse, hired a cheap band, bought ten kegs of beer, and threw a party! He had napkins printed with a short résumé and his telephone number. He got a bunch of interviews from people he didn't know and three or four job offers. He had a great time, too!

Along this same line, go to lots of parties, especially around the holiday times. Be highly visible. Let lots of people know that you are looking for a job!

Rent a Billboard

Put a picture and a brief description of yourself on a billboard. It could be a little pricey depending on where the billboard is, but it sure is effective.

Following the Script

This part of the instructions needs to be followed to the letter. Most people will read this, get the meaning of it, and then go off and do it their way. And that is where the mistakes will begin. Here, and in other places, I'm going to give you a carefully researched script that is likely to work. If you follow the instructions and do it exactly the way I teach you, the system will work. If you don't follow the script and end up ad-libbing on your own, you won't be as successful. These scripts will work 90 percent of the time. So, please, for your own sake and for the sake of those who love and support you, follow the instructions exactly like I'm teaching you.

I will provide for you the same kind of script to be used in different scenarios. Unless you have been using this kind of script on a daily basis, you need to practice this script before you use it. At first, the script isn't going to sound natural to you. To many people, some of this script is going to appear to be very pushy and aggressive. No matter how difficult it might be for your personality to be this aggressive, the sooner you do it, the sooner will you be successful in your job search.

Eventually, the pain of either not having a job or of needing to change jobs is going to get so great, most people will opt to be painfully pushy in getting themselves interviews. All of the scripts I recommend take lots of practice. Most of them will be ones that you are going to deliver over the telephone. So, it is simple enough to practice them with someone who is supporting you in your effort. They are simple but very specific. So, practice the scripts to the point where they sound natural to you.

Throughout this book, I am teaching you to sell yourself. I am teaching you to sell yourself very, very, hard. The kind of aggressiveness and assertiveness that I recommend is necessary in these days of a changing economy. To the vast majority of people, this kind of aggressive selling of oneself does not come naturally. It may be uncomfortable at first, but needing to find a job or change jobs is uncomfortable too. It all depends on what you find to be more uncomfortable.

Contacting People You Know

It is important that you record the telephone number and date you call people. *You may be calling the person back again in thirty, sixty, or ninety days.* Many people will not respond to you positively for a month or two. *You want to remind them that you need a job!*

PREVIOUS EMPLOYERS, PEERS, SUBORDINATES, AND ACQUAINTANCES

Name _____ Phone# _____

Date _____

SCRIPT: "Hello, _____, this is ___(your name)___ and I am presently looking for a new job. We know each other from _____. I called to ask you if you might know of any job opportunities available either with the firm you work for or any others that you might know about. For the past ___(period of time)___ I have been working at ___(name of company or what you have been doing)___. I am presently looking for a job doing _____. Can you think of anyone who might need what I can offer? ___(very long pause!)___

(If "no") Then say: "I really appreciate your time. I'd like to send you my résumé, and if you can think of anyone who might be interested, please pass it along to them.

"By the way, I am not sure how long my search will take; I'd like to call you back in a month or so to see if you might have thought of anyone who might be interested. Would that be all right?"

Results:

_____

_____

FAMILY

Name _____ Phone No. _____

Date _____

SCRIPT: Hello, _____. This is ____(your cousin, brother-in-law, etc.)____ and I am presently looking for a new job. I called to ask you if you might know of any job opportunities that might be available. For the past ___(period of time)___ I have been working at (name of company or what you have been doing)___. I am presently looking for a job doing _____. Can you think of anyone that might need what I can offer? ____(long pause)___.

(If "no") Then say: "I really appreciate your time. I'd like to send you my résumé and if you can think of anyone who might be interested, please pass it along to them.

"By the way, I am not sure how long my search will take; I'd like to call you back in a month or so to see if you might have thought of anyone that might be interested. Would that be all right?"

Results:

_____

_____

(I will present a different script for competitors, suppliers, distributors, and so forth when I discuss cold calling in general.)

Finding Businesses That Can Help You Get Interviews

There are many types of businesses that can help you get interviews in your job search.

Private Employment Agencies

This kind of organization is very dear to my heart because it is basically the kind of firm that I am the president of and the kind of organization that I've been with for more than thirty-one years. Over the years, our profession has evolved to the point where applicants are hardly ever responsible for the fee. The fees are paid by the companies that we work with and we work as much for the companies as we do for the applicants.

Our organization, however, is an exception to the traditional employment agency. We do as much recruiting for our clients as we do work for our applicants in trying to find them openings. We earn our fee when we successfully find a candidate who accepts a position with a company to which we referred him or her. Our firm has interviewed close to three hundred thousand candidates on a face-to-face basis in the past thirty years.

Read the classified newspaper ads (as well as yellow page listings and Internet listings) to find the most successful agencies in your area. If the individual who is assigned to help you has any decent experience in the business, he or she will be able to give you a realistic idea about the opportunities that might be available to you. When the employment market is tight and there are many, many candidates to choose from, a hiring company expects to get exactly the experience they desire because they're paying a fee and the kind of experience they want is readily available.

Talk to as many different agencies as you think you can to get qualified interviews. I would not recommend limiting yourself to any one or two, at least in the beginning. You will quickly find out who is going to be productive for you and who isn't. You need interviews! It is in their best interest to get you good interviews because that is how they're paid. If you aren't successful, neither are they.

Executive Search Firms

Traditionally, executive search firms—or search consultants—were never oriented toward a candidate. Their client is the organization that pays their retainer. They do not operate as an agent for the candidate. They are an extension of the client and usually specialize in specific industries or professions. Whereas a recruiting firm that might work in a certain geographic area may work, from time to time, on a retainer basis, executive search firms usually work on a worldwide basis. They usually have offices all over the world and deal with only upper-level management positions. Over the past few years, boutique organizations have cropped up. They may have only one or two offices in a major city but specialize in a narrow category of executives.

A true executive search firm will claim that it is not interested in seeing or collecting résumés from individuals. The firm's stock-and-trade is to reach out and actually recruit certain types of talented people on certain levels that are not actively looking for a change in jobs. Traditionally, they have exclusive arrangements with their clients, and their clients, having paid part of a fee as a retainer, agree to the exclusivity. Along with exclusivity, there is usually an agreement not to solicit executives from the client for a period of time.

If you are aware of these kinds of executive search firms that are specific to your industry or profession, don't hesitate to contact them and see if they might help you. Just don't expect the same kind of results that you might get from a traditional employment/placement/recruiting firm that is more candidate-oriented.

Temporary, Staffing, and Consulting Firms

These used to be called temporary agencies. Traditionally, they were only oriented toward secretaries and other office workers. Along with the secretarial and administrative type of staffing, general labor staffing firms have been around for years. Today, these organizations staff all kinds of professional positions on a temporary basis. There are even staffing firms that place doctors, CEOs, CFOs, accountants, lawyers, technical writers, nurses, all kinds of healthcare professionals from phlebotomists to X-ray technicians to medical insurance clerks, HR professionals, drafters, designers, and engineers.

When you work for a staffing firm, you are actually an employee of that firm and you are contracted out to another business. Liability for payroll, taxes, workmen's compensation insurance, benefits, and so forth are all the responsibility of the staffing firm. The advantage to the client company is that it doesn't have to be bothered with any of these kinds of things and is free to terminate the relationship with the individual at any moment with no serious business or economic consequences.

In recent years, information technology (IT) consulting firms have grown to take on a significant amount of information technology development. These firms hire out their technical expertise, from very narrow and specific types of software development to general software applications. Most of these firms do not see themselves as staffing companies. They see themselves, and present themselves, more as consultants. They often work on specific projects for their clients; often these projects can last for many years. The client pays a high premium for this kind of expertise, and, as with general staffing, does not have the burden of long-term employees. The client can pay for the service on a time and materials basis, a project basis, or a flat hourly basis. Many of these firms spun off from the large consulting firms that developed technical, IT expertise. Business for these kinds of organizations has been difficult for the past few years. The overbuild in the technology arena as well as the outsourcing of many of these jobs to foreign shores has eroded the phenomenal growth of this sector of business.

Advantages to you: Working for most temporary staffing firms has many advantages. Depending on the kind of job you might get through staffing firms, you can often gain flexibility of hours; faster, almost immediate employment; a great entree into a company to experience what working there might be like; and a relatively fast paycheck.

One major benefit of working for a staffing firm and being assigned to another organization is that, 15 percent to 20 percent of the time, the position can become permanent. This happens most often on the secretarial, clerical, and administrative level but it is common in the higher-level consulting types of positions.

Disadvantages: The drawbacks are obvious. A temporary position—even on a very high level of a president or CEO—is still perceived as and is just that—temporary. The attitude toward a person like this is often less than professional. The care and respect that is normally given to a person perceived as a permanent or regular employee is not given. The premium or markup that the client pays is higher than for hiring a permanent employee. That premium is paid for the right to terminate the job for the temporary person at any time.

The major concern from your point of view, however, is that often keeping a temporary position becomes more important than interviewing for a permanent position. It is not uncommon for an individual to have to work interviews around the temporary position. Since a temporary assignment is temporary, the individual knows that it can end at the whim of the client. Therefore, the candidate is often reluctant to schedule interviews for permanent positions during normal business hours while working at the temporary assignment. The immediate short-term benefits become more important than the long-term. So, when accepting a temporary assignment, the thing to do is to be sure the client knows that you are actively seeking a permanent job and let him or her know that your schedule will have to allow the opportunity to interview for permanent positions.

Executive Marketing and Career Management Firms

The existence of these firms ebbs and flows with the economy. Their purpose is to counsel people in their executive career. They supposedly give advice on how to market one's self and provide career management counseling. Because of many scams associated with this kind of consulting, many states have instituted licensing procedures for these types of firms in recent years. These firms often purport to know a hidden job market and have secret connections to job opportunities. These firms charge a fee. I have spoken to individuals who have paid up to $12,000 or $15,000 for this kind of expertise.

Caution: These kinds of firms do not find people jobs. They supposedly provide career counseling. I can only speak for personal experience, but in the thirty-one years that I have been finding people jobs, I have never met any people who used this kind of career consulting service and felt like they got what they paid for. There is no such thing as a hidden job market. Also, paying a fee for advice from someone who is not involved in actually finding jobs for people is a questionable investment.

Résumé Services

There are fewer of these organizations since the advent of online résumé-writing advice sites. An experienced résumé-writing service may not hurt; but unless the organization is involved in helping people find jobs, its opinions about what might be of value regarding your résumé may be incorrect. Chapter 5 will discuss a simple form of résumé writing that is the most effective you can use. The problem with writing a résumé is that just because the individual writing it thinks it is good, does not mean it will be an effective résumé. There is a big difference between what works and what doesn't.

Other Types of Firms

There are other types of employment-oriented firms that provide employment services to employers, but they normally cannot help a candidate actually get an interview.

Employee leasing firms undertake responsibility for an employer's workforce, payroll, benefits, administration, legal obligations, and sometimes other HR functions. They do not, however, recruit, screen, test, or interview prospective employees.

Outsourcing services provide personnel who can handle functions ranging from the mailroom to a telephone call center—all the way to totally revamping a company's information technology system. Over the past few years, *outsourcing* has connoted *offshore*. This often means that the function is sent to a foreign country or the work is done by non-American citizens who are employees of the company itself or employees of the firm that is hired to perform a specific function. The most notable kind of outsourcing has been associated with large call centers in IT functions. The majority of true outsourcing services for U.S. companies are done on the site of the company that did the contracting.

Outplacement services usually provide a facility for use by its terminated employee. This is where the former employee can base a search for new employment. The service may include office space, telephones, fax and Internet access, message center, and so forth. The former employer usually pays the fee for this service.

Newspaper and Internet Advertisements

The odds of finding a job by responding to a specific newspaper ad are probably about one in 350. Although Internet advertising hasn't been around as long, my sense is that the odds are about the same. The sheer volume of résumés that are received from these types of advertisements is astounding. It is common to receive 200 to 300 résumés in one day from a newspaper or Internet advertisement. It is a very deep and wide black hole.

You might respond by actually calling the hiring authority for the position that is advertised. Delivering a résumé to a hiring authority is a great way to respond. Many ads will state that applicants should not phone the company doing the advertising, let alone show up personally, without an appointment. My opinion is that you've got nothing to lose. The probability of getting an interview is close to nothing anyway, so you might as well run the risk of calling or showing up unannounced. Call and ask for the logical hiring authority for that position. If you get the person on the phone, follow the script I have recommended for this kind of cold call.

Where advertisements can help you get a job does not have as much to do with the particular job that was advertised as it has to do with the company or industry that might be advertising. Those in motion tend to stay in motion. If you see a company advertising and expanding in one area, it might very well be expanding in another. So, if you see an organization advertising in one area that may not have anything to do with what you have done in the past, you may consider cold calling the department where your experience would apply.

Getting Interviews with People You Don't Know

We now come to a portion of the process that can make one of the biggest differences in how fast you find a new job. The procedure is simple: You get on the telephone and present yourself to a prospective employer and ask for an interview. It's called a cold call. It is simple and direct. The results you get will be immediate. The cold call will either result in an interview or it won't.

The process of doing this is very simple, but the manner in which you do it is sophisticated and takes a lot of courage. The reason it takes courage is because you are running the risk of being rejected and refused in ten seconds. On top of that, you are going to have to make forty or fifty of these calls before one results in an interview. So, you have to expect rejection and refusal one heck of a lot before you get positive reinforcement.

I prefer to call these *warm calls* because neither you nor the prospective employer are "cold." Keep in mind that when you do this, you are trying to get an interview regardless of whether there is a position opening or not. You are selling an interview, not necessarily selling the idea of getting a job. It is extremely important that you recognize this difference. The purpose of this call, this warm call, is to get in front of that prospective employer so that you can sell yourself and your skills. You are purposely going to ask for a meeting with the prospective employer without asking him or her if there indeed is a need. You are selling a "date"—not marriage. Don't confuse getting hired with an initial interview. All you're trying to do is sell an audience with that person.

The reason that you are just trying to sell the initial audience, or interview, is that, very often, hiring managers will interview potential employees whether they have an opening or not. As you will see, the script does not ask if there are any openings, it asks for an appointment, an interview, and only presupposes a current or upcoming actual position opening.

Whom to Warm Call

If you don't know the name of a hiring manager within a firm when you call an organization, simply ask the name of the manager of the department that you would normally report to. If you are an accountant, call and ask for the name of the controller. If you are a controller, call and ask for the name of the vice president of finance or the CFO or, when it comes down to it, anyone who is in charge of the finances for the company. If you are a salesperson, you should call and ask for the sales manager, the regional sales manager, the vice president of sales, and so forth. If you are an administrative support type person, then you would ask for the administrative support manager. When you call, ask for the manager of the kind of department that your skills and ability would fit. It is that simple.

> I do not recommend calling the HR department unless you are seeking a job in that department. Most of the first-line screeners in an organization are taught to send anyone who is inquiring about a job to the HR Department. People in HR are usually mid-level record keepers. In 97 percent of the companies in the United States, the HR department is not going to help you find a job in the company. The nature of the HR department is to screen out most every candidate, unless he or she is perfect—and who is perfect? The HR department will not normally interview unless there is a specific opening and even then, will only look for candidates who are perfect. Remember, the HR department's underlying, unwritten motto is, "We don't want to look bad." So, don't get relegated to the HR department.

If you have skills that can transfer from one industry or profession to another you can warm call just about anybody. Any kind of administrative experience, accounting experience, bookkeeping experience, sales experience, and so forth can carry over to a lot of different businesses. So, you can warm call from just about any reference book that might provide names of companies and telephone numbers. Don't overlook the telephone book itself.

WARM-CALL SCRIPT

"Hello, who is your (controller, vice president of sales, IT Director, CEO, etc.) Fine, let me speak with _____.

"Hello, _____ my name is _____ and I am _____ with (feature) _____ and have a great track record of (advantage and benefit) _____.

"I would like to meet with you to discuss my potential with your firm. Would tomorrow morning at 9 A.M. be good for you or would tomorrow afternoon at 3 P.M. be better?"

If you get a response like, "I really don't have any openings," then your response will be:

"I understand and the kind of people whom I want to work for probably do not presently have an opening.

"I would just like to take fifteen or twenty minutes of your time because I am a top-notch performer. I am the kind of person whom you would want to know to either replace your 'weakest link' or to know of my availability when the next opening does occur. Now, would tomorrow morning be good for you or is tomorrow afternoon better?"

You will either get the appointment or a more insistent response of, "I really don't have any openings. There is no reason for us to meet."

Your response:

"I understand that you don't have any immediate openings, but I have a great track record of _____.

"Mr. or Mrs. _____, I am the kind of professional who is better than 90 percent of the employees that you might have now. It is to you and your company's best interest that you at least talk to me and be aware of my availability. If not for now, then maybe in the future. My experience has taught me that, often, great talent comes along when you don't need it. But, it is always a good idea to be aware of talent on a face-to-face basis. I will only take a few moments of your time and it may wind up being beneficial for all of us. Would tomorrow morning or tomorrow afternoon be better?"

If the response is, "Well, can you e-mail me a résumé?" Then your response is:

"I can, but my résumé is only one-dimensional and it is of value for both of us to associate a face and a personality with a résumé. I'd like to bring it by, hand deliver it to you, and spend maybe fifteen minutes of your time so that you know what my accomplishments are and how they can benefit you and your company. Is tomorrow morning good or would tomorrow afternoon be better?"

If the response is an emphatic, "Just e-mail me the résumé!" (which is just a nice way of saying no.) Then, your response is:

"I will, right now. I will call you back tomorrow to be sure you have received it, and then we can set up a visit."

If you get a very emphatic "no" and it is clear that you're not going to get any kind of face-to-face interview, you then need to pause for two or three seconds and say:

(*pause*) "Do you know of any other opportunities that might exist in your firm with any other manager?"

If you get a person's name, ask:

"May I use your name as a reference?"

If you get the name of another manager, also ask for his or her phone number. If the answer is "no," then ask, after a two or three second pause:

(*pause*) "Do you know of any other organization that you might have heard of through the grapevine that might need someone of my experience?"

If you get the name of an organization or a person's name, ask:

"May I use your name as a reference?"

Script for Following Up on a Referral

If you get a referral to a particular person or organization and the person who referred you said you could use his or her name (this is an indication of how strong the ties the people might have), here is the script:

"Hello, Mr./Ms. _____ . I was referred to you by _____ . I am _____ with _____ and a great track record of _____ .

"I would like to meet with you to discuss my potential with your firm. Would tomorrow morning at 9 A.M. be good for you or would tomorrow afternoon at 3 P.M. be better?"

You will be amazed at the number of job opportunities you will uncover this way. Controllers know other controllers. Vice presidents of sales know other vice presidents of sales. Engineering managers know other engineering managers, and so on. It is not uncommon for one type of manager to know a number of other types of managers both within and outside of their own company. These managers are often asked by their counterparts in other organizations if they indeed know somebody to fill vacant positions. You may get a productive response once out of every forty times you try this approach. But don't be discouraged. *The one interview you get as a result of asking that question is worth the forty or fifty times of asking.*

Whether you get a referral or not, it is a very good idea to end the conversation with the following:

> "Thank you for your time, I would at least like to e-mail you my résumé in case something might change with you or someone you know."

Nine out of ten times, the person on the other end of the phone will be willing to receive the résumé. No matter what the person's response, whether it be positive or not, end the conversation by saying:

> "I'd like to give you a call back in thirty days or so to see if there might be any openings there or if you might know of any with friends of yours."

Again, nine out of ten people will agree to your doing that. To a certain extent, that lets people off the hook for the moment; but they know, in the back of their minds, that they could easily have a position open up at any time.

Key point: *Warm calling is a numbers game. The more calls you make, the more likely you are to get an interview.*

If the hiring manager just plain dismisses you or insists that you deal with the HR department, you can say:

> "My experience with company HR departments, (as far as identifying top talent when there isn't an immediate need), just hasn't been good. I am sure they are wonderful people; but I need to be talking to decisive managers who can make immediate decisions. Is there any other decisive manager in your firm that has an opening?"

Analysis of the Script

This is very simple but very strong stuff. The idea is to sell a face-to-face interview whether the hiring manager has a position opening or not. You are not asking if there is a job opening or asking to be hired; you're simply getting a face-to-face interview. The script is meant to be forceful and to the point.

There are a few crucial aspects of this script. First, you do not ask the person answering the phone who might be doing the hiring. If you ask who does the hiring, nine out of ten times you'll be relegated to the HR department and that for the most part is a dead end.

Once you get a hiring authority on the phone, you have to provide *features, advantages,* and *benefits* as to why you should be interviewed. This is very important! If you simply call and ask for an interview without giving specific features, advantages, and benefits to the prospective employer, you won't get to first base. This is, again, simple stuff if you are aware of what you are doing. Here are some examples:

> "Hello, Mr. or Ms. _____ . My name is _____ and I am (*features*) an accountant. I passed my CPA exam in one sitting and I have fifteen years of very stable accounting experience. I have worked my way up in two organizations from the ground floor to an assistant controller position. The *advantage* that I bring is stability and performance. The *benefit* to you and your organization is that you would have a long-term employee with a great track record.
>
> "I would like to meet with you to discuss my potential with your

firm. Would tomorrow morning at 10:00 A.M. or tomorrow afternoon at 2:00 P.M. the best for you?"

Or, another example would be:

"Hello, Mr. or Ms. _____ . My name is _____ and I am a (*features*) salesperson. I have ten solid years of experience with two Fortune 500 firms and have never been less than 110 percent of quota. I continually (*advantage*) perform in the top 2 percent of the sales organizations that I've been with. I would like to (*benefit*) continue this kind of a performance with an organization like yours.

"I would like to meet with you to discuss my potential with your firm. Would Tuesday morning at 9:00 A.M. or Wednesday afternoon at 3:00 P.M. work the best for you?"

The purpose of this script is to briefly and succinctly tell a hiring authority your personal features and advantages so that they can be perceived as benefits to the hiring authority's company. So, your job now is to come up with a features, advantages. and benefits statement on yourself. The question is, and always will be, on the part of that hiring authority, "Why should I hire you?" The whole interviewing process centers around this question.

Keep in mind that features, advantages, and benefits regarding you and your possible employment do not have to be mystical, miraculous, or mesmerizing. They can be simple and rather uncomplicated. In fact, simple and uncomplicated reasons for hiring somebody are the best. So, the next exercise is to come up with a features, advantages, and benefits statement about you.

A *feature* is an aspect of you or your career that makes you unique. It can be the number of years of experience. It can be grades in school. It can be things like hard work, determination, persistence, and dedication. A feature, in a job-seeking situation, is simply a unique aspect about you that is going to be translated into being a good employee.

An *advantage* is something that the feature does to set a person apart from the average. So, if a person graduated cum laude from college and worked his or her way through college with two jobs (features) that person demonstrated hard work and commitment way above the average person (advantage).

A *benefit* would be the gain that a company would realize from hiring a person who brings unique features and advantages. So, the features of graduating at the top of your class as well as working two jobs demonstrated your advantage to perform on a higher level than average, therefore you will perform in the same way for whoever you work for and the company will benefit from your work.

So now, write out your own:

Features: _____

Advantages: _____

Benefits: _____

Now, remembering that you are selling yourself and that you are briefly giving a prospective employer a reason for why he ought to interview you, write a features, advantages, and benefits statement about yourself:

"Hello, Mr. or Ms. _____. My name is _____.

"I am a _____. I (features) _____ , which are (advantages) _____ and, therefore (benefits) _____ you and your firm."

Practice writing this and in just a few minutes you can write three or four features, advantages, and benefits statements on yourself to fit just about any situation. *Remember, the purpose of this statement is to intrigue a hiring authority enough to want to interview you.* Do not try to sell the whole idea of hiring you in one phone call. The purpose is to get the interview by giving a hiring authority a brief statement about what you can do for him or her.

The closing question of, "Could I see you tomorrow morning or would tomorrow afternoon be better," is a minor choice resulting in a major decision, which most salespeople learn in their first training class. This concept is so simple it is almost too good and yet a phenomenal number of people will avoid using it because it appears to obviously manipulative. It definitely is simple, but it definitely works! At the end of your features, advantages, and benefits statement, ask the minor choice and major decision question. It works. Do not ask questions such as: "Would you be interested in talking with me?" or "Could I come by and see you?" or "Can we set a date for an interview?" None of these questions are nearly as effective as:

> *"Could I see you tomorrow morning at* _____ A.M. *or would tomorrow afternoon at* _____ P.M. *be better?"*

Please, please don't try to be coy or cutesy by making this more complicated than it needs to be. Simply make the features, advantages, and benefits statement and ask the alternative choice question. Then, *shut up!* Don't say another word until you have a response.

Now, most people who are not in sales, and even some that are, will have a difficult time using this statement and question, especially in the beginning of their job search. I have been using this format for finding other people jobs for more than thirty-one years. It works better than anything you can imagine. So please, you want to start getting results, or interviews, as fast you can. It works—don't fix it!

So, there you have it. A features, advantages, and benefits statement followed by an alternative choice question that will get you the results that you need. Now all you need to do is to *practice!* You have nothing to lose but your anonymity.

USE THIS FORM FOR EVERY CALL

Company _____ Phone _____ Date _____

"Hello, who is your (controller, vice president of sales, IT director, etc.)? Fine, let me speak with _____.

"Hello, _____. My name is _____ and I am _____.

"I (features) _____, which are (advantages) _____ and, therefore, (benefits) _____.

"I would like to meet with you to discuss my potential with your company. Would tomorrow morning at 9 A.M. be good for you or would tomorrow afternoon at 3 P.M. be better?"

Response: **"Well, we really don't have any openings."**

"I understand that you don't have any immediate openings, but I have a great track record of _____. I am the kind of professional who is better than 90 percent of the employees that you might have now. It is to your and your company's best interest that you at least talk to me and be aware of my availability—if not for now then maybe in the future. My experience has taught me that, often, great talent comes along when you don't need it presently. But, it is always a good idea to be aware of talent on a face-to-face basis. I will only take a few moments of your time and it may wind up being beneficial for all of us. Would tomorrow morning or tomorrow afternoon be best?"

or

"I understand and the kind of people whom I want to work for probably do not presently have an opening. I would just like to take fifteen or twenty minutes of your time because I am a real, top-notch performer. I am the kind of person who you would want to know to either replace your weakest link or to know of my availability when the next opening does occur. Now, would tomorrow morning be good for you or is tomorrow afternoon better?"

Response: "Well, we just don't have openings and there is no need for us to meet."

(*pause*) "Do you know of any other opportunities that might exist in your company with any other manager?"

If you get a person's name, ask: "May I use your name as a reference?"

or

(*pause*) "Do you know of any other organization that you might have heard by the grapevine that might need someone of my experience?"

If yes, get the person or organization's name and ask: "May I use your name as a reference?"

If you get the name of a person or organization, use this script when you call the person:

"Hello, Mr./Ms. _____. I was referred to you by _____. My name is _____ and I am _____."

"I (features) _____ that are (advantages) _____ and, therefore, (benefits) _____."

"I would like to meet with you to discuss my potential with your company. Would tomorrow morning at 9 A.M. be good for you or would tomorrow afternoon at 3 P.M. be better?"

Results:

_____

_____

If the conversation does *not* result in an interview, ask:

"May I call you back in thirty or sixty days to see if the situation in your firm has changed?"

Call back on _____. "Thank you for your time!"

Keeping Track of the Process

This may not come as a surprise, but you absolutely must keep good records of all these calls. Your job search, whether you like it or not, may take six, eight, or nine months. I hope, for your sake, that it doesn't, but you need to be prepared for that possibility. If you follow my advice properly, you're going to talk to numerous people whom you have warm called many times. Just because a company, or an individual within the company, says there is not an employment opportunity today, it does not mean that there will not be an opportunity in the future.

The probability of you discovering a vacancy when you initially warm call like this is about one in fifty. You will almost double those odds by calling back a second, third, or fourth time. So, it is important to recognize that warm calling the individual or organization is not simply going to be a one-time thing. Your odds of getting a face-to-face interview at the second or third call are much greater than they were on the first call

> Out of every fifty calls that you make, in the manner I suggest, you are only going to reach an average of ten hiring managers. This depends on the kind of hiring managers to whom you need to talk. Vice presidents of sales are not in their offices as much as accounting managers, controllers, and so forth. You're going to discover one opportunity, on average, for every thirty to forty managers with whom you talk. This, again, depends on the level of job that you are looking for. Engineering manager positions are a lot harder to find than design-type jobs. But, these numbers are about right. So, you're going to have to make 150 to 200 calls to hopefully get one interview. That is what it takes to be successful at getting interviews this way. Do yourself a favor and don't complain about it one way or the other. If that is what you have to do to be successful, then that is what you have to do.

simply because the person that you're calling is more aware of who you are and what you're doing. Even if it was slight, you made somewhat of an impression on the person the first time you called. By the second, third, or fourth time you call, the person has become more aware of possible employment opportunities that might be available in the organization. If you are going to make the investment of the warm call to begin with, you will reap greater rewards by following it up with subsequent calls.

. I suggest simple manila folders to keep records of each organization that you approach or interview with and a daily planner that you can make notes in every day or into the future. Although there are computer programs that can probably help, simple manila folders to store records and a large daily planner will suffice.

When a person first starts out looking to either find or change jobs, he or she usually has no idea how long it is going to take to be successful. There is a tendency to have a lot of activity in the beginning of the process: however, the process may carry on for a lot longer than a person would imagine. Good record keeping helps the momentum in the beginning to be sustained over however long it takes.

Should You Leave a Voice Mail Message?

Somewhere along the line you're going to be faced with leaving a voice-mail. You diligently practice a warm-call presentation and then you get voice mail! Well, there is a lot of debate as to whether or not you should leave a message on a hiring authority's voice mail. Try your own experiment and see what works. I recommend doing it.

First off, I would call the same hiring manager two or three times, trying to make a presentation to him or her before I would leave a message on voice mail. If I concluded, after even the second time, that I'm not likely to catch this hiring authority answering the phone, I would leave a voice mail message. The script for the voice mail message isn't much different from the script used when a live person answers the phone. The ending, however, is slightly different. It goes like this:

"Mr./Ms. _____ . My name is _____ . I am a _____ . I have (features) _____ that are (advantages) _____ , which would be (benefits) _____ to you and your firm.

"I would like a chance to meet with you. My phone number is _____.
Again, that is ____(your name)____ and my phone number is _____."

Be sure to repeat your telephone number at the end of the message at least once, and repeat it very s-l-o-w-l-y so the person can write it down as you record it the second time. Many people find it too hard to go back and listen to your voice mail message a second time just to get your telephone number. If you say it slowly and repeat even more slowly at the end of the message, people are more likely to write down the number and return your call.

If you don't get a response the first time that you leave a message on voice mail, don't hesitate to record a similar message two or three times for the same person. This sounds a bit excessive, but my experience has been that if there is even the slightest pain of needing someone now or in the near future, this kind of message will get the attention of a hiring authority.

After leaving four or five messages similar to this and not getting a response, you should stop calling, at least for now. If my experience had been with a similar kind of organization where my value might be greater than the average candidate looking for a job, I would certainly call back a number of times down the road. But, for now, I would stop calling after four or five messages.

If you don't get the courtesy of a call back from a hiring authority, don't take it personally.

The In-Person Cold-Call Visit

One great way, and one of the most effective ways of getting an interview and the attention of a hiring authority (the person with pain), is to simply show up in his or her office and ask the administrative person if you can have a few moments of the hiring authority's time. Then you just wait in the office until he or she sees you.

Once you are meeting the person face-to-face, even if it is a brief moment in the lobby, you state the following as you hand the person your résumé:

"Mr. or Mrs. (Employer), I understand that you are looking for an excellent candidate to fill your position of _____. I am an excellent candidate and would like to spend a few moments with you to discuss my qualifications. Do you have a few moments?"

Do not expect that you are going to get an interview right then. That will only happen occasionally. If the hiring authority says that he or she does not have time right then, ask when there will be a better time: be persistent about setting a specific time.

When you have the boldness to do this kind of thing, you have everything to win and nothing to lose.

Jeff and Amy's Thoughts on Getting Interviews

Neither Jeff nor Amy ever thought it would take so long or be so difficult to find a job. Since Jeff had always been able to find a job easily in the past, he confused activity with productivity in looking for a job. He did many things, especially in the beginning of his job search, that really didn't have any bearing on him getting interviews. He spent hours, days, and weeks sending résumés over the Internet and responding to newspaper ads. This activity is common for people when they first start looking for a job, especially if they haven't looked for one in a few years.

Even though Jeff performed well in interviews when he got them, he didn't get enough of them. I mentioned earlier that when people start out looking for a job, they use all kinds of different approaches. After a while, they often stop working most of the approaches that they used at the start and resort to only one or two ways of getting interviews. Jeff did exactly that. At first, he was excited about the opportunity of finding a new job, but when it didn't happen after a long period of time, he basically shut down most of the process.

The part in the chapter about approaching family, friends, and acquaintances was especially pertinent for Jeff and Amy. They found many friends and family members simply couldn't understand how someone as talented as Jeff could be out of work for any length of time, if he was really trying to find a job. People just don't know how hard it is to find a job until they need one.

Jeff did seek out some permanent recruiters before he came to us, but they didn't get him many interviews. He was approached by a consulting firm that wanted $2,500 to rewrite his résumé and give him advice. Jeff was besieged with all kinds of other huckster angles like, "for $69.95 we will post your résumé on 10,000 sites" and numerous pyramid marketing programs that required up-front investments.

The concept of how many calls it takes to get a face-to-face interview was not a revelation to Jeff and Amy after all they had been through. They wished they had known this in the beginning. Understanding the numbers and how they work prepares people for the process that they are going to go through. It is a process of getting in front of as many people as you can to eventually get hired. Rejection is part of this numbers game. Jeff and Amy were amused at the idea that counting the rejections was just one more way of keeping score toward the successful interview.

Amy suggested that people read this chapter twice before they even start looking for a job.

4 : The Stark Realities of Your Potential Employer's Hiring Process

I told you earlier that 97 percent (or close to 12 million) of the businesses in the United States employ fewer than one hundred employees. These companies run like the people who own them or manage them.

None of these owners or managers could be called a "people person." They focus on what they do, rather than who does it. They think that if they do what they do well enough, they will have a model business. In general, they are unfocused, grossly disorganized, illogical, ignorant about most things, ambitious beyond their realistic abilities, fearful, without clear goals, impatient, and vain. They do not have a real system of doing business; they operate with a seat-of-the-pants mentality. When a recession comes along, things become even more complicated. For the most part, these are messy companies, surviving tough economic times, squeezing every bit of effort and work out of all their employees, as well as themselves, wondering when the recession will end. If you *really* get the message of this chapter, 90 percent of the emotional strain that typically goes into changing jobs will be alleviated.

Hiring authorities in business organizations are just as stressed over the hiring process as the job candidates. The process of hiring people is riddled with uncertainty, great doubt, and fear. Most hiring authorities feel as though they are being personally and professionally judged by the people whom they hire. There is as much fear of making a mistake while hiring someone as there is fear in the mind of the person being considered for hire.

Recognizing that hiring authorities and managers often "go emotional," will empower you, as the job seeker, to more easily and effectively manage the process and get the results you want. The key is managing the process of your job search. How you emotionally deal with the crazy components of the job search process will determine to a great extent what outcome you achieve.

Why People Get Hired

It is important to learn early on that the most qualified candidate for a job often is not the one who gets hired. In the more than thirty-one years that I've been doing this work, I have placed people who were hired for the most illogical, crazy reasons you can imagine.

The primary reasons that people are *interviewed* are different from the primary reasons why they are *hired*. There is a big difference between the candidate's qualifications and his or her ability to get hired. People are often hired—or not hired—for all kinds of reasons that have nothing to do with the job, the company or their previous performance. Over the years, I have seen people being hired for the following strange, but primary, reasons:

- They were tall and the hiring authority believed that the best salespeople were 6 feet 2 inches or taller.

- They were short and the client thought short people would try harder proving themselves to others.

- They were pretty faces, which was a plus to the hiring person.

- They were average-looking females who supposedly (according to the client) would not distract the male-dominated organization.

- They were very handsome men, so the hiring female managers were swayed in their favor.

- They were average Joes, making others feel comfortable around them.

- They were young and theoretically had more energy.

- They were "old" and the client felt that older people didn't have the distractions of family life, such as little kids or becoming pregnant, or having to go through all the problems of growing up.

Key point: *The primary reasons that people are interviewed normally have to do with their qualifications. The primary reasons that they are hired usually have nothing to do with qualifications.*

Your task in finding a job therefore becomes two-fold. The first thing you need to do is demonstrate sufficient qualifications to get the interview. Then you need to be ready to deal with a whole different set of criteria in the process of getting hired. This is the reason that the most qualified candidate is not usually the candidate that is hired. Selling yourself in the interviewing process is the most important aspect of getting a job.

How a Hiring Authority Sees the World

The majority of hiring authorities in 97 percent of the businesses in the United States cannot see their companies as people companies. Not only does the hiring authority need to find a person to fill the vacant job but he must also find someone whom he and the others are going to like. The ideal candidate is someone who can do the job; someone who fits in; someone who is going to make the hiring authority look good; someone who doesn't represent a big risk; and someone who will work for the right salary.

Most candidates do not consider all the peripheral issues the hiring authority will take into account. Candidates usually assume that the hiring authority sees the qualifications (including the ability to do the job) and nothing more. The candidate does not maintain the same perspective as the hiring authority.

Next to finding a candidate with the right qualifications, the biggest concern that most hiring authorities have is *the fear of making a mistake.* That is why hiring people becomes such an emotionally charged event. No one likes to make mistakes, but making a mistake in hiring is one of the greatest fears for most managers. Anyone looking for a job must be aware that the fear of making a mistake is a great driver in the decision-making process of any hiring authority.

What does this mean to you in looking for a job? It means that you must be as aware of the reasons why you might not be hired as you are of the reasons why you should. You must know your perceived liabilities to a hiring authority. A major part of your job in interviewing is to assure the hiring manager that he is not making a mistake; and that, to the rest of his world, he is going to look good by hiring you!

What They Care About

Most organizations really don't give a darn about you as a candidate.
Once an individual becomes an employee, there may be a little more re-

gard for the person and his or her contribution to the organization. However, get it out of your head that a prospective hiring authority or interviewing authority really cares about you. What they care about is the survival of their organization and getting done what they need to get done. Don't expect consideration for the enormous strains that you, the candidate, are undergoing in the process.

When the economy is expanding, companies do not need to be as concerned or nervous about their bottom line, so they can afford to take risks with people who do not have direct experience. When profits are high, companies can afford to take people with no—or relatively little—experience and train them. They can hire "potential." When the economy gets difficult in recessionary times, companies need to hire people who can immediately have an impact on their bottom line.

In a recessionary economy, when most companies believe that there are hordes of people on the market looking for jobs, an employer is hard-pressed to spend money on an unproven commodity when proven commodities are all around. This situation is reinforced by the need for an employer to get someone who can start producing immediately. Employers and hiring authorities simply do not have the time or economic luxury of training a person with "great potential."

It is crucial to recognize in the interviewing process that one of the most important things you need to do is demonstrate how you can bring an immediate, productive value to the organization. The idea that you are simply an excellent worker won't sell. You need to be able to establish *immediate value.*

Expect Lies and Confusion

Within the emotionally stressful process of hiring, you are going to find that hiring authorities lie. They don't intentionally lie. It is not a premeditated intention to lead you to believe something that isn't true. Hiring authorities under stressful situations will tell you one thing and do another.

Prepare yourself for the following lies:

- They're going to call you back.

- They're very interested in you as a candidate (as they're also telling everyone else the same thing).

- They say that you would be excellent at the job and that they haven't seen anyone as good as you (and then they don't hire you).

- They tell you that they are going to hire you (and then you never hear from them again).

- They lead you to believe you are being strongly considered (and then they do not return your calls).

The list could go on and on, but I'm sure you get the idea.

For you as a candidate, next to being rejected and refused, the most frustrating aspect of looking for a job is the indecent manner in which you will be treated by a prospective employer. Some employers don't like to tell people "no." It is a general rule that they tell people what they think they want them to believe at the time in order to make everyone feel comfortable for the moment: This is not always truthful. This process of being led astray obviously takes some getting used to. It is frustrating, especially if you have not changed jobs in a long time. Get used to it.

How should you handle this web of deceit? Start by taking what you hear as the "truth" only for that moment, and realize that it is probably going to change. When you are told that you are a viable candidate, do not go out and spend your first paycheck. When you are told that you are being strongly considered, don't stop interviewing. When you are told that you are going to get an offer, don't shut down all your other job opportunities. Whatever you do, keep the process of finding a job in motion until you have actually accepted one and showed up for your first day of work.

It is not uncommon, at all, for hiring authorities to purposely not talk to their superiors about the kind of candidate who ought to be hired. The average interview process involves three to four members of the hiring company. One person, usually the one with the pain, will have the responsibility of defining the kind of person and experience that are needed. The other two or three people involved in the process are usually peers or supervisors of the hiring authority. The major flaw in this methodology is that the other interviewers do not have the benefit of interviewing all the candidates.

I have seen situations in which three or four candidates have been passed up the line of the interviewing process to three or four levels only to be ultimately eliminated because the different managers didn't know what the other levels were looking for! So expect confusion. Assumptions, innuendoes, and inconsistencies abound. Qualifications and the perceived ability to do the job are usually established by the person doing the initial interview. After that, it almost completely becomes a personality contest or beauty pageant.

Lack of Authority

The lack of authority combined with the burden of responsibility compounds the complicated hiring process. This is especially true for third-party screeners like the ones in human resources departments. Anyone who is involved in the hiring process and seems to be responsible for the evaluation of candidates, but does not actually have hiring authority, will complicate the hiring process. These people are usually placed into this situation to supposedly keep mistakes from being made. The major reason they are brought in is political: If a mistake is made in the hiring process, it will be more difficult to pinpoint the responsible party.

Politics of the Boardroom

We all know that politics plays a role in all business organizations. From the board of directors down to the cleaning crew, when people are involved, so is politics. Because hiring is a personal reflection of many people in the organization, the process itself is political. Candidates will often become pawns in the politics of a company. A candidate who is liked by one camp may be disliked by another camp, simply because of association and ego. This is a basic form of "If I win, you lose" thinking.

Individuals and groups within organizations often exert their one-upmanship games over job candidates. Job candidates are perceived as being expendable—and many organizations believe that there is an endless stream of candidates available at any time. Some individuals will eliminate a candidate just to snub another individual or group within the company. This allows them to flex their authority.

When you are involved in an interviewing process that has you interviewing with more than three people, you should understand that the process is going to be political—and much more than it needs to be. When four, five, six, or more interviewers are involved, the possibility for political activity increases even more dramatically.

In addition, if you have more than one interview with the same people, something political could be going on. While it may be reasonable for the same three or four people to interview you more than once, it could also point to some behind-the-scenes disagreement concerning you and other candidates. Again, there is nothing you can do in this kind of situation except to put yourself in the best light with each interviewer as many times as needed. Stay focused and positive. At least you are being interviewed. Be prepared.

Inflated Opinions

Companies looking to hire often contain people with overinflated opinions of themselves, their jobs, and their companies. There is a tendency for them to think they are the only ones on earth looking to hire. Companies will frequently string things out, by postponing decisions and conducting lengthy, drawn-out interviewing processes. This is because these companies are afraid of making the wrong decision and they suffer from the delusion that there are few candidates actually good enough to work for them.

Some organizations become so wrapped up in the process of interviewing that they forget the actual goal of needing to hire someone to perform the job. In an effort to hire the right person, companies will intentionally complicate the hiring process. So, when you are faced with having to interview with more than three people, trust me, it's "ka-ka."

The higher up you go in the interviewing chain, the more likely you are to encounter inflated opinions. The president of a $70 million to $80 million company who started the business from scratch has a tendency to think of his company as the only one in the world for which anybody would want to work.

Ignorance

When ignorance combines with fear, uncertainty, and doubt, you have a recipe for disaster. Ignorance means knowing that someone must be hired, but not knowing how to go about doing it. The people charged with hiring do not understand the process. It is scary and emotionally charged. They basically fumble around with the process because they are not professional "people hirers."

To make matters worse, they rarely admit their own ignorance and refuse to ask for advice, counseling, or guidance. Most hiring managers in 97 percent of U.S. businesses out there are operating without any real guidance when it comes to interviewing and hiring.

Changing Their Minds

This may come as a shock, but it's safe to say that about 30 percent of the time, when employers need to hire somebody, they wind up changing their minds about hiring anyone at all. They either postpone hiring or they reorganize the current organization so that the "pain" of needing to hire immediately goes away. Now, the pain of needing someone in the job never really goes away; but the fear and emotional strain that goes along with having to hire someone is either eliminated or postponed.

Don't be surprised if you get into the interviewing process—as many as two or three interviews deep—only to find out that the potential employer has decided not to hire anyone.

Situational Interviewing

Most interviewers and hiring authorities are inconsistent in the questions they ask. They rarely ask the same questions of different candidates for the same job.

I call it situational interviewing when the conversation goes off on tangents and misses some of the most pertinent aspects of the candidate's background, experience, or ability. The hiring authority wanders around, asking lots of different—and often unrelated—questions, and becomes immersed in the conversation rather than finding out useful, factual aspects of a candidate to be compared with other candidates.

Your Priority vs. Their Priority

Although finding a job is probably your highest priority, it is not the hiring authority's highest priority. You will be told that it is a high priority for the company. Don't believe it! It's ka-ka. Even if the need to hire is intense, it is rarely going to take precedence over staying in business, making a profit, and day-to-day operations: These priorities are much easier to manage, control, and—believe it or not—a lot less risky.

I have known many organizations that were going through the interviewing process just to convey to their employees that they were trying to provide extra help. In these cases, hiring isn't a priority at all. It's not even a real goal.

Hiring from Within

At least 10 percent to 15 percent of the time companies are going to hire from within. Hiring from within is just plain easier to do. The reasoning used by these companies is "the devil you know is better than the devil you don't know." There is a sense that they know what they are buying.

You might ask, "Why would an organization interview external candidates, if they are probably going to hire from within?" Well, the answer is pretty simple: Nobody wants to look bad. Hiring authorities want to appear as if they have surveyed the market, done their research, and covered all bases. Again, this is just politics. Accept that this will sometimes happen.

Internal candidates are always going to have an upper hand and a much higher probability of being hired. Most of the time, the internal candidate is not nearly as qualified as the external candidate. However, the probability of an internal candidate getting the job is five times as great. So, if you're up against an internal candidate, you have your work cut out for you.

Most organizations want to appear as though they are going to protect and promote their own. Few organizations will admit that their employees are not qualified to do a number of other jobs, including ones that become available. So it is mainly a political move from a company that wants to put forth the message that it supports its employees.

Secondly, some companies fear that if they do not interview and hire from within, people will leave. This fear is warranted. Evidence suggests that many employees who are turned down for positions within their company do, in fact, quit. A company would be better off stating at the outset that it is either hiring internally or externally—but not both. Companies would minimize casualties this way.

Just know that if you are competing against internal candidates, your chances of being hired diminish. Stay focused and be confident that you can still land the job.

Postponing a Decision

"If anything can go wrong, it will."
—Captain Edward Murphy, Air Force Captain, Optimist,
Creator of "Murphy's Law"

Most organizations take far too long in the hiring process. When the average hiring authority says it takes 35 to 40 days to hire someone, it actually takes 90 to 120 days! This comes as a surprise to most job hunters. Don't let it surprise you!

Business priorities get in the way, as does the fear of hiring the wrong person. In many cases, companies need to start the hiring process all over again. This can happen under the following conditions:

- There is a slight reorganization in a company.

- The criterion for the position changes as interviews are conducted.

- Shifts in the business model or business conditions occur.

- People change their concepts of what is needed.

- Customers or clients change.

- A chosen candidate ultimately turns down the job.

The more changes there are in the criteria of what companies look for in a candidate, the longer the process is going to take. For positions that range from $25,000 to $100,000 dollars, it takes an average of sixteen initial interviews and an average of one hundred days for each person who is hired. The hiring process drags on because all kinds of other necessary business issues get in the way.

Expect decisions to take twice as long as you are told. Stay in the game. Many of the successful job hunters I have seen got their jobs because they stayed in touch with the hiring authority much longer than expected—often returning several times to interview with the same or new people for the same position.

What This All Means to You

While I certainly do not want to discourage you about the way you're going to be treated as a candidate applying for a job, the truth is grim. You are going to be lied to, "storied" to, led along (and astray), unfairly encouraged, discouraged, ignored, and made to feel insignificant, as both a person and a professional, in about every way possible. You will be deflated, insulted, forgotten, hurt, pained, treated unfairly, cursed, and blessed in the same conversation; devastated; and put through the emotional wringer.

But keep in mind: *You can control the number of interviews you create for yourself. You can control your attitude.*

What This Meant to Jeff and Amy

Jeff and Amy said that they wished they had read this chapter before they started Jeff's job search. Like most people looking for a job, they had never thought about the fear that might be going on within the hiring authority. "It's just plain enlightening," said Amy. "We never saw the process of hiring from the other side."

Jeff and Amy found it truly revealing to recognize that a company's hiring process is every bit as emotionally stressful and difficult as what the individual goes through. Although it may not make the less-than-positive results easy to live with, it does help to understand the process as being simply human. Candidates have a tendency to think that because hiring authorities and their companies hold the cards when it comes to hiring, they know what they are doing. Here is the truth: They run their hiring just about the same way they run their companies—by the seat of their pants.

Many interviewers had told Jeff exactly what he wanted to hear, but these were non-truths or half-truths. At one point, Jeff was offered a job, but the company instituted a hiring freeze before he received his official offer letter. People focused on finding a job rarely consider the bureaucracy and confusion that go into hiring. My should-be-trademarked statement, "It ain't over till your butt's in the chair . . . and you have been there for a while," was reinforced by the events of Jeff's acceptance of his new job.

Amy suggested that everyone looking for a position cut out the following statement, taken from my words to them during our job-counseling sessions, and put it on the refrigerator as a daily reminder:

> The shock and awe at the way you will be treated is the first contribution to your disappointment and frustration in looking for a job. If you expect this kind of treatment and you don't take it personally— realizing that it isn't directed at you, but simply a result of "spiritual beings acting human"—it will make the experience easier to tolerate.

5　Breaking Down the Popular Delusions About Résumés and Cover Letters

As I mentioned earlier, 97 percent of the companies in the United States are not managed by even one individual who could be called a people person. These managers are not, for the most part, professional résumé readers. This statement may sound mundane and surprising, but the truth is that most hiring authorities really don't know what to look for in a résumé.

Your résumé needs to be addressed to hiring authorities that have "pain"— the actual current need to hire someone. You are trying to get your résumé read by hiring authorities who are accountants, controllers, sales managers, engineering managers, plant managers, officer administrators, and so forth.

Simplifying Your Message

I recommend that you keep the message of your résumé on a level that a high-school senior could understand. If your résumé is more sophisticated or esoteric, it is going to miss the mark. This does not suggest that you cannot explain complicated experiences in your résumé. But it is the difference, for example, between explaining the splitting of atoms to a high-school student or to a nuclear physicist. A high-school student may not know anything about the companies that you have worked for, or the kind of businesses that you have been in, or the kind of duties and responsibilities that you have had, but the message you communicate must be on a level that a high-school student can understand.

Most people write résumés that *they* understand. They describe events and experiences in ways that make sense to them, so what their résumé says is usually clear to them. Let me stress again that the hiring people at 97 percent

94

of the companies in the United States probably do not even know what they are looking for in a résumé. If they come across something they don't understand, the easiest thing for them to do is just discard the résumé.

I advise writing your résumé using the K.I.S.S. method: *Keep it simple, stupid!* Just as your telephone presentation must communicate features, advantages, and benefits, your résumé needs to do exactly the same thing. It is being read by people who want to know what this person can do for them.

Your résumé must reflect in quantifiable, real, specific terms what you have done before, who you have done it for, how long you did it, and how well you did it. And the communication of these factors must be so simple that anyone who is in a hurry; who is trying to run a business; who really doesn't want to read résumés; who is doing this because he or she has to; who sees it as an annoying means to an end; who is doing it "between" everything else, maybe over lunch or a coffee break, can understand it clearly. It is going to be a ten-to-fifteen-second scan by someone who is very busy and would much rather be doing something else.

Overrating the Value of a Résumé

The first big issue regarding résumés is that people have a tendency to think that there is some kind of magical tool that is going to get them a great job. A résumé never got anybody a job—and it never will. The idea that there is some secret science to it is simply untrue.

Another reason that people tend to overrate résumés is because people can control what they write in one. It is one of those activities that can be confused with productivity. I encounter people all the time who devote three or four days to writing a résumé. It may take five or six hours if a person starts from scratch, but beyond that, it is a waste of time. Because it is one of the things in a job search that an individual can control, people have a tendency to think that if they devote enough time to it they will get a better job.

If you are changing jobs or looking full-time for a new one, of course you need a well-written résumé. I will show you how to do that in this chapter. However, even a well-written résumé is simply just a résumé. Getting interviews and managing the process of interviews are one hundred times more important than having a good résumé. Most people looking for a job would be better off to devote half the time they normally do in writing a résumé and spend the other half of the time cold calling to get themselves into an interview.

A poignant example about how a résumé is overrated occurred with a phone call that I received from a man in Detroit after my second appearance on the *Dr. Phil* show. He called and asked me to review his résumé. He was convinced that a poor résumé and the fact that he was fifty-six years old was standing in the way of his getting a job. This fellow had been out of work for a year. He had been a programming manager in the advertising business for thirty years. He told me there were one hundred people for every advertising opportunity in Detroit. His inability to find a job had absolutely nothing to do with his résumé or, probably, his age. The problem was that there just wasn't a big need for his experience. His résumé had nothing to do with the simple supply and demand of his expertise. He was overrating the value of a résumé.

Key point: *The purpose of a résumé is to get you into the initial interview and to give the interviewing and hiring authorities an aid to help them decide in the interviewing process if you are a person they should hire.*

The average résumé is read for ten seconds. When you couple that with the fact that hiring authorities are literally receiving a hundred or more résumés for each opening they have, you might begin to appreciate what happens when they look at a résumé. Think about it— *ten seconds!* If your résumé cannot interest somebody in calling you in for an interview in ten seconds, all of your artful, miraculous, cosmic, inventive, or unique formatting or wording isn't going to matter.

So, what do most hiring authorities scan for initially in the ten seconds they look at a résumé? They want to know for whom you have worked, how long you were there, what position or positions you held, and your accomplishments and successes. Those four things are what everybody looks for. If the initial scan is palatable, the résumé gets read further—maybe even read two or three times. The initial scan deals with who, how long, and what.

Writing the Most Effective Résumé

The clear message of an effective résumé needs to be: "You need to interview (and subsequently hire) ME because this is what I have done in the past FOR OTHERS and therefore THIS IS WHAT I CAN DO FOR YOU!" Prospective employers don't care about what you think of the résumé and your track record. They care about what you can do for them.

The most effective résumé for finding a job is a simple straightforward chronological history of your employment.

Length

A résumé should never be more than two pages. A résumé that is more than two pages is simply not going to get read in any kind of detail. One-and-a-half pages are ideal; but if your experience is more than fifteen years, you might end up with a full two pages.

Name, Address, E-Mail Address, Telephone Numbers

Your name, address, e-mail address, and telephone numbers are the basic things that should appear on the top of a résumé in black, bold printing. Simple printing! No fancy script. Nothing cute. Just plain, black, simple, bold type.

Objective

I do not recommend writing an objective. The person scanning the résumé just wants to know where you've worked, how long you were there, and what you did. Prospective employers don't care about what *you* want, they only care about what *they* want.

About the only time I might recommend the use of an objective is if you are customizing your résumé for a specific job. If you know exactly the particular requirements of a particular position with a specific organization, you might be able to write the objective meaningful to the hiring authority.

Summary/Highlights of Qualifications

I do not recommend a summary of qualifications for the same reason that I don't recommend an objective. Any meaningful summary is either too general and broad to fit a specific need, or so specific that it would eliminate you for other possibilities.

Chronological Format

Always use a chronological format. Don't let any supposed authority convince you that you should use any kind of format other than chronological.

A functional format communicates that you are trying to cover up something—too many jobs, gaps in your work history, and so forth. As a result, a functional format communicates distrust and deception. When a hiring authority receives more than a hundred résumés, and is in the middle of reading them, as soon as he or she comes across a functional résumé, it gets pitched.

Accomplishment formats feature a list of supposedly impressive career achievements. This dog don't hunt either. This format is just as bad as the functional format. Without relating to exactly when, where, and with whom, these so-called impressive career achievements are meaningless. An accomplishment of being the "#1 salesperson in the U.S.A." probably won't get you an interview. Did that accomplishment happen last week or twenty years ago?

Dates

Starting with the most recent position, it is advisable to write the dates of employment clearly, both month and year. This should be done for every job that you have had for at least the past fifteen years. The dates, companies, and functions older than fifteen years can be consolidated.

If you were out of work for more than three or four months or in-between jobs more than twice, it is probably to your benefit to record the years rather than months. After all, the purpose of the résumé is to get you in front of a hiring authority. Just be aware that you might run the risk of not being interviewed by not reporting the months and years of your employment.

Names of Employers

You should state in black, bold letters the names of the companies that you currently work for or have worked for in the past. If a company is not well-known or easily recognized, state next to the name of the company what the organization does. Even if you work for a large, well-recognized organization, it's advisable to specifically name the division of the organization that you work for and what that division does. You need to be certain that the person reading the résumé clearly understands at a glance for whom you worked and what they do. Just because you know exactly whom you work for does not mean your reader will.

From time to time, I receive résumés where a candidate writes "confidential employer" in the place of the name of his or her current employer. Don't do this. Again, this comes across as having something to hide. You communicate that you are worried that your job search is going to be discovered. Well, any decent candidate is going to run this risk. The truth is that hardly anybody will interview a candidate who doesn't name the organization that they work for.

Titles

It is appropriate to list your job title after the name of the company where you work. If it is not clear in the job title what you do or did, or if the title is confusing, change it to something that is more accepted or consistent with what other people might recognize. If you have or had an oddball title that practically no one can recognize but you feel like that you have to use it, put in parentheses next to the title in bold black letters what a traditional title might be. For example, a title of "client advocate" might be the same as "customer service." You be the judge. But just remember that because you know what you did at a company and understand the function of your job doesn't mean that other people will.

Prior Experience

After the date and title of each job, describe in three or four sentences exactly what you did. Again, do this in terms that anybody who reads it can understand. Keep it on a high-school level of understanding. It may be appropriate to spend more space on your recent jobs, especially the one that might be most applicable to the position that you might be applying for. However, if you have been in your current position for only one year and spent fifteen years in your previous position, whoever hires you is going to be more interested in the previous fifteen years than the past year. Use good judgment; the longer you worked at an organization and the more recent the experience, the more you need to describe it.

Stories sell . . . numbers tell. Anything that can demonstrate statistical improvement in any aspect of the businesses you have been with show up well on a résumé.

Education

Some people leave education for the end of the résumé, while some put it at the beginning. Baccalaureate degrees and graduating with high honors from a prestigious school may be worth putting at the beginning. Advanced degrees from prestigious schools should probably be noted, as well. If you have graduate degrees such as a Ph.D., you may want to consider having one kind of résumé that includes this information and one without it. (I will address next how having two or three different résumés may be useful for different situations.)

A Ph.D., as well as other advanced degrees, can often communicate that a candidate is overqualified for a job within some businesses. So, I recommend that you have one type of résumé highlighting all the advanced degrees that you might have and another one that understates the education. A bachelor's degree and an MBA are reasonable to report. However, more advanced degrees scare some employers, because they think, "Why would someone with a Ph.D. want to work here?"

By the way, always include the dates that you received your degrees when you report them.

Personal Information

I do not recommend writing personals. The reasons are simple. Anything that you write about may work for you, but it also might work against you. Being married with three kids might sound great to you; but to a hiring authority who needs somebody to travel 70 percent of the time, that kind of personal information might keep you from being interviewed. Having a hobby of golf might communicate to a prospective employer that you're going to try to spend two days during the workweek playing golf. The point is that there's just no real good reason to write about personal things that may keep you from being interviewed or from getting the job.

Reasons for Leaving a Previous Job

Never write down why you left or why you are leaving an organization. You leave yourself open to too many reasons why you shouldn't be hired. I am not sure of the psychological reason for this, but when a prospective employer asks about why a candidate has left or is leaving his organization, a verbal explanation seems to satisfy the question. However, a written explanation never seems to work in favor of the candidate.

Hiring authorities are looking for just as many reasons *not to interview* as they are looking for reasons for why they should. So, it's in your best interest not to explain in your résumé why you are leaving or have left your present or past organizations.

Money

Don't ever put your past, present, or desired earnings on your résumé. You will eliminate yourself from too many opportunities.

Confidentiality

When you write a résumé, e-mail it or send it to at least one person and you run the risk of your job search being discovered. This issue has become more complicated over the past few years with the advent of the Internet and the posting of résumés on literally thousands of Internet sites. No matter how confidential you try to be, if you are looking for a job while you presently have one, you run the risk of being discovered.

If you are worried—and rightfully so—about the confidentiality of looking for a job, then you need to send your résumé to specific hiring authorities only after you have spoken to them on the telephone. Unless you are out of work or don't care if your present employer finds out that you're looking for a job, I would be careful about where you send the résumé. Writing the word *confidential* all over your résumé doesn't help.

References

In most traditional business environments, there is no need to include references in your résumé. With some academic curriculum vitas, political, or scientific and research-oriented résumés, it may be appropriate to provide a list of references. It is appropriate to just state, "References Upon Request." Besides, depending on the situation, you may want to give different references for different positions. There are exceptions to this guideline. If your references are high-profile people, they may be of value to put on your résumé. Frankly, most of us don't have those kinds of references, so leave references off your résumé.

All Galactic/All World

There is a tendency for people to confuse selling themselves in the same way that they would sell any other kind of consumer product. These people present themselves in what I call "all-galactic" fashion. It means that people are trying to present themselves as though they are and can be the "biggest bang for the buck." But, most of the time, candidates *overstate* how wonderful they are and actually ace themselves out of many good, solid opportunities.

If you are a vice president of finance for a multimillion-dollar Fortune 500 telecommunications firm and you are at laid off, it doesn't matter how "all world" you are. There are damn few positions out there for which you will be hired. It doesn't matter how wonderful your experience is, how much responsibility you had, how many millions of dollars you have managed, or how many hundreds of people you have supervised. You cannot do anything about the availability, or should I say, lack of availability for those kinds of jobs.

Creating Several Different Résumés

I would advise having several different résumés that you can use in different situations and for different opportunities. This is simple to do on a computer, which allows you to add or delete information in your résumé within just a few minutes, then save each version you create.

In fact, I recommend that you try to customize your résumé every time you send it. This is especially true when you might be sending a résumé in response to a particular need that a company might have. For instance, if you're an accountant and you are applying for a finance or accounting position with a business (where cost control might be an important aspect of the company's accounting function), you might emphasize cost control in your résumé. If you're the administrative support person and you are applying to an organization that has to meet tight schedules and deadlines, you can emphasize in some of the job descriptions your ability to deal with the pressures of deadlines.

I encourage you to send a résumé to a hiring authority *only after you have spoken to him or her on the telephone.* If indeed you accomplish this and you then e-mail or send a résumé, you will have found out specific information, or "hot buttons," that will be of interest to the hiring authority. You will then highlight those parts of your résumé that reflect those interests. You might need to put a different spin on your résumé before pursuing each specific opportunity.

The point is to think creatively and be prepared to target certain positions with the exact experience that might be requested.

Dumbing Down Your Résumé

This is a practice of positioning your résumé so that you can reasonably apply for opportunities that might be one or two levels below your current or most immediate past position. So, if you are a controller of a hundred-million-dollar company with a staff of five people, you may want have one résumé that reflects the full-blown, all-galactic aspects of your job where you describe every bit of leadership and accomplishment that you ever performed and another résumé that reflects your experience as simply an accountant or accounting manager. The latter might downplay the amount of your leadership experience and focus on the simple accounting, budgeting, and finance responsibilities that you had.

I have personally placed numerous vice presidents of sales, sales managers, directors of sales, and so forth over the years in individual contributor, regular sales jobs. Especially in a difficult market, the kind of management positions that most of these people were looking for just plain weren't available.

So, as you will see, I not only recommend having several different résumés for a number of different kinds of positions, I highly recommend that you have an all-galactic management résumé as well as a frontline, in-the-trenches, worker-bee résumé. Sometimes, the earnings associated with a first- or second-line position are not much less than those of higher-level managers. Only you can judge the viability of a particular salary or earnings relative to the job you have or, in some cases, the job you don't have. Most people would agree that being an employed accountant is better than being an unemployed controller who has been looking for a job for ten months.

Does Everybody Lie on Résumés?

Now we come to a sensitive part of writing a résumé. No one is ever going to admit to lying on a résumé. Yet a large number of studies show that people embellish or outright lie at least once every time they rewrite their résumé. Lies on a résumé can range anywhere from an embellishment of duties and responsibilities all the way through to factual issues such as job titles, length of time at a position, or degrees. The most common lie is to cover up jobs that a person might have had that they don't want to put on a résumé for whatever reason. These fabrications are the most difficult to detect or discover.

Now, as a good consultant, I must tell you that lying on your résumé isn't very smart. I have had people tell me that they lied on their résumé simply because everybody else does. And the truth is the majority of people probably do lie, everywhere from a lot to a little, every time they write a résumé. So, I can warn you all I want, but the idea of lying on your résumé is going to tempt you. If you decide to embellish or stretch the truth to the point that you are outright lying, you run a great risk being fired after you've been hired, if the lies are ultimately discovered. We preach this in our organization on a daily basis. In spite of all of the warnings that we give about lying on a résumé, we experience at least thirty-five to forty situations a year where a candidate is about to be hired and lies are discovered on his or her résumé.

You'd be shocked at the number of times lies on a résumé are discovered—either during the hiring process or later on. So, my duty is to tell you not to lie.

A Standard Résumé Example

This is a standard form of a chronological résumé. Read it, study it, see how it compares with your current résumé, and adapt it to your situation, if necessary.

YOUR NAME
Your Address
landline phone number   cell phone number   e-mail address

OBJECTIVE:
(Again, I recommend *not* including an objective on your résumé. You don't want your objective to discourage the reading of your résumé. If you have some reason for wanting to include it, use only general terms such as *sales, accounting, engineering, production, administrative,* and so forth.)

EXPERIENCE:
April, 1998–Present NAME OF COMPANY (Short explanation of what the company does or explanation of the division of a large company, so that anyone can clearly understand its function).

TITLE: (Make sure the title is commonly understood; if not, explain it in common terms.)

Write a specific, understandable explanation of your *duties* and *responsibilities*, as well as specific *accomplishments* that are highlighted. Write all the way from one margin to another so that you can get as much information on one page as possible. Write no more than a three- or four-sentence paragraph that a high-school senior could understand. Remember, the résumé is to communicate why you should be interviewed.

January 1992–April 1998 NAME OF COMPANY (Same as previous example)

TITLE: (Same as previous example. If your title is "odd," you may want to change it to make it resonate better; just be sure to explain to an interviewing or hiring authority what you have done during the interview.)

Again, explanations of duties and responsibilities need to be clear to anyone who would read them. Remember, that *numbers* and *statistics* get recognized and paid attention to. So if you can quantify what your successes and accomplishments have been with numbers or statistics, do so. Percentages of sales quotas, cost savings, size of a department, even amounts of budgetary responsibility are noticed. Highlight or bold any outstanding numbers that will set you apart from other candidates.

August 1985–January 1992 NAME OF COMPANY (same as previous example)

TITLE: (same as previous example)

The farther back you go in your job history, the less you have to explain about what you did and how you did it. Highlight the outstanding success or performance, but one or two lines of information will suffice. A hiring organization is most interested in what you have done in the past few years.

How to Handle Previous Experience: If your experience goes back more than fifteen years, you could summarize all of it in two or three sentences. You may want to highlight the names of the companies and the success you had with them, if it is appropriate to do so. For example, if you began your career with a prestigious organization that is noted for its training programs, such as IBM, Xerox, Procter and Gamble, or Perot Systems, you may want to feature that fact in this part of the résumé. Some people simply leave off their résumé anything before fifteen years of recent experience. Remember, the résumé is supposed to help sell you into an interview, not get you a job. Don't feel like you have to communicate your whole life story. On the other hand, don't leave out important facts that might help you get an interview.

EDUCATION: College or university, type of degree, beginning with the graduate degree first and year of graduation. If no degree was conferred, simply put the years of attendance. Any honors such as high grade point or scholarships should be noted. Any formal school less than college does not need to be reported. Any continuing education (such as certifications, sales courses, or negotiation courses) could be mentioned here (stay away from any personal growth programs that might be religious or political—mention nothing controversial).

Making Your Cover Letters Concise and Powerful

Cover letters are as overrated as résumés. A well-written cover letter needs to be short and to the point. If a résumé is read for only ten to fifteen seconds, a cover letter probably gets five to ten seconds, at best. My experience is that cover letters just don't get read unless they are brief and full of impact.

The purpose of a cover letter is to briefly introduce the highest points as to why you should be interviewed, as well as accentuate the facts in your résumé that might be most important to the prospective employer to whom you are sending it. If you have not spoken to the hiring authority, then you might highlight in boldface one-liners of two or three things that you believe would be most important to know about you, what you would want to know if you were in the hiring authority's shoes. It should read something like this:

Mr. or Ms. _____:
You should read my résumé and interview me because:

- **I have ten solid years of experience in your business.**

- **I have been a top performer.**

- **I give you dependability, leadership, passion, and commitment.**

Read my résumé and interview me this week.

Sincerely,
Candidate's Name

If you are e-mailing or sending a cover letter to someone you have previously spoken to—which is what I recommend—then your cover letter should mention your brief conversation and highlight the discussion points that you might have had with this person. A previous conversation before the receipt of your cover letter or résumé makes all the difference in the world as to whether or not your cover letter or a résumé is read. A cover letter in this situation would read:

Dear Mr. or Ms. _____ :

Our discussion today was brief but informative.

You stated that:

- **You *wanted* someone who had at least ten years of experience in your business—I have twelve!**

- **You *wanted* someone who was a top performer—I have been one for twelve years!**

- **You *wanted* someone with leadership skills, dependability, passion, and commitment—I have all of these!**

Read my résumé where I have highlighted my **experience, performance, leadership, dependability, passion, and commitment**. My résumé documents the proof of my attributes.

I will call you tomorrow about arranging a personal interview.

Sincerely,

Candidate's Name

Following up this type of cover letter and résumé with a phone call is more likely to secure the interview.

Learning When the Résumé and Cover Letter Work Best

This fact is so simple and yet rarely advised: a résumé and a cover letter are most effective when they are supported by *a previous telephone conversation* with the hiring authority. Your résumé is 85 percent more likely to be read if you have had a previous phone conversation with the prospective hiring authority. It is just like the warm call discussed in Chapter 3. A résumé associated with at least a voice has a better chance of being read.

Getting your résumé read is a function of the same threshold as getting an interview—the pain threshold. The greater the pain of needing a new employee, the more likely your phone call and résumé will get the appropriate attention.

The most effective way of using a résumé and a cover letter is:

- "Warm call" the prospective hiring manager and uncover pain or interest.

- E-mail your résumé and cover letter, highlighting hot buttons you heard in the conversation; be sure to use the exact words or phrases the hiring authority used.

- Follow up with a phone call confirming the hiring authority received the résumé and ask for a face-to-face interview.

Don't be surprised if you have to call several times. Most people have a tendency not to want to call at all, let alone call as many times as might be necessary. Well, being a pest is a lot better than being out of work and needing a job.

It is possible to secure an interview by sending a cover letter and résumé without the telephone calls. In a very narrow profession, where there are few people with the experience that you have and the kind of organization that you're going to distribute your résumés to receives so few of them that each one probably gets read, this whole process doesn't apply.

Picking out a group of companies to simply e-mail your résumé to, when you have no appreciable experience that would be of great value to them, is probably nothing but a waste of time. Now, picking up the telephone and selectively calling potential organizations and speaking directly to potential hiring authorities, and then e-mailing a résumé, will have a much greater statistical probability of getting you an interview. So, get on the phone and discover a potential employer's pain!

In the case where you know that a company has an opening for someone of your kind of experience, you'll follow a similar process. Don't just sent a résumé to the e-mail address for the response. Probably five thousand other people are doing exactly that. Pick up the phone and call the person who would be the logical hiring authority. Even if you have to leave several voice-mail messages for that person, this tactic is going to produce better results than simply e-mailing your résumé to the e-mail address posted on the advertisement.

As I mentioned in a previous chapter, one of the best ways to distribute your résumé is to go to an employer's office and physically deliver it as you request a face-to-face interview.

How This Strategy Affected Jeff and Amy

Jeff and Amy were already practicing the information in this chapter. Jeff's résumé was already excellent. Other than coming up with a version of the résumé that emphasized his accounting experience, as well as another one that emphasized his technology experience, there really wasn't much to be altered.

The problem that Jeff had in regard to his résumé was, like so many other people, he spent a great amount of time e-mailing it to all kinds of people and getting no response. Lack of response to his résumé had nothing to do with the quality of the résumé. It had to do with the lack of opportunities for people with his experience that existed out there. There was nothing he could do to control that situation. The issue wasn't the quality of the résumé, but finding an employer with pain.

6 : Common Myths and the Realities About Hiring

There are many myths about hiring that can lead job candidates off in the wrong direction. If you are prepared, your search will be easier. This chapter will discuss the myths and realities of the hiring process.

Myth #1: "Hiring authorities and companies really know what they're doing when it comes to hiring." A good part of this book addresses the fact that most hiring authorities, managers, and companies don't really know what they're doing when it comes to hiring. They have a vague idea of a process—some do it better than others, and some are even surprisingly successful. You should expect idiosyncrasies, inconsistencies, and relative chaos.

Myth #2: "Companies approach hiring with common sense, logic, and good business acumen and consistency." Consistency in hiring, even from day to day, is a myth. Don't expect common sense, logic, or consistency. There is nothing you can do about this reality, so you need to accept it and deal with it because that is the way it is. Common sense isn't very common.

Myth #3: "The human-resources department streamlines the hiring process." Most people running HR departments in U.S. businesses are not decision makers. They are record-keepers and their presence blossomed in the late 1960s when the push for Equal Employment Opportunity began. At that time, the function of the HR department was to keep track of interviewing and hiring and to be able to answer any governmental investigations about hiring practices. Over the years, human resources gained tremendous responsibility

110

and, since the department was keeping records about hiring, the initial functions of recruiting and hiring fell into HR's purview when hiring authorities were just too busy or too inept to do it themselves. Because the initial stages of interviewing and hiring are an interruption in the flow of everyday business, it was easy to rationalize someone else doing the activities.

The problem with an HR department initiating the hiring process is that its personnel don't normally know or understand the give-and-take of experience and background that a particular department might need. Most HR departments are not capable of assessing the total package of a less-than-perfect candidate. The bottom line is: *You do not want to seek a job through the efforts of a human resources person.*

I am not saying that no one ever gets hired through the HR department. It happens occasionally. I have known many wonderful people who work in HR departments. However, they are not hiring authorities.

Myth #4: "I can find a job on the Internet." In my humble opinion, posting your résumé on the Internet or chasing a job on the website of a company that posts on the Internet is mostly a boondoggle. Do the math. If the studies are correct, only 2 percent to 5 percent of the people pursuing a job on the Internet get interviews, so your odds are very poor. So don't be misguided into thinking that you can post your résumé on the hundreds of job boards that are out there and expect to get interviews or be hired. (I discussed posting your résumé in Chapter 3.)

Where the Internet can help you is by giving you a lot of information about companies that you might approach. The Internet can give you wonderful background information about companies, their competitors, their industry, their growth or lack of it, and so forth. It can help you find the names and telephone numbers of hiring authorities in those organizations. Then, armed with that information, you can pick up the phone and call them. Use the script I've given you earlier in this book.

Now, if you are in a profession that is in high demand, like the medical profession, healthcare, or certain types of narrow, niche professions, just posting your résumé on any one of a number of professional job boards will get you lots of activity. But unless you are in one of those very rare professions, the probability of you finding a job on the Internet isn't good.

Myth #5: "There is a time formula for finding a job." For years there used to be all kinds of time formulas predicting how long it would take a candidate to find a job based on the amount of money he or she made. Whoever came up with this idea wasn't living in the real world. How long it takes to find a job depends on what you do and the market for it. Duh! If you did software maintenance and made $90,000 in 2000 and your job got shipped off to India, you're probably still looking for a job and delivering pizza at night. There is absolutely no way of anybody being able to predict how long it's going to take anyone to find a job.

Myth #6: "You can find your dream job." There have been more than twenty-five books written, nine that I have read, that address how to find your dream job. I cannot tell you the countless number of candidates I have interviewed over the years who have read books about finding their dream jobs. These candidates honestly, seriously thought that just because they described their perfect job, it exists and—what's more—they were going to get it. For any job, your probability of getting it depends on your ability to perform. My dream job is to play basketball for the Dallas Mavericks. I know that I am fifty-seven years old, 5 feet 11 inches tall, and flat-footed, and can't dribble with my left hand; but, by God, that's my dream job, and I want it!

Just because someone dreams about being in a particular type of position doesn't mean it will automatically happen. Now, if people are in the economic position where they don't have to work to feed their family, pay a mortgage, or pay a car note, and they wish to pursue their dream of being an actor, stunt pilot, writer, musician, or whatever, that's okay, I guess.

So, if your dream job has nothing to do with your ability, experience, or aptitude, you aren't going to get it. If your ability is commensurate with your dream, like, say a basketball wunderkind like LeBron James, then dream on and don't stop. I assure you that if LeBron James changed his dream to be the CFO of J.P. Morgan Chase next year, he'd have the same luck I would playing for the Mavericks.

Myth #7: "I've paid my dues, so now someone will pay me what I'm really worth." This idea ranks close to the top of egocentric self-centeredness. It usually comes from people who are told they are underpaid and underappreciated by everyone except the people who really matter—their present employer.

Employers are going to hire you based on what *they* need, not what *you* need. Other people care only about what you want to the extent that they get what they want. What you deserve and the dues you've paid couldn't be farther from their mind.

Myth #8: "Since I'm looking for a job anyway, this is probably a good time to change careers." In this scenario, a candidate has usually been in a particular type of business or a profession for a number of years. For one reason or another, this person thinks it is possible to change careers and somebody is going to pay him or her on the same level of his or her previous or current employment.

Well, some people might be able to change careers, but they have to start all over learning a new career in the same way they learned the current one. And that is assuming that their ability to perform in a new career will be equal to their ability to perform in the old career. It doesn't always follow. Just be aware that if you change careers, you are likely to start taking a very significant—if not huge—setback in earnings and start your business life all over.

Myth #9: "If I change jobs, I need to make more money." Well, depending on the economy and the market for your particular skills, this may or may not be realistic. If you are out of work in a tough economy, finding any job at all, regardless of the pay, may be a necessity. But it is a bit misguided to insist that in changing jobs you will always get more money.

Myth #10: "An MBA or graduate degree makes me a better candidate." It is a myth that an MBA or any other kind of a graduate degree, in the business setting, will automatically get you a better position or more money. This may be true in academic circles or pure scientific organizations where a Ph.D. can get you a promotion. In the majority of businesses in the United States, however, having an MBA or graduate degree doesn't get you a better job or more money.

In thirty-one years of doing this line of work, I have never seen a candidate hired just because he or she had an MBA or any other graduate degree. Now, I have seen situations where an MBA was preferred and since the employer suggested the advanced degree as a criterion, the company limited itself to interviewing candidates with an MBA. However, the MBA was not the reason that the successful candidate was hired.

Universities sell the idea that an MBA is going to make you a better businessperson. Universities love MBA programs because these programs are cheaper to run than any other kind of graduate program. The ratio of student to professor is extremely high so these kinds of graduate programs pay for the scientific and technical graduate programs where the student/professor ratio is very low. MBA programs help universities pay for all of the graduate programs that do not make money.

The truth is that people who get graduate degrees are also people who are diligent about many other things, including their jobs and their careers. These kinds of people would get ahead anyhow, with or without the graduate degree. People with MBAs make more money than employees who don't have one. But it's not *because* of the MBA. They are the kind of people who want to do better, and, since America seems to promote the idea that more education is better, these people get MBAs. They would wind up being successful anyhow, with or without the MBA.

Myth #11: "The most qualified candidate gets the job." The candidates who get the jobs are the candidates who sell themselves the best in the interviewing process. More often than not, the most qualified candidates are not hired unless they sell themselves better to the hiring organization.

I cannot overemphasize that qualifications are the 10 percent to 20 percent threshold that needs to be crossed over to get the interviewing opportunity. But 80 percent to 90 percent of getting a job comes down to the people who are not only reasonably qualified but who sells themselves the best in the interviewing process.

Myth #12: "I know I'm good; just get me in front of them." This is the egotistical approach to interviewing. These candidates usually assess their success and ability based on the job they are in currently or the one they had been in most recently. Unfortunately, this kind of attitude does not take into account the competition candidates are going to encounter in the interviewing process. Candidates with this arrogant attitude have no idea how difficult the interviewing process is going to be. They may well be in for a rude surprise.

Myth #13: "Interviewing and hiring is a two-way street." The idea that interviewing is an equal give-and-take on the part of the candidate and the employer is simply not true. The interviewing process is a one-way street, at least for most of the process, and that one-way street belongs to the hiring authority. The reason is simple: In most interviewing situations, the employer has several qualified candidates who are available to do the job. The objective is for the candidate to sell himself or herself as hard as possible to the offer. The candidate can then qualify the opportunity. Then, and only then, does the interviewing process become a two-way street.

Myth #14: "Offshoring and outsourcing are killing jobs in America." This is not a myth but a very misguided statement. Every fifteen years or so, we hear that America is going to be devastated by outsourcing jobs to companies that use cheap foreign labor or by offshoring, which is when domestic companies establish divisions in another country to take advantage of the same cheap labor. While it is true some people lose their jobs to cheaper foreign labor, the predicted impact has never been as devastating as feared.

Today, especially in the technology sectors of business, the fear of U.S. jobs being lost to India, Russia, or Brazil runs rampant. However, outsourcing has always been with us. It is part of American free enterprise. The manufacturing and call center jobs that were moved in the late 1960s and early 1970s from major metropolitan cities to many rural cities in the United States, where labor was cheaper, are now being sent to foreign countries.

A cheap labor market will attract a lot of demand. When the demand for that cheap labor market increases, wages go up here in America or anywhere in the world. Eventually the cost advantage of so-called cheap labor is no longer cheap, so the jobs either come back to the United States or move to another part of the world. Then the cycle repeats itself.

One of the reasons that offshoring and outsourcing are currently such a large issue is that because of technology the practice can take place in more countries faster than we ever dreamed. Therefore, it affects more people than ever before.

America taught the world free enterprise, ingenuity, hard work, and innovation—and now these principles are being used to compete with the United States. We have a choice. We can curse the darkness that we perceive the world to be doing to us by using the principles we taught them or we can take those same principles of free enterprise, ingenuity, hard work, and innovation and use them to compete with the rest of the world. In order to compete though, we have to be better and work harder.

Myth #15: "If you're really good, people will want to hire you and you will always have a job." Try selling this myth to most of the IT, telecommunications, electronics, and manufacturing people who have been either laid off or downsized in recent years. Some of these people have been looking for jobs for two or three years. They're really, really good people. There is just no market for their skills.

Myth #16: "I want to find the last job or company for the rest of my career so I'll never have to change jobs again." Unless you are sixty-two years old and plan to retire at sixty-five, this concept is really misguided and borders on mythical. The average job is going to last from two to three years—either within the same company or at a new one. Now, you may beat the averages; and the opportunity that you find may last for the rest of your working career. Probabilities of this scenario are not very great. So, you need to be prepared to change jobs every two to three years. You may not like it, but that is reality.

Myth #17: "I know the market for my skills." This statement is usually followed by one that states that since the candidate keeps up on his or her industry or profession by reading and keeping in contact with people in the same profession, he or she knows exactly what the market will bear in looking for a new opportunity. This is a misguided concept.

There is a large difference between knowing a general, broad, overall market and actually finding a specific job opportunity that might be of value to both parties. Since people don't look for jobs that often, they really don't know what the market for their skills is.

Myth #18: "Networking is the only way to go." Concentrating on any single method of finding a job is misguided. Most people begin looking for a job in several different ways. They will start out doing networking, contacting recruiters, talking to previous employers and subordinates, and so forth. By the fourth week, however, most of these people will focus only on one or two means to get interviews. This is a big mistake. The key is to work as many different angles as possible to get interviews.

Myth #19: "Being employed while looking for a job gives a person leverage." This is definitely another misguided concept. Trying to find a job while you have one does not give you any kind of advantage at all. Most hiring authorities have pain, and, therefore, they really don't care whether the person who can alleviate their pain is currently employed or not.

If you are currently employed and don't have to change jobs that badly, it may be less risky to negotiate and run the risk of being refused because of demands that you might make. It is comforting when you have a job—even one that you may not like—to know that you aren't desperate and have to take a job just because it's offered.

A hiring authority with pain needs that pain alleviated by the best-qualified candidate he or she can find. Unemployed candidates feel that they are at a distinct disadvantage in the hiring process because they do not currently have a job; but it is more of a psychological and emotional inferiority complex than reality.

Myth #20: "I'll 'stick my toe in the water' and casually look for a job, just to see what's out there." I have known candidates who approach finding a job this way for years and they've never found one. They are still at the same job they've had since they started "looking" for a job. There can be nothing casual about looking for a job. You're competing with people who are not casual about looking for a job. You are going to lose out to someone who really wants to go work—and acts like it.

Myth #21: "If I'm recruited, they have to sell me. After all, I'm not looking for a job." It is true that if you are happily employed and an organization—either through a recruiter or on its own—approaches you about changing jobs and joining the company, you have somewhat of an advantage. Just be aware that once you get into the interviewing process, you have to sell yourself just as though you were going after the job on your own.

Myth #22: "When companies 'stroke' you, they're signaling that you've got the job." "You're by far the best candidate we've seen. . . . We'd love to hire you. . . .

We'd love to have people like you in our organization. . . . You're exactly what we want." These are some of the most misleading statements that you will encounter in the job-finding process. They can also be the most emotionally debilitating, especially when an offer does not formally materialize. Even the statement, "You've got the job," means nothing, unless it is accompanied by an actual job offer. I have known hiring authorities who told three or four candidates simultaneously that they would like to hire them for the same position, and then never hired anyone.

Myth #23: "Big companies have more security; I can be more effective in a smaller firm." Both of these statements are myths. There is no more stability in large organizations then there is in small ones. The average job is going to last two to three years, whether you are with a big company or a small company. It really doesn't matter.

The only difference between a big company and a small company is that people have a tendency to have more understanding when they lose a job at a big company. I've never figured this out. When a big company lets a person go, it is called a layoff. When a small company lets someone go, there is a tendency to think, "The SOBs fired me!"

Myth #24: "It's not what you know, but whom you know." It is true that the more people you know, the more opportunities for interviews you may get. It is true that the more people like you, the more opportunities you might have for going to work. However, who you know can often backfire on a qualified candidate. I cannot tell you the number of qualified candidates I have seen not get hired because of familiarity.

This is a difficult concept to communicate and even a little harder to accept. What it comes down to is that your friends, or people who you think are your friends, don't really want to hire people who know them. When people get to know people, they get to know their strengths *and* their weaknesses, the positives and negatives about their personality. Often people who you know fairly well really don't want you around in their organization because you know *their* positives and negatives, too. The old adage of "familiarity breeds contempt" comes to mind. Don't trust people you know to help you any more than people you don't know.

Myth #25: "I asked around and got great advice from _____ about the kind of job I should take." You fill in the blank! I love it when candidates talk to (two or three or five or fifteen or twenty people) who have changed jobs in the recent past and gave them advice.

Unless these people have a "skin in the game," take all of the so-called advice they give you with a big chunk of salt. Unless someone is willing to offer you a job, most of the opinions that you will get from people are just that—opinions.

Myth #26: "I changed jobs a few years ago, so I know what I'm doing." Job markets change. Just ask Jeff Mills. Like many other people who changed jobs in the recent past, Jeff thought that finding a new job was going to be much easier than it turned out to be. It was two years before he found a job this time. Now, the skills necessary to find a job were no different than they were a few years ago. But the market itself had changed.

Myth #27: "Finding a good job is more luck than anything else." Many people think that finding a good job is more luck than anything else. Luck is *preparation meeting opportunity!* The harder you work, the luckier you get.

If selling yourself into lots of interviews, knowing what to say when you get there, and getting a good job because of it is luck, then I guess some people are just lucky. This is a numbers game. Babe Ruth hit a lot of home runs, but he also struck out a lot. Was he any more lucky when he struck out as when he hit the ball? Hard work creates a lot of luck.

Myth #28: "I'm too shy to thrust myself at a prospective employer." Well, I really understand. Many people are just not good at pushing themselves onto other people. I read one book that stated the alternative to thrusting yourself at a prospective employer was to use the Internet. You may be more emotionally comfortable hitting that SEND button; but it isn't going to get you a job.

If you practice all the scripts that I recommend, you will become confident in your ability to secure and perform well on an interview. You can overcome your shyness with practice. I didn't say it would be easy; but it is necessary.

Myth #29: "I don't want a job like the last one; I really got burned." This misguided concept is a result of people running away from what last hurt them.

There is a tendency to globally generalize those companies or people with whom you have worked in the past when it didn't work out. Just because one business or one organization burned you, it doesn't mean another one will. People always have a tendency to be most sensitive to their last bad experience. It doesn't always follow that just because you work at one organization that was poorly run, everyone else in that profession or industry is of the same ilk.

How Jeff and Amy Were Affected

Jeff and Amy were realistic about most of the things that they did after not finding a job for six or seven months. They just didn't know what to expect. Jeff became anxious and hopeful every time he had in interview, only to become disappointed by most of them. "We expected common sense, logic, and consistency," lamented Amy, "and we hardly got any of it." Jeff became tremendously burned out after sending hundreds of résumés over the Internet and never getting anything for his efforts. "We did all the right things and it just didn't seem fair," said Amy.

In the final analysis, it was networking that got Jeff the job he has now. As I stated, there are many, many ways that everyone needs to explore to get a job. The point is that you have to be realistic about every activity you engage in to find a job, taking every action you can. Explore every possibility with tempered expectations.

7 · The Benefits of Practical Spirituality

"What lies behind us and lies before us are tiny matters compared to what lies within us."
—OLIVER WENDELL HOLMS, PHYSICIAN, POET, HUMORIST

Practical spirituality is a way of feeding the spiritual side of your being so that it can reinforce and support your physical, mental, and emotional side during the trying time of changing jobs.

I have seen job candidates in all kinds of difficult situations: being fired, being laid off, suffering bankruptcies, battling illnesses, and in some cases, facing extremely drastic circumstances. Yet some of these people dealt with everything in ways that actually helped them find a better job faster and more easily than some of the other candidates whose experience, background, and track record were just as good, if not better. I found that these particular kinds of candidates were doing certain things either as a practice before they had had to look for a job or started doing these things after they started looking for a job, and these practices were making the process easier for them.

Some of these candidates prayed a lot; some of them read spiritual books; some practiced meditation. Some of these people volunteered their time to charity while others became involved with charitable organizations. Some mentioned that they just simplified their lives. The more I started noticing what these people were doing, the more I began to see that these activities they were involved in were actually helping them find better jobs—faster than most candidates who weren't doing these things. So, I started asking candidates what they were doing, especially when I found them to be dealing reasonably well with the trials and tribulations of finding a job.

Why These Things Work

I must admit that I am not really sure why these kinds of things—what I call *practical spirituality*—work. I can't give you any scientific proof, but I absolutely stake everything I own that it does. It could be the Buddhist Law of Karma, which states that "for every event there follows another event whose existence was caused by the first and the second event will be pleasant or unpleasant according as its cause was skillful or unskillful." It could be a Christian philosophy of "seek and ye shall find." Or the quantum theory that relates to the spirit, "everything affects everything else." It could be the humanistic approach of treating others the way you would want to be treated. It could be the Zen teaching that there is a time and a place for everything and that things always work out just as they should. It could have to do with the theory of flow as we see in the Eastern arts of feng shui, tai chi, qigong, and many other practices.

We all know that there is a mind/body connection. We have all had a so-called sixth sense about things. There have been double-blind prayer studies where people who don't even know they're being prayed for recover from illnesses faster than those who were not prayed for. Psychic phenomenon, remote viewing, premonitions, hunches, and the like are all part of the mind, body, and spiritual connection. We all know that stress affects the immune system. Is not stress simply an idea that is turned into an emotional reality that is turned into a physical effect? Studies in biofeedback strongly suggest that when we become aware of our physical conditions we can affect them through mental exercises.

So What?

So, now you ask, "Tony, what the hell difference does this make in my search for a job?" Well, if you are aware of the spiritual facet of life, it's going to make your job-seeking strategy much easier. Conversely, there is a dark side to all of us. When we are faced with the stress and strain of physical or emotional challenges, like finding a job, our dark side can override our normal nature. For most of us, that dark side may cause us to be self-centered. Combine emotional strain with self-centeredness, fear, and rejection and we have volatility. We can have a tendency to be negative and express our unhappiness to just about anyone who will listen. On top of that, if fear overcomes us we can even become hostile, if not overtly, in subtle passive-aggressive ways. This is definitely *not* the state that you want to be in when looking to change jobs.

You must avoid this state at all costs (if you're already there, you need to shake yourself out of it) because it will negatively affect every aspect of your job search. Be aware that in order to:

- Get people to give you the benefit of the doubt, you must give them the benefit of the doubt

- Get people to listen to you, you must listen to them

- Get people to understand you, you must understand them

- Get people to appreciate you, you must appreciate them

- Get people to have empathy for you, you must have empathy for them

- Get people to give you a chance, you must give them a chance

- Get people to give you a job, you must convince them of what you can do for them

In other words, you have to get out of your self-centered, emotionally painful state and focus on what you can do for others.

What to Do

I know of many things that people have done while looking for a job that have reinforced the spiritual side of their being and literally helped them find a job with less emotional stress. People can do all kinds of additional things, but here are some very important ones:

Be Grateful

I mentioned in an earlier chapter about waking up every morning with an attitude of gratitude. I know you say, "But, Tony, you don't know the troubles

I've got." You're right! I don't! However, just as Norman Vincent Peale stated, "The only people that don't have problems are dead." Just try it! It works! Even if you have to convince yourself over and over to be grateful—do it!

Be Nice

Sometimes it is really difficult to be nice to people, especially when you are in a stressful situation. But even when you are emotionally hurting, it helps to go out of your way to be really nice to people when you don't necessarily feel nice.

When I started in this business in 1973, we had an office in the tallest building in Fort Worth, Texas. Back then, the elevators had operators. These people actually operated the elevator and worked the mechanisms to get it from floor to floor. At that time there were four or five employment agencies, including ours, in that building. I can still hear the lady who founded this company in 1952, Mildred Babich, telling us to be really nice to the elevator operators because when people came into the building and wanted to go to "the employment agency," the operators would bring them to our floor and our offices.

I have known hundreds of employers over the years who purposely kept candidates waiting in their reception area just to see if they were going to be nice to the administrative personnel. I can't tell you the number of candidates over the years who were not hired because they were rude to the support people in the organization where they were interviewing. So, it may not necessarily be your nature to be an outgoing, nice person, but do it anyway.

Create Flow

Get rid of the clutter in your house, your garage, your office, your car—in any space that you occupy. Get rid of all those old clothes in your closet that you hope to fit into one day. If you haven't used it or worn it in the last year, give it away. You'll find that the seemingly symbolic act of uncluttering your various spaces actually unclutters your mind, creating flow and energy that will help you in your job search.

Practice Forgiveness

There are few things that are as spiritually uplifting as forgiving. First, forgive yourself for all the stupid things you have done to yourself and others.

Contemplate the lessons you learned. Make a list of all the people you can remember whom you may have transgressed. Even if the transgression was an accident, call, write, or e-mail those people and ask them for forgiveness.

At the same time, make a list of all the people who may have committed transgressions against you. Call, write, or e-mail these people and forgive them. Don't expect a return call or letter or e-mail. That's not the point. Your spiritual growth depends on your ability to forgive others and seek forgiveness.

Start a Prayer or Intentions List

As you can probably tell, I am a real big fan of praying. But on this particular issue of having a prayer or intentions list, you don't have to believe in prayer to make it work. The purpose is for you to pass along positive intentions to specific people. It is a form of giving. After all, you are a person who wants to receive; so, in order to receive, you're going have to give and this is one of the ways of doing it. It is great to begin this list with people whom you care for, maybe close members of your family or friends. However, it is also of great value to pray for or pass along good intentions to people you don't know.

One thing about prayer as regards your job search that I have found to be essential and most successful is to pray, not so much for an *outcome*, as to pray for guidance in the *process*. Praying specifically for a good job or a certain job doesn't seem to be as effective as praying for spiritual guidance and help in the process of finding a job.

Volunteer

This is a tremendous way to get out of yourself and really help other people. Now, I'm not recommending that you volunteer during the time that you should be interviewing. However, there are plenty of opportunities in the evening or on weekends to volunteer. There are hundreds of volunteer organizations that go out and help people who really need to be helped. This is a form of giving and asking nothing in return: serve food at the soup kitchens, build homes for Habitat for Humanity, visit senior citizens in nursing homes, children in hospitals, and so forth.

If you're not a "joiner," or can't fit volunteering into your schedule, you can organize by yourself to do things like pick up trash on the street, clean up your alley, or mow and trim the lawn of an elderly person in your neighborhood.

Seek Peace

Your life is going to be stressful enough with just looking for a job. I would recommend staying away from newspapers (other than to look at the classified ads), negative people, violent movies, television, and other emotionally draining activities. While I recommend seeking solitude and quiet, especially in the morning, finding moments of peace throughout the day, however brief they may be, doesn't hurt, either.

Let Go

You remember all that stuff you cleaned out, like your trash, attic, closet, office, or car? Well, give it all away. In fact, anything you can give away to someone who probably needs it more than you is a way to build spiritual credit. Learning to give anonymously is truly a great experience. The feel-good you get in giving even a modest gift, without anyone knowing who you are, is tremendously gratifying. I, personally, have $5 gift certificates to one of the fast-food chains in the console of my car. When a street person at an intersection asks me for a handout when I'm stopped at a light, I give the person a $5 gift certificate. It is a really good feeling and it only costs $5.

Release Resistance

This is another form of letting go. It has to do with the fact that emotionally, when we resist any particular feeling, that feeling or idea persists over and over and over. This happens in the job-seeking process, for example, when a person doesn't get a job offer he or she was expecting, or an interview went very poorly, and the person dwells on his or her perceived failure for a long period of time. What we resist persists. The longer we dwell and mull over these negative experiences or feelings and the more we consciously try to resist them, the more they own us. So, the sooner you can release your resistance to any negative event or feeling, the better off you are.

Practice Acceptance

This is the practice of accepting things just as they are. It is the ability to accept even what we don't like just for what it is. It is like being stuck in terrible traffic and talking aloud to yourself about how wonderful it is to be there. "What great traffic this is," you tell yourself. "I haven't seen a wonderful traffic jam like this in years." You will absolutely be amazed at how effective it is.

Laugh a Lot

Read jokes. Watch funny movies. Old family videos or pictures are great for that. If you have kids, get them to tell you jokes every day. A child's laughter is one of the most infectious events there is. Call a friend or relative whom you find particularly funny and just shoot the breeze for a while, allowing the laughs to flow. Studies show that laughter decreases the body's stress chemicals.

Practice Empathy

Ask yourself often, "How does that person see or feel about the world?" We become concerned about ourselves when we look for a job, and rightfully so. It sure helps to put yourself in the mind set of other people. How does that street person or waiter or police officer or soldier see and feel about their life? This is great practice for interviewing.

Sacrifice

The word *sacrifice* comes from the Latin word that means "to make holy." Pass up the ice cream cone or the dessert you love once a week or so. Make a visit to your church, synagogue, or mosque when you don't "have to." Fast one day a week (*not* before an interview). Try consuming only water for that day. You'll be amazed at how good this feels. (Besides, your waistline can tolerate it.) Abstain from meat, sweets, soda, anything like that, for one day a week. Give such things up for the intention of finding a great job.

Other Ways of Feeding the Spirit

Donate blood. Let someone cut ahead of you in line. Be kind to the next person who is unkind to you. Don't criticize anyone for twenty-four hours. When you are upset about something, ask yourself, "What difference will it make ten years from now?" Write or call a friend whom you haven't talked to in a long time. Watch the children play and try to remember what it felt like. Write three sentences that you would like people to say about you at your funeral. Exercise. Write down a paragraph about how you feel about money. Practice awareness. Be quiet for three hours at a time. Pay attention to your attitude. Rediscover rituals in the family. Stargaze on a clear night. Put your closet and garage in order. Slow down and rest. Learn a form of meditation.

The Final Message

There are thousands of books, articles, CDs, audiotapes, and videos that can help all of us to become more spiritual. After all, this stuff has been around since the beginning of history. It can make all the difference in the world. If our spirituality doesn't have an impact on all that we do, it's just theory. In spite of the fact that looking for a job is an emotionally stressful thing, feeding the spiritual side of your being, in the process, can make it a truly positive experience.

Jeff and Amy's Reflections

Throughout his whole ordeal, Jeff felt that he needed to feed his spirit. Jeff had to deal with anger and frustration on a daily basis. His dark side emerged as a mild form of introversion and a feeling of being really down—not quite depression but close to it. Other than Amy, Jeff did not have much of a support system.

Jeff and Amy already believed in the power of prayer. Both of them knew they needed to practice an attitude of gratitude daily. Amy stated, "Even when we did the right things . . . I mean, all the *right things*, Jeff was still out of work; and even though we knew we should be grateful, it was very hard." This is a very interesting point, because it relates to the fact that we all know what we should do to become more spiritual, but it's hard.

Amy mentioned that when they sold nearly all of what they owned in Colorado, they experienced a great deal of relief and flow by getting rid of stuff. They created flow out of necessity; but at the time realized that owning a bunch of stuff was burdensome.

The forgiveness recommendation was especially poignant to Jeff. Jeff's mother and father divorced when he was nine years old. Jeff never felt that he had learned about his father and was never around him very much. Nine or ten months after they had moved from Austin, Jeff's father came to visit for three days. Amy took the kids away during the visit so Jeff and his father could get to know each other again. Jeff's father admitted many of his mistakes and both of them asked for and gave forgiveness.

Jeff and Amy also received counseling through the efforts of Dr. Phil McGraw and his staff. Jeff's initial response was, "How was counseling going to help me find a job and get my life back on track?" Jeff couldn't have been more pleased with the results.

An interesting sidebar to this idea of being on the *Dr. Phil* show is Phil McGraw and his organization's willingness to help Jeff and Amy with counseling. The fact is that Dr. Phil has a whole network of organizations willing to help people beyond what you see on his show. This is a tremendous spiritual endeavor. Dr. Phil and his organization went the extra mile in helping these people and received nothing tangible in return. That is the essence of practical spirituality. Can you imagine the tremendous spiritual return that Dr. Phil and his organization receive?

8 Mastering the Dreaded Telephone Interview

More often than in earlier years, our clients are now asking to interview our candidates over the telephone. Even local organizations will often insist on talking to, screening, or interviewing candidates over the phone first, before they consider talking to candidates face-to-face. With so many candidates to choose from, the telephone interview is a great way to not to have to interview a large number of people. It has now become a de facto terminator of prospective candidates.

Usually, the telephone screener is not the hiring manager. This situation makes the situation even worse. The caller's objective is to pare a large number of probable candidates down to two or three. The screener's job is to *eliminate* candidates. Now, screeners will tell you that their mission is to discover the best candidates; but it becomes more like musical chairs. There is a random stopping point for deciding who "wins" the face-to-face interview. I recently placed a candidate with a company who had been eliminated twice before by two different telephone interviewers from the same company. I got him the interview because he was a good fit and he was eventually hired.

> Some people think that because they have a cell phone, they don't need a land-line phone or an answering system on it. *Wrong!* If you are one of those people, get your landline back, at least until you find a job. Cell phones get lost, sometimes don't work, get poor reception, and so forth. We had a very hard-to-place candidate leave his cell phone in a cab in New York City before he came back to Dallas. It was his only phone. We called him with two interviews, over three days. We couldn't find him. He missed the interviews. He was not only without a phone for some time but also without a job.
>
> When there are so many candidates to choose from, employers will eliminate people for all kinds of insignificant reasons. Not being able to reach someone is not insignificant; but if someone leaves a message for you and doesn't hear back fairly quickly, the person moves on to the next candidate—and you lose.

The skills in getting beyond the telephone screen are different from those used in a personal, face-to-face interview. Here are a few tips we have found that can make a telephone interview successful:

What to Do

If you get a call from a prospective employer from a résumé you sent and you are not prepared or ready for the call, take down the person's number and say you will call back at a designated time. If you've had no previous contact with the organization and you are caught cold, you should take some time to do a quick bit of research on the company and prepare yourself for the interview. Don't feel like you need to talk to somebody just because he or she called you. If you don't know whom you were talking to and what the person is calling you about, I guarantee you won't get to the next step in the interviewing process.

DO remind yourself that this is not a real interview. It is a *screen* and usually the objective for the screener is to *screen out* candidates. It is strictly a "voice" conversation. It does not, as in a face-to-face interview, take into account the candidate's image, body language, and visual communications. Overall, this is an even more difficult situation than a face-to-face interview.

DO sell yourself hard. Since there is more of a tendency for the employer to screen out than to screen in, you must sell yourself a little harder. Remember, the objective of a telephone interview (from your point of view) is to get the face-to-face interview.

DO know beforehand exactly what the criterion for hiring is. Rehearse addressing those needs. If you are being screened by a third-party person who does not have a feel for what the give-and-take might be in a position, the interview is harder to do. This person does not have the personal "pain" of needing someone, so he or she will be more rigid about what is wanted.

DO keep your comments concise and to the point. The more talking on the phone that you do, the more likely you will be screened out. And that is the last thing you want. So, say what you have to but stay focused on getting the personal interview.

DO be fully prepared for the phone screen. Have your résumé in front of you, along with any research you have done on the company. Have a legal pad of paper and pen handy so that you can take notes and a glass of water. If the interviewer, hiring authority, or screener is calling you long distance, there are probably going to be a number of telephone interviews before you get a face-to-face interview. If you are interviewed over the phone by another person in the same organization, you'll come across as more professional if you are able to mention the last person that you spoke to on the phone. You will sound like you really know what you are talking about when you say things like: "Well, when I spoke to _____ last, he/she mentioned that_____."

Make sure that you have time to prepare for the telephone interview. Write out several open-ended questions that show you have done your research about the company. Asking even tough questions about the company's financial statements (if it is a public company) or the success of a product that the company has developed shows that you have taken an interest in being informed.

DO be ready for a psychological time frame of about twenty minutes. Usually, a telephone screen gets old and boring for both parties after twenty minutes. Unless the interviewer has a set group of questions (which most do not), the conversation will tend to ramble around. Just be prepared for this and start closing early for a face-to-face interview.

If you are even a reasonably seasoned professional and you feel like you were being asked stupid questions by a person who knows little about the specific opportunity, you may have a tendency to become frustrated. However, you cannot afford to come across as condescending or too good to be having this conversation with such an ignorant person.

On the other hand, if the telephone interview is being conducted by a hiring authority with "pain," you should be very specific and elaborate on your possible contributions in terms the hiring authority would be familiar with. Be careful though, because you can establish great rapport with someone over the phone and forget to push for a face-to-face interview.

DO try to be the person who initiates the call. The person making the call has a tendency to be in control. There may not be a choice in this, but whenever possible the candidate should initiate the call.

DO set an appointment time for the call whenever possible. It makes the call more important to all parties. Avoid a casual, "call me any time" type of atmosphere. If you initiate the call and need to leave a message, let the person know you called and leave a message that you will call back after five minutes. Do not leave a number. Place the call again. Keep doing this until you reach the interviewer.

> Record your telephone interviews and discussions. Most external answering machines have a feature to record your conversations. Reviewing your conversations, especially telephone interviews, is a tremendous advantage. No matter how good your note taking is, you will always miss something. By listening to your conversation again, you will retrieve some fine points that you can emphasize in face-to-face interviews. It will set you apart from the rest of the candidates.

DO smile. It doesn't hurt to have a mirror in front of you. Be in a good mood, friendly, and in the selling mode. People can "hear" smiles over the phone!

What Not to Do

DON'T leave a "cute" message on your answering machine. You may think your five-year-old sounds great on the answering machine, but a prospective employer will not. Changing careers and finding a job is serious business and so your answering message should reflect serious, too. We have known employers to call a candidate, get stupid stuff on an answering machine, and *immediately* eliminate the candidate. Often, an answering system will state in a computerized voice the phone number of the line. Well, an employer may not be sure it is you. An employer may not want to leave a message unless he or she can be sure it is you. And, by the way, record it slowly and distinctly, so the caller is sure of whom he or she is leaving a message for.

DON'T use a cell phone for a telephone interview. As mentioned previously, some people use a cell phone for all their calls and have discarded their landlines. This is a big mistake, especially in a telephone-interviewing situation. Lines "drop" in the middle of a conversation and service is sometimes not available. The microphones on most cell phones pick up a tremendous amount of background noise, often create echoes, and cause a great distraction. We have known many instances where the telephone interviewer couldn't connect with a candidate after one or two tries, so just moved on to the next person.

DON'T carry on a telephone interview from a busy place or a noisy home environment. If the interview must be conducted from home, make sure there are no kids, dogs, television, or radio in the background. (Don't laugh; we have had that happen more than a few times.) Likewise, don't make the call from the car or on a speakerphone. Speakerphones are especially annoying. No matter what you think, they communicate big ego—too big and important to pick up the phone.

If you encounter a situation where the interviewer, or the screener for the hiring authority, begins to talk to you from a speakerphone, ask the person to pick up the phone by stating that you cannot hear him or her very well. Speakerphones do not communicate a personal, one-on-one relationship. As a candidate, you especially do not want this kind of situation. So, it may come across as a bit pushy, but it is a good idea to ask callers to please pick up the phone so that you can understand them better.

DON'T discuss money in any kind of depth. State what you have made before, if asked, and address money in a "depending on the opportunity" manner.

DON'T ask "what can you do for me?" questions. These kinds of questions are the major cause of telephoned candidates *not* going beyond the phone screen. When asked, "Do you have any questions?" keep the questions open ended, such as "Why is this position open?" or "Mr./Ms. employer, why do you work for the company?" Any question that relates to what the company can do for you will most likely eliminate you as a candidate.

When the interviewer asks, "Do you have any questions?" you should take the opportunity to ask, "When can we get together face-to-face?"

DON'T talk too much. Answer the questions directly and conversationally, but don't ramble. It is easier to become confused in a telephone conversation than it is in a face-to-face one. So err on the "quiet" side. In fact, it is a good idea to end every statement that you make with a question. Even if the question is, "Did I make myself clear?"

DON'T avoid obvious sensitive issues. Things like too many jobs on your résumé, being out of work for an extended period of time, or being fired are red flags. Whatever you do, don't trip over or avoid tough questions. Explain them directly and to the point. Do not appear to avoid them or cover them up with the proverbial "it doesn't matter" excuse.

DON'T say you know what you do not. There is nothing wrong with being comfortable enough with yourself to say, "I don't know" to any question that you shouldn't know. Know the difference.

Prepare for the phone interview or screen in the same manner you would prepare for a face-to-face interview. Take it seriously and sell yourself!

Jeff's Experience with Telephone Interviews

Jeff mentioned that he not only always had his résumé in front of him for telephone interviews but also notes and questions he wanted to ask a telephone interviewer. Jeff and Amy have four little children. If Jeff received a phone call from a prospective employer, he certainly had to call the person back.

During one interview, Jeff sat in a room with one interviewer while the other interviewer was on a speakerphone—calling from India. The system was a quality phone system, but it was very confusing to be talking to one person in real time and another with a bit of a delay on the speakerphone. Under normal circumstances, Jeff said that he would have asked to be taken off the speakerphone: first, so he could understand the conversation better, and, second, to show that he had no hesitation to take control and take the interview seriously. However, this was not a normal situation and Jeff didn't want to antagonize his interviewers.

9 : Making the Initial Interview Successful 95 Percent of the Time

The job interview is a staged, contrived event. It is not an event that has anything to do with a person's ability to do a job. Although the concept purports the idea that the job interview is a mutual evaluation of your past record, talents, and a prediction of how you're going to perform in the future, as well as your personal evaluation of the organization, it is rarely any of these things.

Each party in this process is putting his or her best foot forward, and rightfully so. Candidates are responsible for selling themselves to the employer, trying to convince the employer that they are the best person for the job. The company, (or the individuals representing it), are trying to find the best person to do the job and, at the same time, both selling the company and screening out the candidates they do not think will be capable of doing the job or fitting in.

The essential four-part question to be answered by a hiring company in the interviewing process is: "Can this person do the job? Do we like him or her? Is he or she a minimal risk? Can we work the money out?" That's it! For the employer, it is no more complicated than those questions. The answers to this four-pronged question are the whole reason that individuals go through the interviewing process in the company.

As a job candidate, you must turn these questions around by asking yourself: "Can I do this job? Do I like them? Are they a risk? Can they afford me?" That's it! For you as a candidate, it is no more complicated than answering those questions. That is the essence of the interviewing process.

The best experience that money can buy, the most significant accomplishments that an individual can attain, and all the knowledge attained from the best MBA schools in the world will never be investigated or revealed (or, more importantly, hired) unless you can sell yourself in the interviewing process.

So what this means is that, in spite of the fact that interviewing is a staged, contrived event, it is absolutely necessary that it be done, and preferably done well. The better your ability to interview is, the better your opportunity to get a good job.

Key point: *You are going to get a job based on your ability to interview well, more than on your ability to perform in a job.*

Sell Yourself Through to the Next Interview

"Find a system and stick to it."
—Douglas MacArthur, World War II General

I'm going to offer you a format and script that I have developed. It is the most successful technique that can be used to make your initial interviews successful 95 percent of the time. This is a bold statement, but it is true. If done correctly, you will be successful in at least the initial interview, if not beyond. Remember, you are trying to sell yourself through to the next interview. That is all you're trying to do: get from one interview to the next interview to the next interview—so that you can be in the final group of people who are interviewing for the job.

There are two variations of this format. The second one is not quite as effective as the first one, but in some instances, it might work. Always begin your interviewing process with the first technique. It is going to get you to subsequent interviews 95 percent of the time. But, *you need to execute this technique exactly the way I demonstrate*. It is easy, and amazingly uncomplicated, but it does require lots of practice. That is what you have a coach for; and that is why you should videotape yourself making a presentation.

Successful Technique Number One

You walk into the interviewer's office or interviewing environment. You are rested, refreshed, and prepared. You sit down and lean forward a bit. After you share a few ice-breaker comments, you hand the hiring or interviewing authority your résumé (*even if he or she already has it*) and state:

(Phase 1) "Mr. or Ms. _____, I'm here to share with you why you should hire me.

"First of all, I am (ten or twelve descriptive adjectives to explain your work ethic):

_____

_____ "

(Transition Phrase Number One) "And here in my background is where these *features have been benefits* to the people whom I have worked for:

_____

_____ "

(Phase 2) "I am presently (or most recently have been) at _____ company. I have functioned for them in the capacity of

_____

_____ "

(Give a thorough description of exactly what you did, how you did it, whom you did it for, and how successful you were—in terms a high-school senior could understand.)

(You then emphasize *how much you love the job and the company, the reason you have to leave or why you left* in very positive terms.)

"And before that, I was at _____ company. There, I functioned in the capacity of

_____

_____ "

(Give a thorough description of exactly what you did, how you did it, whom you did it for, and how successful you were—in terms a high-school senior could understand.)

(You then emphasize *how much you loved that job and why you had to leave it* in very positive terms).

"And before that, I was at _____ company. There I functioned in the capacity of

_____

_____ "

(Again, give a thorough description of exactly what you did, how you did it, whom you did it for, and how successful you were—in terms a high-school senior could understand.)

(You then emphasize how much you *loved that job and why you had to leave it,* in very positive terms.).

[Continue in this manner for at least three jobs, if you have that many. If you've had a series of short stints at jobs, like one year or less, you may want to go back further than three jobs.]

(Transition Phrase Number Two) "Now, tell me Mr. or Ms. _____, how does what I have to offer stack up with what you are looking for?"

(Phase 3) You now pull out a legal pad, unless, of course, you have one in front of you already, start asking questions of the interviewer, and start taking notes. If you do this correctly, one question will lead to another question, which will lead to another question, which *will lead to a conversation,* which is exactly what you want.

As the conversation progresses, the hiring or interviewing authority is going to tell you more of what the company is looking for in an individual. As the interviewer does this, you weave into the conversation any important information that *pertains* to the job that you can extract, also expand upon the information about where you have been, what you have done, and how you did it in the second portion of your presentation.

As the conversation/interview winds down, when you feel the time is appropriate, you say:

(Phase 4) "Based on what we have discussed here, Mr. or Ms. _____ my ____(background, experience, or potential)____ makes this a good fit for both of us. What do I need to do to get the job?"

(*Then be quiet and don't say a word.*)

Now, the conversation may go off in a number of different directions. If you have to repeat your enthusiasm and interest in the position, you may have to push harder and repeat the fact that you are an ideal candidate for the job and you have to know what you need to do to get it.

Script Analysis

Tell 'em what you're gonna tell 'em . . . tell 'em . . . then, tell 'em what you told 'em.

Let's analyze this technique, and then I'll tell you why it works so well. I'll write out two specific scripts that have worked in a recent practical application.

Phase 1

What you say in Phase 1 is really simple. You state ten to fifteen basic intangible traits of a hard-working, successful, committed worker that you possess. In the final analysis, all hiring or interviewing authorities want to see is somebody who is going to possess the traits of a committed, hard-working employee. It is that simple.

What you're doing in this phase is simply communicating that you understand what hard work is. You would be shocked and amazed at the number of people who go into an interviewing situation and just assume that the interviewing or hiring authority already knows that they are a committed worker. Remember that your hiring or interviewing authority is scared of making a mistake. This person is afraid of risk. When you communicate the ten to fifteen intangible traits of a hard worker that you possess, it provides assurance in the interviewer's frightened state that you not only know what the traits of a hard worker are but also possess them. What I recommend here is stressing traits such as hard worker; determined to go the extra mile; get up early, stay late; accomplished; passionate about your work; committed to the customer; love what you do; intelligent; great work ethic; and so forth.

I cannot emphasize enough that prospective employers hardly ever hear these words from the typical candidate. You are simply communicating basic attributes that every employer wishes he or she saw in every employee.

Transition Phrase Number One

The transition phrase leading to Phase 2 of your presentation is, "Now, here in my background is where these *features have been benefits to the people I have worked for.*" This is a powerful phrase. You are using the terms *features* and *benefits.* It is implied that these features will be benefits to the hiring authority and his or her company. This transition phrase allows you to lead into an explanation of every job you have had, what you've done, how you've done it, and how successful you were.

You are doing their thinking for them! They don't need to ask that stupid question, "Well, tell me about yourself."

Phase 2

At this point, you are going to work backwards and give a short, but very thorough, description about exactly what job function you had, how you did, whom you did it for, and how successful you were, as well as—and this is very important—that you loved the job, and why, in very positive terms, you're looking to leave or why you left. The execution of this phase of your presentation is very important. There are clear key parts to this phase.

Explain your job function. First of all, you need to you explain *exactly* what your job function is now or was in the past so that the hiring or interviewing authority understands exactly what you have done before. I can't tell you the number of times over the years that candidates have walked away from interviews thinking that they had done a really good job on the interview— only to have the hiring authority, in giving us feedback, explain that he or she really didn't understand what the candidate did (either in his present job or the jobs he had before).

Why this happens: Hiring authorities are just as nervous as you are in the interviewing process. They feel like they have to get a deeper understanding about you and your background in order to evaluate you. They usually have to do this with a large number of people. Most of the time in the interviewing process, when a hiring or interviewing authority asks a question, partway through your answer they are thinking about the next question, and then partway through that answer, they're thinking about the next question, and so forth.

On top of that, most hiring or interviewing authorities don't want to look stupid or ignorant. Like most people, they are uncomfortable saying, "I don't understand, could you explain it to me in layman's terms so that I really get it." After all, they are the hiring authority. They are supposed to know and understand everything as the so-called authority. So, they will act like they know exactly what the candidate is talking about, and nod their head in complete agreement and understanding as the candidate speaks in terms foreign to everyone but himself. Then, after the candidate leaves, rather than admitting they had no idea what the hell the candidate was talking about, they will claim that the candidate's skills, experience, background, or personality isn't what they were looking for.

Explain why you want to leave your job. Next, you need to explain, in very positive ways, why you are seeking to leave the company you're with now and why you left other jobs. I cannot overemphasize this point. You are going to weave into your explanation along with what you've done and how you have done it, all of the positive reasons that you left the companies and the jobs that you had or the one that you are leaving now. If you bring up why you left in positive terms—even if it wasn't under the most positive circumstances (for example, you were fired)—the whole scenario has a tendency to be more palatable to a hiring authority.

The reason(s) that you want to leave, and the reason(s) that you have left other positions, have to be very specific and as detailed as necessary. Saying things like, "It was a mutual understanding; it was just time to go; we grew tired of each other; management changed; the company was bought; the company was sold"—or any broad generalization—will not help you be successful in the interview. Remember that the interviewing or hiring authority is concerned about taking a risk. Nebulous, unclear, broad generalizations have risk written all over them.

This is one of the many situations in the job-finding process where you absolutely need to see what you are communicating through the eyes of the interviewing or hiring authority. There is a tendency for all candidates to see the reasons that they're looking to leave, or the reason that they left other opportunities, only from their own point of view. What matters is how the hiring or interviewing authority is going to react to the reasons you give. If those reasons communicate risk, you're doomed.

This is going to take much thought and practice on your part. You always want to tell the truth; but you might have to put a spin on it, that, if nothing else, neutralizes any negative connotations. Do not think that an interviewing or hiring authority is going to see things from *your personal* point of view.

Communicate your positive feelings about previous employers. The third idea that you are going to communicate in the second phase is that you absolutely loved every job you ever had. You don't have to use the word *love* in every instance. But you need to communicate that you had a very positive experience with every job that you have ever had; that you learned a lot from each one; and that you really appreciated the people you worked for. You can communicate this by saying things like, "You know I really love the organization that I work for now but unfortunately. . . ."

The point is that you talk positively in every way you can about the organization that you're currently with and every organization that you ever worked for. No matter how difficult the circumstances are or were, you have to put your present or previous employers in a positive light. Even if you were laid off or fired, you have to say something along the line of, "Although I'm disappointed by not being there, I understand what took place from their point of view." Remember, employers identify with employers.

Both the second and third points in this phase of your presentation must never communicate an adversarial relationship between you and your current or previous employers. No matter how difficult the experience was or is with your past or present employers you have to communicate a "we're all in this together" type of attitude.

> Try to weave as many *stories* about what you have done as you can naturally throw into your presentation. People love stories. People remember stories. People remember *you* when you tell them stories about your past. Stories bypass conscious resistance and preconceived notions. Stories, analogies, and metaphors about you that pertain to the hiring authority's need are absolutely the best way to be remembered. Of course, they need to be short, to the point and, above all, pertinent to the opportunity for which you are interviewing.

In this phase of your presentation, you only need to go back three, maybe, at the most, four jobs and describe what I have suggested here. If you had jobs before that, unless they are germane to the position that you are presently applying for, you can lump them together by just saying something like, "before that (meaning the third or fourth position back) I was in sales or accounting or engineering (insert your job area) for a number of different firms."

In this phase of the interview, you want to make sure that you don't ramble for so long that the interviewing or hiring authority gets bored. Stick to the high points in your background that are applicable to the job for which you are interviewing. It should not take more than five to seven minutes.

Transition Phrase Number Two

This is a transition phrase to the third phase of your technique. You simply ask, "Now, tell me Mr. or Ms. _____, how does what I have to offer stack up with what you are looking for?"

Phase 3

"He who asks the questions, controls the interview."

—Anonymous

When the interviewing or hiring authority starts answering your question of how you stack up with what he or she is looking for, take notes. When the interviewer stops answering that question, you want to have a prepared set of questions ready. Some questions that you may ask are:

- What are the most important qualities that a successful person in this position should possess?

- How would you measure the success of the last person that was in this job?

- Why was he or she successful? or Why was he or she not successful?

- In your opinion, Mr. or Ms. _____, what is the most difficult part of the job?

- Mr. or Ms. _____, how long have you been with the company?

- Why do you like working here? What is the most difficult part of your job?

- Where do you see the company going in the next five to ten years?

- As I was doing my research on the company, I found that _____. Could you give me your opinion about that?

- What is the biggest challenge that the company is going to face in the next five to ten years?

- I believe your competitors are doing _____. How does your company respond to that?

- How will you know when you have found the "right" person for this job I'm interviewing for?

- How would you describe the culture of the company?

- What do you, Mr. or Ms. _____, like most about working here?

- How many people have you interviewed for this position? Have you seen anybody whom you felt was qualified to do it? Have you offered the job to anyone before my interviewing here?

I could go on and on but you get the idea. Ask enough questions to engage the employer or hiring authority in the conversation. You want this person to open up to you as much as he or she possibly can about what they want in the person whom they are going to hire. You then have a better idea of how to sell yourself into the job.

Now, the following is very important. As the conversation progresses and you write down some of the highlights of what the employer is looking for, you will reinforce the fact that you are a qualified, excellent candidate by going back to some of the jobs that you had, or the job you presently have, and talk in even more specific terms than before. As the interviewing or hiring authority is sharing with you his or her exact needs, you need to be able to relate exact experience, responsibilities, duties, and successes that you have had that *specifically address* the particular issues being discussed.

In the presentation you made (in Phase 2 of this technique), you talked about each job that you either currently have or have had, your duties and responsibilities, and your successes. But you did it in a very broad, descriptive way. Now you are going to use the information that the interviewing or hiring authority is giving you and bring up examples in the job that you have now or the jobs you had before that specifically demonstrate your ability to do the job under consideration. Whereas your initial presentation about your experience and background was detailed enough for the interviewing or hiring authority to understand what you have done, you now get specific about particular things that would be of value to the interviewing or hiring authority—based on the conversation that results from the questions you ask.

Phase 4

After the conversation has begun to wind down and you can see that the interview is nearly over, you "close" the interviewer or hiring authority by stating that your background and experience fit what the employer is looking for and you need to ask, "What do I need to do to get the job?" This is the hardball part of the interview. You are either a candidate or you're not, and you need to know right now!

"No" is the second-best answer you can get. More often than not at this point in the interview, candidates will become afraid of being rejected. So they will say stupid things like, "Well, what's the next step? Where do we go from here? When should I hear from you?" These kinds of weak questions are the ones that most interviewing and hiring authorities expect. They get them from 98 percent of the candidates they interview.

Interviewing and hiring authorities want to hire an individual who wants the job. I cannot tell you the number of candidates over the years who failed to ask this essential question in the interview and ended up being dismissed by the interviewing or hiring authority. I know that this is terribly unfair. But life is unfair. This is a part of the interview that truly is a contrived event. The truth is, there is no real way of knowing whether or not you really want this job right now. But, unless you ask for the job, you're never going to get beyond first base.

Whatever you do, don't fall into the trap of thinking, "Well, I'm not really sure that I want the job so, before I commit, I better think about it." Remember, while you are "thinking about it" somebody else is getting an offer. *You don't have anything to decide about until you have an offer.*

Asking the question "What do I need to do to get the job" takes courage. That's okay. But if you're serious about finding a job, you will use this question at the end of every interview, especially the initial one.

I will now provide two detailed examples of how to use this interview technique, so that you can really understand this strategy.

EXAMPLE #1

Sally is a software salesperson who has ten years of sales experience, two years as a technical support person and two years as a systems analyst. She has been at her current company for less than a year and the company is experiencing financial difficulties as well as product deficiencies. She was at her previous job for three years, the job before that for two years and the company before that for six years, two years in technical support and four years in sales. Before that, she was a systems analyst for two years right out of school.

Sally arrives early. One minute before the interview, she takes a deep breath, relaxes, closes her eyes, and envisions herself performing well in the interview. She goes into the interview with a hiring authority, a regional manager for another software firm that is somewhat of a competitor to the company that currently employs her. They break the ice with casual conversation and even though he has a copy of her résumé, she hands him one. Sally then states:

(Phase 1) "Mr. _____, I'm pleased to be here and to share with you why you should hire me. First of all, you need to know that I possess all the skills of an excellent salesperson. I am aggressive, assertive, get up early, stay late, don't take 'no' for an answer, and understand the ratio of calls to presentations to sales. I love to cold call, and have taken a number of excellent sales training programs. My clients see me as consultative, I'm there to help them 'get' the right product for their needs—rather than 'selling them' something they don't need. People like me. People trust me, I work independently and I have demonstrated success in every position that I've had."

(pause, as she looks him in the eye)

(Transition Phrase Number One) "Here in my background is where I can document that these features have been benefits to the organizations that I've worked for:

(Phase 2) "I am presently at _____ company. We sell an integrated suite of developmental tools and professional services. My territory is here as well as the five surrounding states. I am presently at 95 percent of a $1 million quota. Of all of the salespeople around the country, and there are fifteen of us, I rank number three. I really love what I do and all my customers really appreciate the hard work and service that I've provided them. Our average sale in the company is about $85,000 in revenue and $100,000 in implementation services. However, I am only compensated for the license revenue. We target telecommunications companies and financial institutions $500 million or above.

"Unfortunately the company is experiencing serious financial difficulties. They have developed a product that is only 80 percent functional and users, in some applications, are beginning to complain. I really appreciate the people I work with. In fact,

I followed a previous boss over to this company. Unfortunately, he didn't realize a year ago the financial difficulties that the company would have nor could he foresee the product issues. The applications work in only about 50 percent of the environments that we sell them to. I usually begin my sale by contacting the CIO or the CTO. I have excellent relations with about 110 of these managers throughout my territory, and a deeper business relationship with 35 of them. I am certain they would all buy from me again if I were representing a solution to one of their technological problems. (*This is an excellent example of appropriate storytelling*.)

"It's very unfortunate, but I'm not going to be able to solve my clients' problems and, therefore, not be able to maximize my earning potential. I love what I do, and I have performed well, but unfortunately I'm going to have to leave.

"Before that, I was at _____ company. We also sold developmental tools and professional services. My territory was the same as it is now, and every year I was there I was at least at 110 percent of quota and as much as 128 percent of quota. I made the President's Club every year and, in my second year, I made the largest sale in the history of the company to Hertz Rent-a-Car Corp. It was a great sale for the company and me. It started out after two of my predecessors had tried to penetrate the account. It's a great story about how I did it and resulted in my being named salesperson of the year. (*Here she can tell the story if the hiring authority asks to hear it.*)

"I really loved this company, and the people in it, and I was really doing well. But when my current, and then, boss left to go to the start-up I am with now, I followed him. We both were going to receive a tremendous amount of stock options because we got in on the ground floor; and it was our opportunity to reach for the brass ring. Neither one of us had to leave this organization; but the lure of a start-up with lots of stock was too difficult to pass up. I trusted him and he trusted me, and we both thought the opportunity was going to be excellent. (*Another great story.*)

"Looking back, it may have been a mistake to leave _____ for the start-up. But I sure learned a lot working in a small, start-up organization and wouldn't trade the experience for anything.

"I have been very successful before and I will be again.

"Before that job, I worked for two years at a software development firm selling an integrated suite of Human Capitol Management Software. My quota each year that I was there was $2 million. That was a great job and I really loved it. Our product was difficult to sell and I was very good at finding big opportunities, which I closed. We sold to HR departments of large Fortune 1000 firms. Most had tight budgets and the competition was difficult. I was 120 percent of quota the first year and 150 percent of quota the second year. I made the third-largest sale in the history of the company to Ryder Truck Corp., and they still ask about me five years later.

"This was a great company and a great group of people. Unfortunately, the company was sold to our largest competitor. That competitor, _____ company, already had a tenured salesperson in the territory that I was in. They gave me the opportunity to relocate or to take a severance package. I decided to take the severance package. They were very nice; but, after all, for two years they had been our fiercest competitor and I just didn't feel comfortable working for them—so that's why I took the package.

"Before that, I was with _____ company. They were wonderful people. The company was small and they developed turnkey healthcare management software applications for clinics, hospitals, and HMOs. I spent six years there, the first two in product support and the last four in sales. I was always in the top two or three salespeople in the company because I was technically competent and really understood the application from a technical point of view. That is a great advantage I bring to all of the software sales jobs that I've had or will have. I don't get bogged down in the technical aspect of things; but I do know what the stuff does from a technical point of view.

"This was a very small company of about $20 million in revenue. The owners were absolutely wonderful to me but they were never going to grow beyond what they could easily control. Both they and I knew that I was experiencing limited growth, both personally and professionally. They blessed my leaving, even encouraged it, because they knew that my potential was well beyond what they might be able to offer me. I still keep in touch with them. They're wonderful people. (*Another good story.*)

"Before that job, I spent two years in the technical and software development arena."

(Transition Phrase Number Two) "As you can see, I have been successful at every place that I have ever been and am looking to continue that success. Now tell me, how does what I have to offer stack up with what you're looking for?" (She then takes out the legal pad.)

(*This presentation took eight minutes. I will discuss the positive points in a moment.*)

The prospective employer explains to Sally about the job, the territory, and the product. She takes notes as he talks.

(Phase 3) After listening to what the hiring authority has to say, Sally asks the following questions:

- "I noticed in doing research on your company that your competition claims that they have a similar type of product for a much lower price. What is the company's stance on that?"

- "What do you think is the biggest challenge in this job and in this particular territory?"

- "I noticed in doing my research that your company had to restate its earnings two years ago. How has that affected your customers and your sales?"

- "What is the average tenure of each one of your salespeople? How would you describe the best ones, and what are they doing that the unsuccessful ones are not?"

- "It seems, based on what research I have done, that your company might be a target for a takeover by your largest competitor. What is your feeling about that?"

- "How long have you been here?"

- "Why did you come to work here?"

- "Whom do you report to, and how would you describe their management style?"

- "How would you describe your management style?"

(Well, you get the idea about questions to ask. Notice that *none* of them are "What can you do for me?" questions.)

At the end of the interview, Sally states:

(Phase 4) "Based on what you have told me, I am a good fit for your company. I have sold a similar product. I know the customers you are selling to, because I sell to some of those people now. I really understand your technology, and since I have been successful in this environment before, I will be successful here. *What do I need to do to get the job?*"

Looking Closer at the Spin

The following is the *whole story behind* why Sally wants to leave the job in the previous example. The reason that I'm sharing this with you is to show the way in which a candidate has to put the right light on his or her situation and has to communicate everything in as positive a way as possible.

The real truth is that Sally can't stand her boss. They have had yelling and screaming matches over just about everything. It is true that she followed him over to her current company; but she would admit that it is one of the biggest mistakes she ever made. Her payroll checks have barely cleared the bank and they still owe her a large commission check that is three months overdue.

Sally is mad as hell at her boss because she thinks he lied to her about the company before she went to work for them. She had worked for him in the previous organization, really didn't care for him that much one way or the other, but simply followed him out of pure greed and the lure of becoming rich with stock. She really didn't do research on the company she's presently with very well at all; or she would've found out, rather easily, the poor quality of the product and she could have predicted how difficult it was going to be to sell it. She simply stayed with the company for a year to make it look good on her résumé. Now, it is true that Sally was the number three salesperson in the country for the company, but all but two of the salespeople have been with the company for less than six months. Her quota production is correct, but since she was the first salesperson in the company, she got a lot of "blue-bird" sales that came to her because she was the first, and for a while, the only salesperson in the company. She is desperate to get off a sinking ship.

Sally presents her leaving the previous organization to follow her ex-boss as though she were a positive risk taker. The whole truth was that they had cut her commissions and her boss's commissions by 25 percent and increased their quota by 50 percent right before she left. So, she wasn't going to make anywhere near the amount of money she wanted. She did run a risk, but it was nowhere nearly as educated and calculated as she presents it. She could have stayed at this organization, but would have taken a significant cut in earnings.

Most everything else that Sally says about her previous employers or positions was mostly correct. The reason that I bring all of this up is that once you see the *whole story*, you realize that selling yourself correctly in an interviewing situation is as much putting a positive spin on things as it is anything else. Everything that Sally stated was true, but she presented it with a positive spin to every prospective employer she interviewed with.

EXAMPLE #2

Joe is an accountant with more than fifteen years of experience, but unfortunately, he has been with seven companies. He is currently in a senior role reporting to a CFO with whom he had worked before, knows, and trusts. Unfortunately, he has only been there for ten months and the company is now in poor financial condition. His earnings are quite a bit below even today's market value and the company is probably not going to make it. So, he needs to find a new job.

He arrives early at the interview, dressed conservatively, and, a minute or two before the interview begins, he takes a deep breath and imagines how well he is going to do in the interview.

(Phase 1) "Ms. _____, I'm really pleased to be here. I've heard a lot about you and your company and am excited about the possibility of going to work for you and your firm. I'd like to share with you why you should hire me. I am a very hard worker, I get up early, I stay late, and I go the extra mile when it comes to accounting and detail type of work. I am technically very competent, and not only keep up on the latest software technologies but have also actually implemented and installed complicated accounting packages. I am very detailed in my work, and I am known for being accurate and careful about even the most complicated accounting reports. I've been fortunate to have had very good mentors, even some managers who were impossible for anybody else to work for."

(Transition Phrase Number One) "Here in my background is where these features have been benefits to the people whom I have worked for:

(Phase 2) "I am presently at _____ company. I have been there for ten months. I really love what I do and I love the people for whom I work. I work for a $40 million tax process and services firm. I was hired by the CFO with whom I had worked before. He is a great CFO, and it is a compliment that he sought me out to work for him again. He trusts me and knows me and he gives me a lot of authority to make decisions regarding the business applications needed to produce the most effective reports. I am responsible for the total tracking of the financial operations and making sure that it is done accurately. I had worked for Blake before . . . a few years ago. He is one of the brightest people in accounting and financial planning that I know. The accounting department was a mess in this organization until he got there and it was a real compliment to be called and asked to come there and help him straighten it out. (*Story*.)

"Unfortunately, we find ourselves in a difficult financial situation and because the CFO respects me and feels somewhat responsible for bringing me there, he has informed me that it might be better for me and my future to find another job. He is going to stay on and try to weather the storm; but the essence of what I needed to accomplish has been done and he can maintain without me. He is probably going to retire at this organization so I will not be following him again; but I will get an excellent reference from him and he is available for that. (*Story.*)

"Before going back to work with Blake, I worked for two years in the insurance business for one of the most difficult CFOs that most anybody can imagine. He was brilliant when it came to accounting, but impossible to get along with. He had been through a series of accountants who lasted no longer than six months, but I was able to weather this CFOs personality storm. I was there for twenty-six months. People were surprised that I stayed for as long as I did, but I really loved the work. We implemented a total PeopleSoft enterprise-wide application from scratch and I sure learned a lot doing that. (*Story.*)

"Before that, I worked a couple of years for Blake, which was the first time that I worked for him. We both joined one consulting organization and, after about a year, it was bought by another firm. We both stayed on for about another year. Then the company was sold and the accounting function was moved to the corporate office of the company that bought us, out of state. It was a start-up company and we really learned a lot by helping the company grow from the ground up. It was a great experience.

"Before that, I was with a radiator manufacturing company as a plant accountant. It was a typical accounting type of position where I was doing the expense and cost analysis for fifteen domestic locations on a monthly basis. I did everything from budget preparation to analysis of capital expenditures and maintenance expenditures; and I served on the operations management task force. I was recognized within this company as the Employee of the Quarter and received a cruise as recognition for my contribution. I also received numerous customer compliments because of my ability to resolve complex issues internally so that the customer received better service. I really liked this job and could probably have stayed, and maybe even still be there, but there wasn't going to be much personal growth beyond the job I had. Not to mention the fact that the owners were near retirement age and let it be known to everybody that they were going to sell or close down the company within a few years. The opportunity came along to go work in the consulting business—and that's what I did. (*Story.*)

"Before that, I worked a number of years in Oklahoma as an accountant with a couple of different organizations there. I'm from Oklahoma City and I graduated from the University of Oklahoma with an accounting degree and began my accounting career there. These were the gritty accounting types of jobs that handled everything from payables, receivables, fixed assets, preparing the month end closings, general ledger analysis, bill of materials, and collections. They were great basic training types of jobs."

(Transition Phrase Number Two) "Now tell me Ms. _____, how does what I have to offer stack up with what you're looking for?"

(This presentation took five minutes.)

(Phase 3) After listening to what the hiring authority has to say, Joe asks (while pulling out the legal pad to take notes):

- "I noticed in doing research on your company that you took some huge financial write-offs last year. Can you share with me the circumstances for doing that?"

- "What is the biggest challenge in the accounting department now?"

- "How long have you been with the company?" and "What is the most stimulating part of your job?"

- "How long have you been looking for someone and what have you not found in other candidates that you would ideally like to find?"

- "In doing my research, I've found that you recently implemented a PeopleSoft enterprise-wide financial and human resources application. I would be of real value to you because of my experience with this package. Are you finding the implementation to be going smoothly, because I can sure help with that effort."

(I'm sure you get the hang of the kinds of questions that are good to ask.)

(Phase 4) "Based on what you have shared with me, I am a very good match for what you need. Now please tell me, what do I need to do to get the job?"

The Spin

There really isn't so much spin that needs to be put on this because Joe's background is pretty simple and to the point. His primary problem is that he has had too many jobs. He has been on the job he has now for only ten months. The one before that was twenty-six months, the one before that was nineteen months, and the one before that was twenty-five months. That isn't really bad; but it is going to cause some concern with mostly conservative CFOs that ordinarily like to see ten- to fifteen-year stints.

Joe "sells" around this by going to work for Blake twice and, after all, it is a compliment to be hired back by a previous employer. Joe actually sought Blake out in this last job because the person whom he was working for in the position previous to this had a horrible personality and was just very difficult to work for. It is true that Joe lasted there longer than any other accountant the organization had, but it was not a very pleasant experience at all. When Blake told him that he might have a position for him, Joe jumped on it.

Joe needs to be careful when he talks about having worked for Blake two times. If a candidate has worked for a particular employer more than one time, it crosses the mind of a new, potential employer, that if he hires the candidate, the candidate may leave if that previous employer recruits him or her away. That is why Joe had to communicate that it was likely that Blake was going to retire from the company that they're both with now—because he doesn't want a prospective employer to think that Blake will recruit him again. (Interestingly enough, Sally could face this same perception problem in Example #1, even though she can't stand her boss.)

Other than the issues of too many jobs and following Blake from place to place, Joe makes a good presentation of himself. He gave a really good overview of what he had done and what his strengths were; and then he can get more detailed about anything else the interviewing or hiring authority might need.

What They Didn't Talk About

It is important to remember not just to enhance the positive aspects of what you've done but also minimize risk by not talking about the negative things that might put you at risk. People often shoot themselves in the foot by thinking a prospective employer will understand the situation from the candidate's point of view. Wrong! Hiring authorities are more sensitive to the negative stuff than they are to the positive.

Sally did not talk about how she felt like she had been misled by her former boss who brought her over to the company she is with now. She did not emphasize what a big mistake it was to take the job or that her paychecks have barely cleared the bank or that she's mad or that she didn't do enough research on the company or that she stayed just to complete one year. She did not talk about how her bluebird sales helped boost her quota production. And she did not mention that her previous company had cut her commissions, meaning that her move was less of a calculated risk and more of a financial imperative.

Joe did not talk about the short stints that he has had at various companies—if anything, he actually put a positive spin on them. He did not talk about the fact that he sought out Blake, hoping for a job offer, instead playing up the positive aspect of being rehired by a former boss to help at a new company. And he stresses the fact that he won't be following Blake again.

I emphasize all these points to be sure you understand that it is just as important to not present some things as it is to sell yourself. Most people might think that a prospective employer, for instance, would understand and empathize with Sally's plight in following her previous boss. This couldn't be farther from the truth. A hiring or interviewing authority is looking for just as many reasons not to hire you as there are reasons to hire you. In fact, the negative reasons not to hire you will carry more weight than the positive reasons to hire you. So, when you develop a presentation on yourself, be sure you're just as aware of what not to talk about as you are aware of what to emphasize.

Customization

This whole process of presenting yourself in an initial interview is simple. While there is some work involved in putting the presentation together, once you get the hang of things, it's very easy to keep doing. After all, you're going to give the same basic presentation to just about everybody you interview with. As you do your research for particular organizations, you will end up customizing your presentation when you know there are certain things that might be of value to the particular employer.

It's important to try to find specific differentiators that might put you ahead of the other candidates for a particular employer. This is one of the things you want to do when you ask questions after your presentation of yourself. If you ask the right kinds of questions, you will be able to get even more detailed information about what the employer might need; and then you can go back over your previous positions and emphasize your relevant experience.

Successful Technique Number Two

This technique is for those people who feel more comfortable with trying to find out what an interviewing or hiring authority might be interested in before they talk about their experience. I offer this technique because it does work in some situations. I personally don't like it as well. But it has been successful for many candidates over the years, so I will offer it.

It isn't much different than the first technique. You ask the question: *"What would you like to find in the ideal candidate?"* before you talk about your intangible attributes and other experiences and background. It works like this:

You sit down in the interviewing or hiring authority's office, take a deep breath, and affect the pleasantries, then you say:

Phase 1: (as you put the legal pad down in front of you) "Tell me, Mr. or Ms _____, what kind of candidate would you ideally like to find?"

(As the hiring or interviewing authority speaks, you take notes about what they're looking for in an ideal candidate. You may ask a number of questions, but the idea is to find out, in the employer's words, what they're looking for.)

Phase 2: "If you will allow me Mr. or Ms. _____, I would like to explain why I would fit what you are looking for and how I could do the job.

"First of all, I am (ten or twelve descriptive adjectives to explain your work ethic):

_____

_____."

Transition Phrase Number One: "Based on what you said you wanted in a candidate, I would like to demonstrate where these features have been beneficial to the people whom I've worked for, in the light of what you need."

Phase 3: "I am currently (or most recently have been) at _____ company. I have functioned for them in the capacity of

_____

_____ "

(Give a thorough description of exactly what you did, how you did it, whom you did it for, and how successful you were—in terms a high-school senior could understand.)

(You then emphasize *how much you love the job and the company and the reason you have to leave or why you left* in very positive terms. Tell a story, if appropriate.)

"And before that, I was at _____ company. There, I functioned in the capacity of _____ "

(Give a thorough description of exactly what you did, how you did it, whom you did it for, and how successful you were—in terms a high-school senior could understand.)

(You then emphasize *how much you love the job and the company and the reason you have to leave or why you left* in very positive terms. Tell a story, if appropriate.)

"And before that, I was at _____ company. There I functioned in the capacity of _____ "

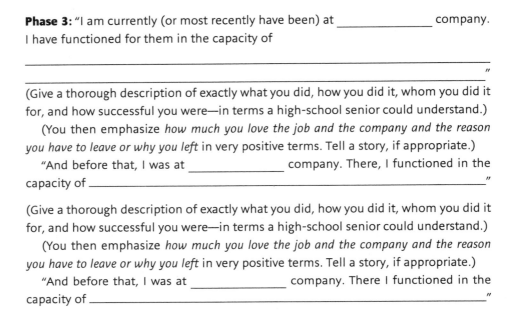

The slight advantage that you might have in using this technique is that you will get a really good idea about what the employer is looking for. This slight advantage does not, I believe, offset the drawbacks. The major drawback to this technique is that once the interviewing or hiring authority starts talking about their position, and starts asking you questions, you may not get the chance to take control by talking about your features, advantages, and benefits—and the successes that you had in your previous jobs. This technique does work, but I don't think it is as consistently successful as the first one. Do what you and your coach think is best.

(Give a thorough description of exactly what you did, how you did it, whom you did it for, and how successful you were—in terms a high-school senior could understand.)

(You then emphasize *how much you love the job and the company and the reason you have to leave or why you left* in very positive terms. Tell a story, if appropriate.)

(Continue in this manner for at least three jobs, if you have that many. If you've had a series of short stints at jobs—like more than one in the last year or less—you may want to go back farther than three jobs.)

Note: The only difference between this and the first technique is that you ask up front what the employer is looking for in an ideal candidate. With this approach, you might be able to be more specific about the things that the employer wants in a candidate in the descriptions of the jobs that you had.

Transition Phrase Number Two: "Based on what you said you wanted, I'm an excellent match. What do I need to do to get the job?"

Ending the Initial Interview

Once you and the hiring or interviewing authority have reached the end of the interview, you're probably going to get an idea of what the next steps might be. Don't be afraid to be assertive about pushing yourself into the next steps.

You may be surprised to discover that a lot of interviewing or hiring authorities are not sure of what the next steps might be. Most often, even though you have pushed for the next interview, a hiring or interviewing authority is going to say something like, "Well, we have a number of people to interview, we're going to complete that process and then we're going to set up second interviews."

This is a perfect time for you to again ask, "Based on what our conversation has been here, I would think that I would be in that group, would I not? So let's set up that second interview now." Then you pull out your note pad or calendar and ask, "When would be good for me to come back?"

You will probably still get from the interviewing or hiring authority the standard, "Well, we'll get in touch with you." Again, this is an excellent time for you to find out how you really stand, relative to the other candidates, by asking, "Well, Mr. or Ms. _____, you must have some idea how I stack up with your ideal candidate or the others whom you have interviewed. Please tell me what you think."

This kind of questioning (and statements) will usually get you a good idea of how you stand. It is relatively aggressive and it does not necessarily come naturally or easily. But if you practice asking these kinds of hardball questions, they will wind up becoming very easy for you.

If you don't get the chance to set a date and time for the next interview at the end of this initial interview, you need to ask for and get clarification of exactly what the next step might be. Most of the time the interviewing or hiring authority will give you an idea about what the next steps are, but most likely will not commit to your coming back, at least at this moment. Don't worry about this too much. Remember, I'm emphasizing process. Getting an answer as to how you stack up relative to the others is merely part of the process.

The Follow-Up Activity

The first thing you should do after the interview, when you get into your car, is take out the notes you took during the interview and write down a summary of the interview on the form on the facing page. Write down the high points of the interview: the major issues or topics that you spoke with the interviewer about. Summarize for yourself where you think your strengths are and where you think your weaknesses are—relative to the interview. Write down your interpretation of the things that seemed the most important to the hiring authority; and make sure that you understand them clearly. Often, in the initial interviewing situation, we think we completely understand what a hiring authority is looking for, and we actually do not! The major reason you want to collect your thoughts immediately after the interview is so that you remember the important points; you cannot rely on your memory. It may be a two- to four-week period of time before the second round of interviews. You need to be able to refresh your memory with detailed notes.

The important issues and criteria for hiring may change as the interviewing or hiring authority interviews more and more people. It is not surprising that hiring/interviewing authorities become confused about the candidates whom they have interviewed. Likewise, I have had candidates become confused and supposedly remember the wrong issues and embarrass themselves during the second interview. So, take very detailed notes after every interview on the form that follows and use them. Keep them in the folder for that particular employer and refer to them, where appropriate, in your e-mails and letters. Keep them handy for when you go back to the follow-up interviews: use them wisely and to your advantage!

The Immediate E-Mail

You have gotten the business card of the interviewing or hiring authority at the time of the interview. Immediately after the interview, or as soon as possible, you want to e-mail the interviewing or hiring authority. You don't

1ST INTERVIEW

Date _____ Interviewing Company _____

Interviewing/Hiring authority _____

Was this an interviewing or hiring authority? _____

How long was the interview? _____

Summary _____

What are the most important aspects of my background to the interviewing/hiring authority? _____

What were the major concerns about my candidacy? _____

How could I have sold myself better? _____

What do I need to do to get to the next step? _____

Follow-up activity: _____ e-mail? _____

Overall impressions and thoughts _____

Next steps _____

2ND INTERVIEW

Date _____ Interviewing Company _____

Interviewing/Hiring authority _____

Summary _____

What are my strengths and weaknesses as a candidate? _____

(My impressions if I'm in their shoes) _____

What do I need to do to get to the next steps? _____

How could I have sold myself better? _____

Follow-up activity _____

3RD/4TH/5TH INTERVIEWS

Interviewer _____

Summary _____

What questions should I be asking? _____

How can I better my chances? _____

just want to thank the person for his or her time. More important, you want
to reinforce all the reasons that you should be hired.

Every interviewing book in the world is going to tell you to send a thank-
you to the interviewer. You would probably be shocked at the number of
candidates who don't. One out of every seven or eight, even when they're
coached by a professional, either don't do it or do it so late after the interview
that it is ineffective. Of course, thanking someone for the interview is obviously important. But what is most important is that you reinforce the high
points of what the interviewing or hiring authority said he or she wanted and
restate where or how you address those issues *better* than anyone else.

The e-mail needs to be short and to the point. Do not ramble about how
much you appreciated the interview, how much you like the person, or how
you appreciate the conversation. This letter is going to be read, like the résumé, in ten seconds. So this is what it should look like (remember to make
it look like an actual letter):

> Dear Mr. or Ms. _____,
> Thank you for taking the time to speak with me today, regarding
> the position with _____. Your needs and my qualifications
> are compatible.
> You stated that you wanted someone who has:
>
> - (Experience or attributes that the employer said were wanted.)
>
> - (Another experience or attribute the employer said were wanted.)
>
> - (Another experience or attribute the employer said were wanted.)
>   I have given a lot of thought to what we spoke about. I would like
>   to reinforce the confidence you can have in me to deliver what
>   you need.
>
> - When I was at _____ company last year, I _____
>   (accomplished the first thing that you wrote previously).
>
> - When I was at _____ company, I _____ (ac-
>   complished or proved the second thing you wrote pre-
>   viously) _____.

- And, when I was at _____ company, I _____ (accomplished or proved the third thing you wrote pre-viously) _____.

I'm an excellent fit for you and your company. I would like to go to work for you and your firm. This is a win/win situation for both of us.

Sincerely,
Your name

When you reinforce what the interviewing or hiring authority said he or she wanted, you need to do it in quantifiable terms. State things that can be measured objectively such as percentages of quota, longevity on the job, grades in school, stability, being promoted consistently—anything that can be measured in a quantitative manner. Make sure that you address specific issues that the interviewing or hiring authority stated was of value to them.

Follow-Up Phone Call

Once you have e-mailed the letter, you need to be aware that interviewing or hiring authorities, after initial interviews, have a tendency to move on to other things and don't think about the interviewing and hiring process as much as you think they do; unless, of course, their pain is extremely severe. Interviewing or hiring authorities will have a tendency to tell you things like, "Well, we'll get back to you in a couple of days," and then go on vacation for a week.

With this in mind, it is advisable for you to follow up with the interviewing or hiring authority two to three days after the interview with a phone call to check in and see how the process is coming along. Interviewing and hiring authorities have to at least act like hiring is a top priority. And sometimes it is. Hiring is something that everybody knows they should do with decisive-ness and real business acumen, but they mostly don't. So, your call reminds them of the task at hand. It is often a timing thing; but you may catch the person and all of a sudden, since you have him or her on the phone, the person will make an appointment with you for a second interview. This is also a great time to ask about anything you might have discussed in the initial interview that you didn't fully understand or that you need further clarification on.

If you don't get the person on the phone, and often you won't, you'll have to deal with voice mail. In spite of the fact that I have a ton of experience in this profession, I'm never really sure of how many times to call someone back when they don't return your call. My best suggestion is to call until you get them. You may say, "Well, Tony, don't I run the risk of irritating them and making them angry and, therefore, they will not be interested in hiring me?" Well, my answer is that you have absolutely nothing to lose. After all, until you have a job offer, you really don't have anything to decide about.

Most hiring authorities don't intentionally think, "I'm not gonna call that sucker back. She's a schmuck and I'm not going to hire her anyhow." The truth is that their intentions to do what they are supposed to do are sincere, but the activity just doesn't get done. The process of hiring often just slips further behind in favor of other more pressing issues. So, a timely call, and many of them after that—if you have to—may put you on top of the list of potential candidates.

Now, after ten to fifteen days of calling an interviewing or hiring authority, with no response at all, you might wind up with the conclusion that you should pursue other people and other opportunities. Never, never, never take this result personally and do something stupid, like calling the hiring authority and leaving a mean, sarcastic voice mail about what they can do with the job and that you didn't want it anyhow. There is always a tendency to take perceived rejection personally. Now, the odds are that if you have not heard from a prospective employer in a couple weeks, you were probably not on the list of candidates to be considered. But you never really know. Always leave the door open, so that if a prospective employer wants to still consider you, even after weeks or months have gone by, you could resurrect the opportunity.

How This Affected Jeff and Amy

Jeff and Amy both admitted that the initial interview could be much more scientific than Jeff knew it to be, but his real challenge in finding a job wasn't interviewing. In fact, Jeff interviewed extremely well. Even without any previous instruction in interviewing, he did an excellent job of presenting himself and his skills, as well as he could, for a hiring authority.

The major difficulty that Jeff had regarding interviewing, as we've spoken about a number of times, is that he just wasn't getting enough interviews. He spent a lot of time before coming to Texas, and even when he did come to Texas, trying to get interviews, but just wasn't having much luck. Most of his interviews either had pretty flaky deals or he was grossly overqualified. Again, the issue wasn't how he performed on the interviews; it was just getting them.

The idea of "thrusting oneself upon other people" that I recommend in this chapter does not come naturally for most people. This was especially true with Jeff. He's such a mild-mannered, intelligent young fellow that he just assumed everybody knows what a good guy he is and the idea of aggressively forcing himself upon a prospective employer is just not something he would think of doing.

However, Jeff's personality lent itself very well to the interviewing process. His skills and mind-set were very analytical; after all, he had an accounting degree, a master's degree, and experience as a programmer analyst. Also, he has an expressive personality. Selling his features, advantages, and benefits was not difficult for Jeff. Once he became conditioned to the practice, he had no difficulty tooting his own horn.

10 Follow-Up Interviews: A Whole New Challenge

So, you think because you made it past the initial interview and have been called back for a second one that you're well on your way to getting a job offer and going to work? Wrong! Frankly, your quest has just begun. Now, it is true that you should be congratulated for making it past the initial interview; 90 to 95 percent of the time, candidates don't make it that far. But the race is far from over. In fact, I liken these next steps in the process to the playoffs in sports. The regular season is competitive and entertaining to all; and you have to go through it to get to the playoffs. And, it is true that the initial interview stage was necessary for you to get to this level of the interviewing process. But once you've gotten through the initial interview, the competition really heats up—you've made the playoffs.

The people who write books and articles about finding a job rarely, if ever, enlighten people to the fact that interviews beyond the initial one are most often a very different experience from what you expect. That is because most of the people who write these books and articles don't really find people jobs.

The process of follow-up interviews actually involves asking the same questions; but the number of people asking these questions increases and the detail involved is much more significant and intense. Most candidates aren't ready for the kind of intensity and complication that goes on in the follow-up process. The intensity, depth, and complication in this part of the process are much less predictable and patterned than any other stage in the interviewing process.

What to Expect

You absolutely must be aware that the follow-up interviewing process is going to be very different from what you experienced in the initial interviewing

166

process. You're going to basically sell yourself in the same way; but there are going to be a greater number of variables in this process than there were in the initial interview. Just be ready and know that it is a brand-new day and a brand-new process; *just because you made it past the initial interview, you can take nothing for granted.* Be prepared for playoff intensity, because now it's all on the line; and, just as in the playoffs, you have to bring your "A game" and ratchet it up tenfold.

> Studies have shown that successful hires are just as likely if *only* the hiring authority is involved, as opposed to several people being involved in the process. In fact, one study I read documented that in certain industries and professions, it's actually better to have only one person—the hiring authority—who is responsible for the position, involved in the interviewing process. But nobody is ever going to be able to convince the businesses of corporate America that they are just as well off when one person does the interviewing and hiring as they are when several people are involved in the process.

Why do companies go into follow-up interviews and involve more people in the process than there probably need to be? Remember, I stated that the interviewing process was a staged and contrived event. Well, the reason that most organizations involve so many people in the hiring decision is to *spread the risk.* Yes, you read it right. Corporate America will tell you that the reason so many people interview a candidate for a job is that the more people involved in the decision, the better the decision. Employers say they want to make sure of the candidate's qualifications, that he or she can do the job, that everybody likes the person, and so forth. But the truth is that no one individual wants to take on the responsibility of making a hiring decision and personally living with the possibly bad consequences. People in the hiring process are so afraid of making a mistake, that if they do, they want other people to share the responsibility for the screw-up.

When the First Interviewer Is Not the Hiring Authority

If your initial interview is conducted by a third party or simply an interviewing authority, and you make it past this person to the second stage of interviewing, you are most likely one of the safest candidates to be interviewed. The interviewer who does not have hiring authority is usually going to screen out far more candidates than he or she screens in. This person is going to look for more reasons why a candidate should not be considered rather than reasons why the candidate should be considered. As I've stated before, these people don't want to look bad.

Recently, I worked with a candidate who was eliminated by the internal HR department interviewing authority because he had three jobs in the past three years. The interviewing authority was given overall instruction by the ultimate hiring authority not to consider people with too many jobs or with short stints of employment. In general, that is a valid request. The particular candidate that I was representing, though, had an exceptional track record in pretty much the same business as my client. After the interviewing authority eliminated my candidate for having had too many jobs, I called the hiring authority directly and explained the situation. Not only did this get the candidate an interview, but he was subsequently hired.

Now, I'm not suggesting that you go around every interviewing authority that you encounter; just be aware of their strengths and limitations.

Once the interviewing authority has told you that you're going to be promoted to the next step in the process, you need to be sure that you get this person's support for future interviews within the company. Do what you can to get the person to promote you throughout the process. The way you do that is to simply ask if he or she will help you in every aspect of the subsequent interviews. In fact, it doesn't hurt to simply ask in this fashion, "Mr. or Ms. _____, I really want this job and am convinced that I am the best candidate you could hire. I would like you to help me as much as you can through the interviewing process." Even if you have to suggest meeting a second time before you go on the subsequent interviews, you want them to "load your shotgun" so that you perform well in the rest of the interviewing process. You want to ask this person about the backgrounds of everybody you will encounter, what their positions are, how long they have been with the organization, what their role might be in the interviewing process, and so forth. The more you get this third-party interviewing authority to help you, the better off you are.

When the First Interviewer *Is* the Hiring Authority

This is a much easier situation to deal with than when the interviewing authority is not a hiring authority. When the hiring authority does the interviewing, he or she takes on a long-term, personal responsibility for the decision. Most of the time, this person is going to be responsible for not only hiring you but also contributing to your success or lack of it in the job. This person's reputation is really on the line.

When hiring authorities decide to move candidates up in the interviewing process, they are getting other opinions in order to protect themselves. Since hiring is a personal thing and these people have a personal, vested interest in whoever is successful in getting the job, they are likely to help you as much as they can. It is important that you ask this person how many people are being interviewed; how you stack up in their eyes with the other people who are being interviewed; who you are going to be interviewed by; the perception the hiring authority has of these people; how long the process is going to take; what the people involved like and don't like; or anything else you can glean from the hiring authority.

Once the hiring authority tells you that you are going to be promoted to the next step, it is not a bad idea to request another meeting with this person so that you can get as much information as possible about the other people you will be talking to. A hiring authority wants to hire someone who goes the extra mile and wants the job.

Multiple Interviews—Watch Out!

Mark my word, and you better remember this, *the more people who are involved in the interviewing process, the more difficult it is going to be to get hired.*

I am constantly amazed at the number of interviewing authorities above the hiring authority who have a completely different idea about what kind of candidate should be hired than the initial hiring authority does. You would think that once an organization decided it needed a particular type of individual, all the people involved in the hiring decision would be reading from the same page, and have some consistent idea among them about what kind of person they ought to hire. Unfortunately, most of the time this just isn't the case.

I recently had the vice president of sales for a company interview one of my candidates. After a three-hour interview, he came to the conclusion that she was what his company really needed. Frankly, what he told me that they wanted was a fairly difficult experience to find. The woman didn't have the exact experience, but what she didn't have in experience she made up for in a tremendous track record in a similar business. The vice president, within a day, arranged for her to fly to the corporate office to interview with two executive vice presidents and the president of the organization.

So, on a bright Wednesday morning, she flew from Dallas to Boston and then drove an hour-and-a-half to the company's corporate office. When she got into the interview with the two executive vice presidents and the president, she was asked one question. Then she was immediately informed that she really didn't have the right kind of experience that the organization needed; she did not have a track record in exactly what their business was; and, on top of that, she was just too young and inexperienced to do what they wanted done. The interview lasted no more than twenty minutes and she was sent back home to Dallas. Obviously, these people hadn't agreed on what they were looking for. They spent $2,000 and wasted people's time simply because they didn't communicate with each other.

> You have been interviewing with one or two people in an organization. Now you're told that the next interview is simply a rubber-stamp interview—or something like, "Our boss just likes to kick the tires." Whatever you do, don't believe anyone who tells you this. Nobody, I repeat, nobody, interviews anyone if they can't say no.

Time Is Your Enemy

The longer that the interviewing process takes, and the more people who are involved in it, the less likely it is that you, or anyone else for that matter, will get hired. There is no normal time period that is standard for the interviewing process. I have experienced interviewing/hiring processes that took fifteen minutes and I have experienced ones that took eighteen months; and some that started but ended with no one being hired.

The time it takes to fill a position and for an interviewing process to run its course usually depends more on the level of pain that an organization or hiring authority has than the level of the position. An executive vice president's position would probably take longer to fill than an entry level accountant simply because there are fewer executive vice president candidates than entry-level accountants; but, again, it really depends on how badly a person needs to be hired.

Key point: *One of the issues you're going to have to deal with in the interviewing process is the paradox of urgency.*

The paradox of urgency states that "every interviewing and hiring authority absolutely, unequivocally, urgently has to fill his or her position . . . someday." Most interviewing or hiring authorities that you will interview with will act as though filling the position that you are interviewing for is the most important thing they can be doing; that it is their number-one priority; and that they are going to set everything aside until they're successful at finding the perfect candidate. Again, I say ka-ka.

An interviewing or hiring authority must act as though there is a sense of urgency in filling the position and interviewing you. This person needs to act as though hiring was a high priority. It is not uncommon, though, for the priority of hiring to ebb and flow over a long period of time.

You cannot afford to get emotionally wrapped up in what interviewing or hiring authorities tell you they're going to do. They will tell you that you are the best candidate that they have seen (until the next one comes along) and you then never hear from them again. You can't control what other people do; you can only control how you react to it. Just don't get excited one way or the other, because time frames in the hiring process are dubious issues.

We have a rule around our place, called Tony's ten-day rule. It states, "If an employer and the candidate don't take some kind of action after the initial interview to move the interviewing process forward within ten working days of the initial interview, the probability of the candidate being hired decreases 10 percent for every day after those ten days." So, if there isn't any substantial activity of an employer getting back to you within the first ten working days after the initial interview, continue to pursue the opportunity, but don't expect many results.

The second guideline, and this as an overall broad guideline that can be applied to many, many things in the interviewing and hiring process, is to *have no expectations.* Go after every opportunity you can as though it was the last opportunity on earth. Prepare well. Interview well. Sell yourself as hard as you can ever imagine. Just don't have any expectations for anything. In other words, focus on the process and don't worry about the results.

Again, interviewing and finding a job is one of your highest personal priorities. However, it is just one of the many priorities within an organization running a business. Hiring or interviewing authorities aren't intentionally rude or unprofessional. They, too, are subject to all kinds of factors that you may not know anything about. People in this situation don't intentionally lie—they just end up lying some of the time. You can't let yourself become overly upset or distracted by it. If you are pursuing enough opportunities, none of these things should affect you. When the hiring authority tells you he or she is going to call you back but doesn't, if you have enough other opportunities to pursue, it won't matter. Remember, it's numbers, numbers, numbers.

> Be ready for the fact that the higher up the hierarchy you go in the interviewing process, the less knowledgeable the interviewing authority is about the job you might be trying to fill. The higher up the ladder you go in interviewing—with people who are removed from the day-to-day function of the job you are applying for—the more likely you are to talk to people who don't know or, at least, aren't sure, of what the qualifications for the position should be.

Success Plan for Follow-Up Interviews

The strategy for follow-up interviews is not far off from the strategy that you used in the initial interview. To a certain extent, you're going to do exactly what you did in the initial interview—with a couple of added steps to give you the advantage. The process, again, is so simple but most people don't think to do it.

Collect All the Information You Can

When you get a call from the interviewing or hiring authority that you interviewed with in the first place to tell you that you are going to come back for a second interview, you need to ask a number of questions that are very important to the success of your subsequent interviews. If you get a call from someone other than the interviewing authority you initially interviewed with, you must call and talk to that person with whom you interviewed. Get out the notes you took after the interview, review them so you can ask any clarification questions and then ask the following questions:

- "Mr. or Ms. _____, I'm excited about coming back and speaking with you all about the position we discussed. Can you please share with me what the whole process will be?"

  _____

  _____

  (Even if you were told what the process would be in the initial interview, you want to take notes and get an exact and detailed idea of what all of the next steps might be).

- "Please tell me what is Mr. or Ms. _____, the next person that I'm speaking to, like as a person?"

  _____

  _____

- "What is his or her role in the interviewing process?"

  _____

- "What does this person look for in a candidate?"

  _____

- "Based on what you know about me, where am I going to be strong or weak in the eyes of Mr. or Ms. _____?"

  _____

  _____

- "If you were me, what are the things from our initial interview that I need to emphasize in my interview with Mr. or Ms. _____?"

  _____

  _____

- "Is there anything in my experience or background that I should emphasize or elaborate about to Mr. or Ms. _____?"

  _____

  _____

- "How many people are moving up in the interviewing process?"

  _____

- "Mr. or Ms. _____, in this next interview, I was going to present myself to Mr. or Ms. _____, in the same way that I presented myself to you. Can you give me any pointers on how I might be able to present myself better as a candidate?"

  _____

  _____

  (This is a very important question because it will give you insights into the next interviewing authority)

- "If you were to personally rank the candidates that Mr. or Ms. _____ is going to talk to, how would you rank me?" _____
  (You hope that the interviewing or hiring authority will be honest with you and tell you how you rank with the other candidates. But most interviewing or hiring authorities don't have the courage or guts to tell you *exactly* how you rank. So, they're usually going to say something like, "Well, we're calling back three or four candidates and you are one of them.")

- *(If the interviewing or hiring authority actually tells you exactly how you rank with the other candidates, and you're not ranked number one . . .)* "Then, please tell me, Mr. or Ms. _____, what do I need to do in order to become your number one candidate?"

  _____

  _____

- *(If you are told that you are the number one candidate . . .)* "That is great to hear, Mr. or Ms. _____, what, in your opinion do I need to do to continue to be the number one candidate?" _____

  _____

  _____

- *(If you were told that you are one of a number of candidates being considered . . .)* "Mr. or Ms. _____, what in your opinion makes me a unique candidate and what do I need to do, in your opinion, to get the job?"

  _____

  _____

- "Mr. or Ms. _____, do I have your support in getting this job?"

  _____

"If it were totally up to you Mr. or Ms. _____, would you hire me for this position?"

(*If the answer is yes . . .*) "Great, what do you think I need to do to get the next interviewing authority to feel the same way?"

_____

(*If the answer is no . . .*) "What are your concerns?"

_____

(*If the answer is "maybe, depending upon what the other people think" . . .*)

"What are my strengths and weaknesses that you think I should emphasize or shore up with the next interviewing authority?"

_____

_____

"If all goes well with the next interviewing authority, are you going to recommend that your company hire me, Mr. or Ms. _____?"

_____

The reason that you want to ask all these questions is that it does absolutely no good to get to the second, third, or fourth stages of interviewing without knowing exactly how you stand or what you need to do to get the job. By asking these questions, you get the initial interviewing or hiring authority on your side of the fence. You are asking the person to support you as a candidate and you want them helping you as much as you possibly can. You will notice that I recommend asking the person to support you as a candidate in two or three different ways.

Keep Doing What You're Doing

Once you go to the second and subsequent interviews, you are going to ask every interviewer who promotes you to the next stage all of the same previous questions after the interview.

Many people get to a second, third, or fourth interview and think that since they have gotten this far they have a lock on the job offer. They relax in their intensity, alter their presentation, and basically quit selling, thinking it's a done deal.

At each succeeding interview, you should present yourself in exactly the same manner as you did with the initial interview. If your system is working, don't mess with it. You should only alter your technique based on what the immediate interviewer might tell you about the next interviewer.

If the initial and subsequent interviewing authorities make suggestions about your presentation, make sure you alter your presentation to accommodate their ideas. Keep in mind that if an interviewing authority promotes you to the next stage of the interviewing process, he or she has at least stated that you might be a viable candidate. If you ask the right questions as I have suggested, you'll not only get their support, but you will get their input and suggestions on how you might be able to interview successfully up the ladder.

If you don't get any substantial suggestions or input, the only way you should alter your presentation in the second and subsequent interviews is, instead of asking, "What do I need do to get this job?" at the end of the interview, you should ask the interviewer this question:

"Mr. or Ms. _____, I believe that I have the kind of experience that you are looking for in this opportunity. I believe I am the most qualified candidate you can interview. *Do I have your support? Will you recommend that I be hired?*"

If you ask any question other than this, it's too easy for a second, third, or fourth interviewing authority to say something like, "Well, it's not really my decision, I'm going to leave that up to Mr. or Ms. _____. It's really his (or her) decision." If you ask the previous question, you acknowledge the fact that the decision might really belong to someone else, but that the person you are now interviewing with does have a say in who gets hired. You are not asking the person to hire you, nor asking the person to support you. If the interviewer insists that it isn't really his or her decision, you need to say something like:

"Well Mr. or Ms. _____, your company must think very highly of your opinion or I wouldn't be interviewing with you. I need to be sure that I have covered all the questions about my candidacy with you and that I have your support. If I have answered all your questions, are you going to recommend that I be hired?"

Note: These are blunt and to-the-point closes. If the interviewing authority dances around them in any way and will not give you outright support, you best be aware that you probably will not get his or her support. On the other hand, you may get the person's support but still not get the job. In many instances, interviewing authorities up the ladder may not really choose a candidate to be hired, but they can say no. The idea is that you are being more aggressive and more assertive than most candidates will be.

Once you have completed the second, third, fourth, and so on interview, follow up with e-mails, letters, and phone calls, if appropriate. I would not recommend calling an interviewing authority whose job is to simply "gut check" or provide another opinion in the interviewing process. You want to phone the actual hiring authority and ask him or her about the decision. The more aggressive and assertive you are about selling yourself and closing on being the candidate who should be hired, the better off you are. You can be pushy, assertive, and confident without being obnoxious. Follow your gut, but don't be afraid you will lose the opportunity because you are too aggressive.

Some Interviews Are Worse Than Others

Okay, so we've covered the basics of handling follow-up interviews. You've got to gather support for your candidacy and as much information as possible on those you will be interviewing with as you move on. You want to keep focusing on your presentation, which presumably is working, and tweak it as necessary, based on suggestions of interviewers along the way, to make it even better. But all follow-up interview situations are not equal. Now, let's take a close look at a few interview situations that can really throw you for a loop—if you don't watch out.

The Group Interview—Really Watch Out!

Unfortunately, except in sales situations, the group interview has no likeness to most anything else that goes on in business. The idea is to see how a candidate responds to a group setting. The candidate is brought into a room in front of three or four (I have seen as many as nine) people and he or she is asked several questions. More often than not, this kind of interview becomes somewhat of a forum for personal political strategy among the people who are giving the interview.

Once you find out that it is going to be a group interview, you should ask the previous interviewing authority everything you need to know about the people and the situation. There is not much you can do about the group interview, except prepare yourself to be ganged up on from many directions. If you get into the interview and there are more than three people interviewing you, be prepared for a lot of political undertone in this session. It isn't easy to establish personal rapport with three or four people at one time.

One of the best ways to deal with a group interview is to get involved in telling stories that support the attributes you have applied to yourself. It is likely that in a group interview, especially if it is more than three people, you are going to be addressing people who are drivers, analytics, kinesthetic, auditory, and/or visual. The best way to deal with all those types of people in the same environment is to tell stories. Remember, stories bypass conscious resistance to the listener's own biases.

Immediately after the group interview, make sure you make notes about all the people you spoke with and what their individual questions, issues, or concerns might be. Do not rely on your memory. Take notes immediately, while things are fresh in your mind. You want to follow up with each member of the group in the same way that you followed up with the initial interviewer. If you can, try to remember specific issues that each individual interviewer discussed or brought up to you. That way, in the e-mail or phone call, you can customize your communications.

The Corporate Visit—Really, Really Watch Out!

For some management and sales positions, a visit to the corporate headquarters is often a common practice. Companies send candidates for a corporate visit for the same reason that they have multiple people interview them: *to spread the risk*. It isn't much different from when you interview with two, three, four, or five people in a local organization. You have to plan, be prepared, and get as much information as you can about the people you will meet at corporate headquarters.

There are a couple things that might be of value to note. First of all, rarely does a company send more than one, maybe two candidates for a corporate visit (unless, of course, the corporate office is close and it isn't very expensive to send people there). Usually, if the corporate visit requires a $1,500 to $2,000 plane ticket and a day of everybody's time, it isn't likely that more than one or two candidates are going to be sent at a time. If, however, one of the original candidates is not hired, then other candidates can always be sent.

When local hiring authorities send one or two candidates for a corporate visit, they are essentially telling corporate that they would be comfortable in hiring any of the candidates they send up for those kinds of interviews. Whatever you do, though, don't take that for granted. I have known many organizations that insist on a corporate visit by almost every candidate they hire simply because they don't trust anyone outside of corporate to be able to make the right decisions.

Be prepared to interview with people who, unfortunately, are going to have a say in your hiring but really won't have anything to do with your job, should you get it. This is done so that the company can have enough people interviewing you to make it look like the corporate visit was really of value. Rarely does the corporate visit involve only interviewing with one or two people. It looks rather silly for a corporation to spend $1,500 to $2,000 to get you to go to corporate to talk to only two people. So, they load your day up with a number of people who probably won't make any difference in the job you are interviewing for. However, since you were there to talk to them, they will have a say in whether or not you are hired.

There are going to be two or three key people who you really need to impress about your candidacy when you go to a corporate interviewing visit. The rest probably shouldn't be talking to you at all, but for appearance's sake, they will. Unfortunately, you are going to have to impress them and sell them just as well on your candidacy as the two or three key people. After all, if they're going to interview you, they're going to have something to say about you. I've had many instances where my candidate got to the corporate visit and interviewed with two or three people who even made the statement: "I don't even know why I'm talking to you, I don't really have anything to do with the job you're being interviewed for, but I'll do it." My advice is that since anyone who talks to you could say no to your candidacy, treat every one of them as though they were someone you really had to sell and impress.

Local hiring authorities do have some say in the game when they send you to corporate headquarters. But that doesn't mean you're going to get hired. Most candidates believe that if they are being sent for corporate interviews, they've "got the job in the bag." Don't assume anything! Metaphorically, all you are is on third base. You still have to make the effort to get home and score. Absolutely nothing is certain. So, don't let it go to your head.

Lunch or Dinner Interviews—Really, Really, Really Watch Out!

As you can tell I definitely don't like these things. Most people are not very good at mixing risky business events (like an interview) with social events that involve meals. I would certainly recommend trying to avoid it, but you may not have much choice.

The reason I don't like them is that I have seen candidates lose the opportunity to be hired, when they were the best candidate, because of poor performance in a social situation. So you say, "Well, Tony, we're all social beings and if a person doesn't have the social graces to perform well at a lunch or dinner; he or she may not have the ability to do a job." You may be right. But the truth is that the interviewing process is already an emotionally distressful experience. When you couple the distress and uneasiness of interviewing with having to be graceful in a social setting, it's very hard to do.

If the interview meal cannot be avoided, then there are a few things that you need to remember. First, watch your darn table manners. Slouching over your food, ordering the wrong kinds of food, talking with food in your mouth, or eating sloppily will kill you in a lunch or dinner interview. I have to admit that I am blown away by some of the poor manners that I have seen from both individual candidates and employers over the years. I've had candidates with fifteen to twenty years of excellent experience, MBAs from the most prestigious schools, and track records that were astounding screw up interviews at lunch or dinner because their manners were so appalling. There is no excuse for this.

Second, I would recommend that you never, ever drink alcohol in an interview setting. I don't care if your interviewing or hiring authority sits there and proceeds to get sloshed. Don't you drink. In an interviewing situation, you have to be as mentally and emotionally sharp, congruent, and grounded as you possibly can be. You can't afford to let anything impair your thought process.

Order your food after you see what your host is ordering. Don't appear to be taking advantage of a free lunch by ordering something on the high side of the menu. Let your host lead the way and follow suit. Either order something on the same level that he or she has ordered or something of lesser value.

Stay away from ordering messy foods, such as barbecue or spaghetti. Stick to simple foods that you can cut into small pieces before you put them in your mouth. In an interviewing situation, you are going to be doing most of the talking, especially if you are being asked numerous questions. Stay away from things that you have to pick up with your hands; even sandwiches can be a mess in some restaurants. Pieces of meat like a small steak or a chicken breast are perfect foods to order in an interviewing situation because they can be easily cut.

Get your coach to role-play with you in a mock lunch or dinner interview. Have the person be bluntly honest with you. If your table manners are less than excellent, you are not going to change them overnight. And don't think they're going to change suddenly just because you have an interview. When you get to focusing on interviewing questions, you are going to revert to the normal table manners that you have developed. If you need to change them, it is going to take lots of practice.

Also, it is preferable to eat a little something before you go on an interview that is going to involve a meal. Appearing ravenous or even hungry when you're trying to carry on an interview is very distracting. Order small amounts and eat slowly.

When your spouse, or date, is invited to a social dinner with the spouses or dates of the hiring authorities, you really need to be on your guard. These kinds of social engagements can be very nice, but they have the potential to be disastrous. Whether we like it or not, our spouses reflect on us and they can be either a positive or negative complement. I have experienced all kinds of unfortunate consequences because of a spouse or date who screwed up the social interview for my candidate. I've had spouses of male candidates drink too much, tell dirty jokes, even flirt with the hiring authority—in front of his wife, no less. I have had male spouses of female candidates get into arguments with their spouse at a dinner interview, dominate the interviewing conversation, and, in one instance, inform a hiring authority that he would not let his wife go to work for the company.

The spouse of a candidate who is being considered for job needs to realize his or her role in the interviewing process. We're all judged by the company we keep. Many businesses have lots of social interaction with their customers. Most social engagements with customers or clients will involve an employee's spouse. So, it is not uncommon for an organization to evaluate candidates not just on who they are but who they marry. I had one situation years ago where the wives of the president and three executive vice presidents literally voted on the candidate and his spouse. Yes, the wives of the president and executive vice presidents voted on whether or not the candidate *and* his wife should be hired. My candidate and his wife lost the election, which is why I remember it so vividly.

One issue to remember in the social interviewing situation is to always ask people about themselves. People love to talk about themselves. It's their favorite subject. It is amazing how thoughtful, intelligent, wise, and professional you will appear in a social setting if you let most people talk about themselves. And if you know how to master this skill, you are!

Other Social Events Before You Are Hired—Really, Really, Really, Really Watch Out!

Keep in mind that a golf game or a tennis game might be an integral part of the interviewing process. Remember, you are not yet a part of this organization—you are still being interviewed! When you are involved in a social gathering of the organization, if you are not yet hired, you run a big risk of being eliminated because someone, who probably has absolutely nothing to do with hiring you, isn't impressed with you and voices that opinion to a hiring authority.

Regarding the social events like picnics, Christmas parties, birthday parties, and so forth, if you don't feel like they are the essential to your being hired, gracefully decline the invitation and say that you have other plans. I can't tell you the number of times that I've seen candidates, their dates, spouses—and, even in a couple of cases, their children—screw up the candidate's opportunity to go to work in the company because of the way they behaved at a social function that had absolutely nothing to do with the hiring process.

Remember, This Is the Finals

"Never let the fear of striking out get in your way"
—BABE RUTH, GREAT HOME RUN HITTER IN BASEBALL

You are now in the finals. You're not going to get any other chance. You either win or you lose. It's just that simple. *Whatever you do, play to win!* Go after these opportunities to interview with everything you've got. Leave it all out on the floor, as they say in basketball.

But equally important, don't get overly cautious and play not to lose. Often in the interviewing process, when candidates get into the final interviews, they have a tendency to start operating out of fear of loss rather than the vision of gain. They start to become too careful about what they say and do in the interviews. They start reading into every question they're asked and every interview that they have. They start thinking, "Boy, I've made it this far, I'm really doing well. I really want this job. I really don't want to screw it up . . . I hope I don't screw it up, so I'll just be careful and not run the risk of making a mistake because things are going so well." Then the candidate proceeds to be completely different from the interviews that got him or her this far, and the candidate starts interviewing out of fear of loss rather than vision of gain.

If You Need to Take a Test

Let's spend a few moments on the subject of testing. This would include all kinds of psychological, aptitude, and intelligence tests. After more than thirty years of being in the employment profession, I have seen candidate-testing ebb and flow in popularity. Believe it or not, it seems to ebb and flow depending on the economy. Testing of job candidates can become very expensive, so it is one of the first things that companies stop doing when the economy gets difficult.

Be prepared for what I call the *paradox of testing*. Every company that has ever used testing as a part of its selection process is going to tell every candidate that, at most, the testing only accounts for 25 percent of the final decision. Don't believe a word of it! Whatever kind of test is used, from graphoanalysis to psychiatric interviewing, is a qualifier that you must pass with the minimum standard arbitrarily set by someone or some group in the organization, or you aren't going to go further in the interviewing process. Whether hiring authorities or companies will admit it or not, the test becomes a binary, black-and-white, proceed-or-go-home qualifier.

So, when a hiring authority tells you something like, "Oh, by the way, we have some psychological (or aptitude, or skills, or intelligence) testing you need to do as a candidate, but don't worry about it. Everybody that comes to work here has to take it and it doesn't really account for much more than 10 percent (or 25 percent, or 50 percent) of the decision." Don't believe a word of it! Testing becomes the gate that has to be passed through before you can be considered as a viable candidate.

Testing objectifies the hiring process. When objective tests decide on your viability as a candidate, no hiring or interviewing authority involved in the process of hiring has to have their butt on the line, has to take a stand on your candidacy, or has to run the risk of being the only person who likes you and wants to hire you. Now, a hiring authority is still going to have to make a decision in choosing someone to be hired. But the convenient thing about testing is that it also functions as a cover-your-butt issue. If hiring you turns out to be a mistake, but you did well on the company's battery of tests, the hiring authority can turn to everyone else and say, "Well, she did well on the testing!" It is just another way of passing the buck of responsibility.

First, whatever you do, don't bitch and moan to the prospective employer that testing is a lot of nonsense. In some cases, it very well is; but if a prospective employer does it as a routine part of the selection process, your opinion isn't going to matter. If you voice your negative opinion too much, you'll be eliminated for that reason alone. So, just decide to take the test in stride and resolve to do the very best you can. And, don't say something stupid like, "Oh, my God, I'm absolutely awful when it comes to tests." This may be true, but for goodness sake, don't tell that to a prospective employer.

Second, before you go to take the test, get lots of rest, eat a good meal, and relax. Do the very best you can. Look at it as a challenge. Take it in stride. Trying to prepare for it is useless. Do not be overanalytical and agonize over each answer, nor be flippant about the answers that you give.

While not as prevalent as they used to be, there are still some companies out there that test candidates with a face-to-face interview with a psychologist or psychiatrist. If this kind of thing is involved in your interviewing process, approach it the same way as you would approach a paper-and-pencil or computerized test. Be thoughtful of your answers. Be consistent in your answers and, for goodness sake, don't try to read into every question what the interviewer is trying to get at. That's a losing proposition. Don't become belligerent, challenging, or argumentative with the interviewer.

No matter what you do, no matter what kind of test you're given, whether it be multiple interviews with the psychologist or psychiatrist, written essays, multiple choice intelligence, character, or personality, do not try to outguess the test! If you sit there and ask yourself, "What are they trying to find out when they ask that question? Because if they're trying to find out 'that,' then I will answer 'this' so that they will think 'that' of me," you're finished! You can't outguess them.

Testing creates a great deal of homogeneity within companies. Being included or eliminated in the interviewing process by a testing procedure is just as valid or invalid as any of the other crazy reasons by which you may be included or eliminated.

Drug Tests and Physicals

Drug tests and physicals are part of the hiring process for many companies. I can address these in one short, simple manner: *you cannot avoid them and you cannot argue with the results.* If a physical is required, you probably already know what the results will be. If you have any physical issues that will be discovered, it is best to ask the hiring authority before the exam what criteria are being used and what the concerns are on the part of the hiring organization. Physicals are most often done in relation to the particular job that the company has in mind. These kinds of tests are supposed to be related to the job function. Executive level physicals, for insurance purposes, may not be technically legal. But, legal or not, if you refuse for any reason to take the physical, you will probably be eliminated as a candidate.

I have never known an organization to retest or reconsider hiring a candidate who has already been turned down for failing a drug test. Nor have I heard of a company that will consider hiring a candidate who refuses to take the standard drug test. We even had a candidate a number of years ago that claimed that a drug test would violate his religious convictions! Oh, boy!

How Jeff Handled Follow-Up Interviews

As I've already said, Jeff was very good at interviewing. He came across well once he got in front of an interviewer. His main problem was not getting enough interviews so that the numbers could work in his favor. Also, he would become discouraged when the interviews he got didn't pan out.

It is really interesting that after I began to work with Jeff and Amy, Jeff became much better at interviewing, not just because he was presenting himself in the way that I suggested but also because he began focusing on the process rather than the result. Jeff may not even recognize this, but there was a much more relaxed, confident, in control, and authoritative selling of his experience and ability than there had been in the interviews he had before. He did not come across as desperate and anxious in the interviews. In fact, he approached them with the attitude, "Well, I'm going to go in here and do my dead level best to sell myself because I really am an excellent employee. I sure hope I get the job and I will sell myself as hard as I can; but if it doesn't work out, I will go on other interviews where they will hire me."

Jeff's attitude in the latter stages of the interviewing process became one of, "Well, I'm going to do my best to focus on the process and let the result take care of itself." In interviewing for the job that he has now, Jeff was not called back by the company after the first set of interviews he completed. In fact, he was turned down for that particular job. But he interviewed so well that the company remembered him and called him back on another opportunity they had, which is the one that he accepted.

11 : The Toughest Interview Questions: Be Ready for Pitfalls

I've shown you how to get interviews—the key to your job search—and given you a basic script to follow during the initial interview to sell yourself through to additional interviews. I've also given you pointers on how to handle those subsequent interviews. In this chapter, I'm going to show you how to overcome underlying obstacles that can cost job candidates during the interview itself. Your body language and delivery are important, because they set the overall tone for any interview. However, the critical key is for you to understand the art of answering interview questions.

Body Language

My experience has been that in at least 50 percent of the cases in which an interview goes poorly, it begins to go poorly on the part of the candidate because of his or her body language. Many hiring authorities, during the interviewing process, don't help with their body language either. And there is a tendency to take on the body language of the person with whom you, as a candidate, are interviewing.

One good way to build rapport with an interviewing authority is to assume the basic posture that they are assuming in the initial stages of the interview. If the person crosses his or her arms or leans back in the chair, it isn't a bad idea for you to cross your arms and lean back in the chair, at least in the first few minutes of the interview. As the interview goes on, however, you want to present yourself in more of an open, direct, and assertive manner. It is important that, for the majority of the interview, you have your feet planted flat on the floor, your arms open (at your side or on the arms of a chair), and you lean forward just enough to make good eye contact with the interviewing authority.

Another pitfall is coming across too animated and nervous. This kind of thing happens when the candidate is too intense. He or she leans forward almost to the point of being in the interviewer's face: speaking loudly, nervously, and quickly and waving his or her arms to emphasize a point. Being enthusiastic is one thing, but being so animated that it puts people off certainly isn't going to win friends and influence people.

Remember: If your body language isn't appropriate, your words may never be heard. Practice, practice, practice.

Delivery

Along with body language, you need to be certain that you communicate your answers with enthusiasm, focus, and a high degree of confidence. Most people, especially in the beginning of interviewing cycles, are scared. I can't tell you the number of accomplished professionals I've interviewed over the years who mumbled when they talked, didn't look people in the eye, spoke in a monotone, and seemed distracted and uninterested, when in reality they were scared.

You need to communicate decisiveness, confidence, enthusiasm, and conviction with every answer.

Remember: If your delivery isn't effective, you will never be heard. Practice, practice, practice.

The Art of Answering Interview Questions

Most of the literature (both books and hundreds of articles about finding a job) addresses the kinds of questions that a person needs to be prepared for in an interviewing situation. In fact, some books devote the majority of their pages to providing answers for traditional questions that you will get in an interview. It isn't a bad idea to have answers to most of the traditional questions, but what I am going to do for you is provide *the underlying rationale for all of the questions that will be asked.* If you understand these underlying reasons, you will understand the art of answering interview questions.

Every question that you will be asked, in every interviewing situation, can be categorized under four subjects. If you understand the four subjects, then your answers will be a natural outgrowth of your understanding. The four subjects that all interviewing questions fall under are:

1. Can you do the job?

2. Do we like you?

3. Are you a risk?

4. Can we work the money out?

Look and sound familiar? Yes, it is that simple.

So, let's begin. I will present a number of the most frequently asked questions in interviewing situations and categorize them under each of the four topics. When you catch on to why these questions are being asked, knowing how to answer them will be very easy. I will set the stage for the answer to each question in light of the subject category it falls under and, after a while, you'll be able to figure out your own answers very easily. (As an exercise, at the end of the first three sections, I'll ask you some questions and allow you to answer them.)

1. Can You Do the Job?

These are going to be "What did you do" type questions. The hiring or interviewing authority is trying to discover your skill level, or in some cases, your potential. There are going to be only four or five *factual* aspects of your work history that will either get you to the second interviewing stage or eliminate you from consideration.

"Tell me about yourself and your last few jobs." If you've developed and used the presentation I provided in Chapter 3 on initial interviewing, you will not need to be asked this question. You will have already answered it in the presentation that you gave about yourself. However, if you haven't given your

basic job history and you need to answer this question, it is the perfect time to begin your presentation as I've outlined earlier.

"What kind of job are you looking for?" In other words, "Is what you're looking for the same thing that I'm looking for?" If you have done your research, you will know exactly what kind of position you are interviewing for. If not, then the answer is, "I'm looking for a position that is going to help make a company better and challenge me based on my experience and background."

"Describe in detail your last two positions." Even if you did a good job with your presentation on the last two or three jobs you had, (what you did, how you did it, for whom you did it, and how successful you were), you still may get this question. Give exactly the same description that you gave in your presentation, maybe with a little more detail. Be sure to precede your answers to this question with, "I really loved that job."

"What was the most difficult part of your past two jobs?" Whatever your answer is, you need to say, "Even though that was the most difficult part of the job, I met the challenge every time." Then communicate in appreciative, upbeat tones the hardest part of the job. You can even add something like, "Meeting that challenging part of the job made me a better person."

"What are you looking for in a job?" Obviously, you need to answer this question with an answer that has something to do with the job or position for which you were applying. Make sure that you say something along the lines of, "I've enjoyed the challenge of learning in just about every job I've had."

"Describe the best job that you've ever had and why it was so much better." Whatever you describe, make it similar to the position for which you are currently interviewing. A great way to precede the answer is to say, "You know, there have been some wonderful aspects to just about every job I've had. I have really loved all of them, and they are all 'best' for different reasons."

"How do you define success?" Simple answer, "When I contribute to a successful organization, I am successful—we both grow." Then perhaps relate a

story about how successful you were in your last one or two jobs. Remember, people love stories.

"What is your greatest accomplishment in each of your last three jobs?" Be sure to tell a story about the best accomplishment you had in each job. Whatever attribute was associated with the accomplishment; it needs to be supported by a short, interesting story. (Practice one, two, or three stories that you might use throughout the whole interviewing process.)

"What made you choose to become a _____*?"* It doesn't matter what job title fills in the blank. You need to be able to say that you always had an inclination or a passion for some aspect of your profession. Maybe you had a mentor, parent, or teacher who modeled the kind of profession that you got into. Whatever you do, do not communicate that you stumbled into your profession, it "chose" you, you couldn't find anything better to do, or you figured it was as good as any profession.

"What would be your ideal work group?" "How would you define a 'good-fit' work environment?" "Do you work well with other people?" "Do you prefer to work alone or with other people?" "Do you require and appreciate lots of supervision?" "Do you work best with large groups or small groups?" Any questions related to working alone or with others, in large or small groups, need to be answered with something like, "Well, I've had the good fortune of being able to work in all kinds of different environments. I have worked well alone and with others, in relaxed work environments and in tension-riddled work environments, in big groups and in small groups. I find that, fortunately, I am adaptable and work well in just about any environment."

"Describe the situation in your last one or two jobs where you made a mistake. What was the mistake and how did you rectify it?" Be ready for an "in hindsight" type of answer. Give the example but highlight what you learned from it. Have one or two of these kinds of stories available for this question when you get it.

"What are the things that you find most difficult to do? And how did you deal with them?" If you are an accountant, engineer, a technical person (or any-

body who is analytical or kinesthetic), the answer should center around what your personality is not. For instance, if you are an accountant or an engineer in an organization, you would say that the most difficult thing you have to do is operate in a sales function. If you are a salesperson, then you would say that the most difficult thing you have to do is operate in an accounting or engineering function. This may seem rather obvious, but the answer is very safe.

"Why should I hire you?" As soon as you hear this question, you should be ready to reply, "Because I can do the job, I'm a hard worker, people like me, I'm not a great risk, and we can come to a conclusion about money."

Exercise Questions

Prepare answers for the following basic questions. You're going to get questions like them over and over on interviews. (Where possible, your answers to many of these questions should describe when and how you were successful in the past.)

- Can you walk me through a day in your current or most recent job?

- Are you creative?

- What do you know about the position you are applying for?

- How do we know that you will be successful at this job?

- What is the most recent business lesson you have learned and how did you learn it?

- What specifically have you learned from the jobs that you held most recently?

- What can you contribute most to our organization?

- What do you know about our business? What is our business's biggest challenge or problem? What trends do you see in our profession or industry? What do you know about our competition? What do you know about our company?

- Can you describe a difficult business problem that you had to deal with and how you handled it?

- Where have you made difficult decisions before and what were they about? What makes you think you can handle this position?

- Why did you apply to our company?

- I don't think with your experience and background you are capable of doing this job. What do you think?

2. Do I (We) Like You?

These questions can have a tendency to get under your skin. So the way to prepare for them is to either use the answers that I've given or come up with your own; but practice them with your coach.

"Are you a leader or follower?" Simple answer: "Well, in certain situations I am a leader and in certain situations I am a follower. I can be both." Then reinforce this answer with stories, if necessary.

"What do people like most about you? What do they like least?" Things like being a team player, getting along well with others, dealing well in tense situations, volunteering when you don't have to, perseverance, communication skills, and so forth always work well. Being a perfectionist, wanting to see things done right, assuming control when no one else steps forward, or correcting coworkers when they've done something wrong work well as things people don't like about you (but employers do).

"What are your three greatest strengths? Three greatest weaknesses?" Strengths should be easy for you to come up with. Weaknesses are always difficult. What works well is saying things like, "Well, I'm very impatient with myself . . . I often expect the same passion and commitment from the others that I tend to have . . . I'm working on becoming a better listener." Make sure your "weaknesses" can also be viewed as "strengths." Ask your coach to help you with these because you are going to get this question or something like it.

"What are your hobbies? Outside interests? Books you've read recently?" Don't hesitate to talk about some of your outside interests and hobbies, if they are reasonable and would related well to the business. I would not recommend

talking about your particular involvement with anything controversial. Church groups, political parties, or any organization might be controversial. Talk about hobbies like golf, tennis, running, cycling, gourmet cooking, anything—just be sure it is safe and not controversial. Make sure you are reading some kind of business-oriented book and briefly mention it if you are asked.

"What do you like and dislike about your present (or last) boss?" This question has nothing to do with your boss, it has to do with how you express what you think of him or her. Badmouthing your present or previous bosses or company is the kiss of death. Have something positive ready to say and tone any criticism way, way down. You can begin by saying, "We didn't always see eye to eye," and go on to describe a situation where you disagreed with your boss.

"How do you handle criticism?" How you react to this question is as important as your answer. If you look startled like a deer in headlights, you will be communicating the wrong idea. Just expect to be asked this question and immediately respond by saying, "I really do appreciate constructive criticism; feedback is the breakfast of champions."

"Do you ever lie?" This is another Catch-22 question. The best thing to do is admit that you do lie in some rare instances when telling the truth has no consequences other than to hurt someone's feelings. For instance, you might say, "If I'm invited to a social occasion that I really don't want to go to, I will say that I have other plans. I guess, technically, that is a lie, but I see no sense in hurting other people's feelings by telling them that I don't wish to socialize with them." Then shut up. If the interviewer probes your response, simply say, "It is important to be truthful in every business dealing. I think lying is basically wrong and should only be used in situations as the last graceful alternative where the results are inconsequential."

"If you knew then what you know now, how would you change your life or your career?" This is a really good question and you need to have a really good answer for it. You should mention things that might be obvious. For instance, if you have not completed your degree, you might say that, looking back on it, you would have finished your degree. If you have had a couple of very short jobs on your résumé, you might say that if you knew then what you know

now, you wouldn't have taken those jobs. You should discuss any obvious mistake or misstep in your career, admit to it, and add the fact that you have learned a lot from the mistake. You might also add in summation that "the important thing, for me, is that I've learned from every mistake I've ever made and, fortunately, I haven't made the same mistake more than once. I know I will make others, but I'm going to make the best of what I learn from them." Do not say that you wouldn't change a thing because, even if it's true, not many people would believe you.

"What is your definition of success? Of failure? And how do you rate yourself in these two categories?" This is a loaded question that has no correct answer. But something along the lines of, "Well, success for me is the constant pursuit of a worthy goal where I am personally growing and economically providing for myself and my family. The only definition of failure, for me, would be when people quit trying and give up. Failure is not an option for me."

Exercise Questions
Prepare answers and review with your coach! (Think! Be reasonable! If you didn't know you, how do the answers sound? Rewrite your initial answers if you have to.)

- What are one or two things your present or previous coworkers *dislike* about you?

- What makes you mad?

- How do you make your opinions known when you disagree with management or your boss?

- Rate yourself on a scale of one to ten.

- How would others at your current or previous jobs rate you on a scale of one to ten?

- What makes you better than any other candidate I can hire?

3. Are You a Risk?

These are going to be the most difficult questions you will be asked. They're going to encroach on your character, your judgment, and the quality of your decisions, both personally and professionally. Everyone who has ever been hired is a risk. The real question imbedded in this subject is, "What kind of risk are you?" And along with that, "Am I, as a hiring authority, willing to run the risk and put my reputation on the line with this person?"

A hiring authority is trying to minimize risk and maximize a return on investment. It's a trade-off. A hiring authority wants to minimize his or her risk but get as many benefits as possible from hiring someone. With every risk you present, you have to offset those risks with the benefits you can provide.

Most candidates don't recognize the risks that they present to a prospective employer. In fact, many things that a candidate thinks are a positive attribute might very well be a big liability to most employers. You better analyze and know what the risks are that come with hiring you.

"Why do you want to leave where you are?" or ***"Why did you leave your last position?"*** This is one of the biggest "what kind of a risk are we taking" questions you will be asked. The answer to this question is one that will either effectively end the interviewing process for you or enhance the rest of the interviewing process. The key to this answer is to be as non-self-oriented as you can make it. An interviewing or hiring authority will assume that you will leave the company somewhere down the line for exactly the same reasons that you are leaving where you are now or you've left the last position. Employers identify with employers.

Being currently employed and looking to leave when you have been employed by that company for a relatively long period of time, say five years or more, and you are looking to leave because you are not growing personally or do not have the opportunity to grow beyond your job is a better reason to be leaving the position than new management coming in and not liking you. You have to be truthful in this answer but you also have to spin it so that you communicate a good business reason for yourself and for a future organization.

Again, saying anything negative or disparaging about the company that you are presently with, or are leaving, is not going to do you well. Anything negative about the people whom you were working for or have worked for will shoot you in the foot.

If the hiring authority and hiring company have a tremendous amount of pain, (that is, they really need to hire somebody or they are desperate to fill a position), they are less likely to care about why you are looking to leave or why you left your last employer. So, if you sense that the need to fill a position is great, you don't have to be quite as concerned about how analytical they will be with your answer to this question.

However, few organizations are so desperate to fill a position that they are not going to carefully analyze the answer to this question. Whatever you do, you have to communicate that you like your present job and the present organization that you work with. You are leaving simply because you are capable of doing more for an organization and therefore growing both personally and professionally.

Your answers should be along the lines of "Well, I really love my job, I really like the people I work with, and I appreciate everything the organization has done for me. However, the organization is in the process of being sold (under new management . . . has been contracting for the past few years . . . because of its size, it isn't going to grow, and so forth) and I am personally stymied in my professional challenge and personal growth. I can stay in the position that I am in, and I am not threatened; but for the next few years, I'm not going to be able to grow beyond the job I'm in now."

If you communicate self-oriented answers like, "I need more money or I want a better title or I'm going nowhere in my present firm," you'll be dead in the water.

"You sure stayed short periods of time in your last three jobs. What's wrong?"
The obvious fear behind this question is that, if you are hired, you will only stay at this job for a short time. Your answer has to be one where you do what we call in sales "changing the base."

The answer goes something like this: "While you are correct that I've had three very short stints in my employment, there are two things that are very important. First, I realize that someone like you is going to look at this as a liability. I don't like it any better than you do; in fact, it has really concerned me. I made mistakes in taking a couple of those positions, and if I knew then what I know now, I would have never done that. The truth is, however, that I really learned from the mistakes.

"The fact that I've had three relatively short job stints is one of the very reasons I can guarantee stability. I cannot very well afford another short stint at a job, so I am being very careful about the job I take. Whoever hires me is going to get a passionate and committed employee."

Caution: It does not do any good to try to *justify* two or three short jobs that appear on your résumé. That is a road to disaster. If you have this problem in your background, it will be one of the answers that you have to play down. Practice it.

"You've been the president of a company (or the owner of your own company). How do we know that you know how to work for someone else, or that you will take direction?" This is the underlying fear and concern that all employers have when it comes to hiring someone who has either been the president of an organization, run an organization, or owned his or her own company. The idea that the highest manager of an organization would actually work for someone else scares companies.

It is hard for most presidents or owners of organizations to work for someone else. It is an emotional adjustment that is difficult to make. However, it has been done and it does work. The answer to this question is really simple, "Well, you know as president of an organization (or owner of a company) I worked for a lot of different people and I answered to the entire company. I answered to customers, employees, the government, the IRS, my attorneys, my CPAs, insurance companies, vendors . . . and very often, my spouse (laugh). We all answer to someone. Even the president of your organization or owner of your organization answers to someone. I have never met a good leader who couldn't work within any organization, and be part of a team, as well as be a good follower.

"The truth is that we are all really *self-employed*. In reality, we all work for ourselves within an organization. The organization is simply a group of people working with and for themselves. Someone in the organization signs the paycheck, but the truth is that it is earned by the diligence of each individual. That is the way I've approached business when someone else signed my paycheck or when I was responsible for signing the paycheck. In this opportunity, I may not lead the organization, but I still work for myself. My future earnings will be dependent upon how I perform. In this case, the only difference is that someone else will sign the paycheck."

"This position is one or two levels below the ones you have had in the past. How do we know we won't hire you and then in six or seven months someone calls you

with a position like that and you leave?" To hire somebody and then have them leave, for whatever reason, is a great fear for most employers. Other candidates may stay a short period of time and then leave for all kinds of reasons, but the issue of having held higher positions is so glaring, in the onset of the relationship, that the hiring authority is very afraid.

The wrong answer to this question kills more opportunities for candidates than probably any question that can be asked. You need to really think about whatever answers you are going to come up with and put yourself in the shoes of the interviewing or hiring authority. Ask yourself, "If I didn't know me as I do and I was being compared with a number of other equally qualified candidates, how does my answer to this question make me look?" If the answer to this question makes you look like a dedicated, committed, reasonably well performing employee, who for good business reasons is looking for a job, you'll be fine. If your answer does anything less than that, you're dead in the water.

So, here is your best answer: "Mr. or Ms. _____, in every company in which I've ever worked, I've always started out at a position one or two levels below what I eventually attained. I realize exactly what I'm getting into with this job and the opportunity that you have outlined for me. I have no intention of wasting anyone's time, money, or effort, especially mine or yours. I wouldn't be trying to get this position if I didn't think that it would be challenging, gratifying work and I wouldn't have a really good future with this organization. In the past, when I have been in the lower-level positions with the companies in which I worked, I would get calls from time to time about interviewing at other organizations or other companies for higher-level positions. But I was very happy where I was. I enjoyed the work, I was challenged and, frankly, the compensation followed my being happy, content, and challenged in the job."

"Were you fired? Why were you fired?" If you follow the script that I have recommended about presenting yourself and each job you had (how you performed and why you left), this question may never come up. But, if it does, you must not communicate any kind of emotion or anger.

I strongly recommend that you do not answer this question with something like, "It's the best thing that ever happened to me. . . . It was a blessing in disguise. . . . The job wasn't working out, anyhow. . . . The job just wasn't for me." These kinds of answers have a tendency to come across as flippant and arrogant. The employer thinks, "Well, if getting fired was such a blessing, or the job wasn't working out anyway, or the job wasn't right, why did you keep the job?"

I hope that if you were in a position to be fired, you got your most recent organization to lay you off rather than fire you. The difference between being fired and being laid off connotes an adversarial discharge for cause in the former and an involuntary, at least on your part, separation for usually economic reasons on the part of the company that let you go. There is less of a stigma to being laid off. Different companies have different policies regarding what they will tell a prospective employer about why a person was terminated or laid off. The terminology may not be important to your previous employer, but it is very important to your future employment.

If the last organization you were with formally states that you were "laid off" rather than terminated, you can honestly look the interviewing or hiring authority in the eye and say that you were laid off. It is important to say something along the lines of, "I really loved that job and the opportunity it afforded me. I learned a lot from those people and the time I spent there was gratifying."

Being fired is tricky, but you obviously have to face up to it. It is rare for an employee to do well in a company for two or three years and then suddenly become a bad employee. So, the longer you had been on the job that you were ultimately terminated or fired from, the easier it is to say, "I really loved that company and I was there for a reasonably long time. I performed well, but there came a time for us (the company and me) to make a change." Looking the interviewer in the eye, you can then quickly follow up with, "And before that, I was at _____ company, where I performed very well."

Answering this question, when you have no other choice but to admit you were fired, even for cause, *takes more practice than probably any answer you will ever give* in *an interviewing situation*. Practice! Practice! Practice!

If you were fired for cause (and you're pretty sure that a prospective employer is going to find out that you were fired, rather than laid off), the best thing to do is to explain exactly what happened, in your opinion. You shouldn't criticize or denigrate your previous employer. Communicate the idea that although you don't agree with your former employer's decision, you respect it. In order to overcome the situation where you were fired with cause (and there is no way around having to talk about it in the interview), you are going to have to counter being fired with excellent references.

You may say, "Tony, how can I get good references from a company or individuals that fired me?" Well, you can do two things:

First, find some individual at the company you were fired from who will, on a personal basis, speak to a prospective employer about what you did, how well you did it, and, at least, provide a personal reference that might offset a formal negative reference. In other words, you are going to counterbalance and neutralize the negative reference.

Second, you must have a plethora of positive, glowing references from previous employers whom you worked with before your last job. Being fired, or let go, just doesn't have the same negative impact if it doesn't stand alone.

"If you could start your career over again, what would you do differently?" This is a trick question. Whatever you do, don't go overboard about all the mistakes that you made and what you would've done much differently. Something along the lines of "You know, I've been fortunate, I haven't made too many mistakes in my career and I sure learned a lot from the ones that I made. There aren't many career choices or decisions that I would change." Then have ready some rather innocuous mistake you can own up to and describe what you learned from it.

Exercise Questions

Carefully prepare your answers to the following questions and review them with your coach:

- Where do you see yourself five years from now?

- How does this job fit into your career goals?

- How much time did you take off last year?

- Have you ever had personal financial difficulties?

- If you inherited a lot of money, say $2 or $3 million, what would you do?

- If a personal commitment conflicts with a business emergency, what do you do?

- How long will you stay with us if you are hired?

- How do I know that you will stay with us for a reasonable period of time to be effective?

4. Can We Work the Money Out?

Most people think that these are some of the most difficult questions to deal with in the interviewing process. In my opinion, if all of the other questions about being able to do the job, being liked, and being a risk are answered, even reasonably well, these questions are easy to deal with. In fact, the answers to these questions are merely an outgrowth of all the previous ones. The more an organization would like to hire you and the more you would like to work for the organization, the easier it is to work out the money. So, the better you sell yourself, the more likely the organization is to compensate you fairly.

"What are you currently earning?" or *"What were you earning most recently?"* This is a simple question and requires a simple answer. Just share with the hiring or interviewing authority exactly what you have been earning or currently are earning. Whatever you do, don't inflate the numbers. If you are in sales, do not extrapolate the best month that you ever had and annualize it. If you are asked for a salary history, give it accurately. Over the years, I have had many employers ask this question during the interviewing process, and then after a person is hired, call the person's previous employer to verify his or her earnings—only to find out that the candidate lied. The person is then almost always terminated.

"What kind of money would you like to earn?" You should have some idea about the salary range for the position that you are interviewing for. However, your stock answer in a situation like this is, "Well, I'd like earn as much as I can commensurate with the service that I give. I am just as interested in a fulfilling and challenging position as I am in the money I want to earn. What kind of money for this position did your organization have in mind?"

Always discuss money in conjunction with the relationship it has to the job. What this communicates is that you are just as interested in doing a good job, as you are interested in the money you will receive.

"You have been making $ _____ and the money that is associated with this position is significantly less. How do we know that you will be happy?" In this situation, you have to find out exactly how much of a difference there is between what you have been making and what this particular position pays. If you've been out of work for any amount of time, the truth is, at this point you are making absolutely nothing.

No matter what the difference between what you have earned in the past and what the company is paying, your answer to this question needs to be something like, "Well, I realize there is a difference between what I have made (or what I am making now) and this position. However, I have found that if the opportunity is right and I am able to perform at my best, the difference in the money isn't as important as the quality of the job and the opportunity."

"What is the most money that you have ever made?" Bragging about making a lot of money will never help in negotiations. If you made an inordinate amount of money several years ago, I would recommend not even mentioning it. Again, the answer to this type of question needs to center around not just what you've earned but also the challenge of the job opportunity itself. Try saying, "There have been a few years in which I've been fortunate enough to be with organizations where bonus earnings were sizable. But I realize that those are very uncommon. I am more interested in the opportunity, the challenge of the job and the potential. If those things are taken care of, my earnings will reflect my performance."

"What do you consider most valuable: a high salary, job recognition, or advancement?" Again, combining earnings with job performance is the most important thing you can do. Say something like, "Well, I have found that the better job I do, the harder I work, recognition, advancement (and, especially, money) usually take care of themselves."

"What kind of benefits are you expecting?" In the past few years, benefit plans, especially in the health insurance arena, have skyrocketed in cost—particularly for companies with a hundred people or fewer. So, there is no such thing as standard benefits. Many organizations have drastically reduced their benefit plans for their employees. The purpose of this question is to find out if there is going to be a great deal of difference between the kind of bene-

fits that you have had before and the kind of benefits that might be offered with this company. So, answer something like, "Benefits, like money, to me are not as important as the company, the job, and the professional challenge. I will certainly take the benefits package into consideration if an offer is made, but right now those kinds of things shouldn't be an issue."

Questions About Money

Any questions you are asked about money during the interviewing process before you get to the final offer stages need to be handled gracefully, but postponed until the final offer stages. Once you get to that stage, you have established yourself and the value you can bring to the organization. The greater the value you establish for yourself, the more money you will be able to negotiate.

Remember: Always discuss money in relationship to the value you bring to the job.

Illegal or Inappropriate Questions

With the majority of the companies in this country having fewer than one hundred people, it probably won't surprise you that some hiring authorities just don't have any idea about what is legal and what isn't. Some will simply ask inappropriate questions, thinking that they're trying to help both you and them. Again, I repeat: Most hiring authorities in the United States just aren't very professional. They might be good at their profession, but they're lousy when it comes to interviewing and hiring people.

Interviewers who ask illegal and inappropriate questions usually do so out of ignorance. However, some people's egos cause them to ignore the law and ask whatever they damn well please.

Many of the following questions are illegal and the ones that may be technically legal seem very inappropriate.

- How old are you?

- Are you married?

- Are you single or divorced?

- Does your spouse work?

- Do you have small children?

- Can you work long hours with your family commitments?

- We have a lot of women (men, whites, blacks, Hispanics, Vietnamese, Asians, Christians, Jews, Muslims, etc.). Will that be a problem for you?

- Where were you born?

- What country are your parents from?

- What is your religion?

- Do you go to church?

- What is your race?

I happen to disagree with the experts who will tell you flat out that in an interview you don't have to answer certain questions, especially ones that are illegal. I'm going to tell you to do what you think is best. I'll be the first one to tell you that illegal and inappropriate questions are completely out of line. However, if you really need the job, the legality and inappropriateness of any question is probably way down on your list of priorities. Getting a decent offer is more important.

Even if you think that the hiring or interviewing authority is aware that what they're asking is illegal, it may not be a good idea to say, "That is an illegal question and I don't have answer it" or "That is an illegal question and I won't answer it."

You may want to consider answering the question, depending on the context in which it is asked. If you feel like someone is asking your age, or if you were married, because the person will probably use that information to eliminate you from consideration, then you might say something in a startled, surprised but very *kind* manner like, "Oh, goodness, I didn't know you could ask that question, but . . ." Then answer the question in a way that you think is appropriate.

You might also answer the question with a question, such as, "How does the answer to that question have an impact on my performance of the job or my ability to get it?" This is a very nice way of saying, "That's an illegal question. It has nothing to do with my ability to do the job, so I'm not going answer it." If you feel that the question is being asked out of genuine interest and in sincere empathy—like in a casual conversation after a formal interview—feel free to answer it in any manner that you wish.

Again, follow your instincts and answer these questions in whatever way you are comfortable doing. If you think it is appropriate to "set someone straight" about the legal questions, feel free to do so. Just don't get your nose out of joint over it. If the questions insult you, don't work there.

Jeff and Amy's Experience

As I've said, Jeff's personality lent itself very well to the interviewing process. He is smart, personable, and could communicate ideas extremely well to just about anybody. He sold himself extremely well when he got into the interviewing process itself. Performing well on interviews wasn't a problem for Jeff.

However, like most people who rarely look for a job, Jeff lost sight of the basic questions that a candidate needs to remember that the employer is asking, "Can this person do the job, do we like him, is he a risk, and can we work the money out?" Jeff mentioned that because he had not had to look for a job very often, he never really focused on those questions.

One area that tripped up Jeff during interviews was the fact that he had become overspecialized. His recent experience focused on valuation software—a narrow application that was not relevant to the work needed at other companies. Also, most of his accounting experience was three years old, which put him at a decided disadvantage to the other candidates whose accounting experience was more up to date. When questions were raised in these areas, it was hard for Jeff to overcome the facts.

When Jeff first began looking for a job, he thought there was a silver lining in his needing to look for a new one. He was convinced that he would find something better, as he had found before. When this didn't happen within a reasonable period of time, he tried to find what he and Amy called survival jobs. He applied to retail types of positions and fast-food types of positions, but felt that when people looked at his résumé they knew that he was only going to be temporary until he found a better job. Of course, he couldn't claim that this wasn't the case, so none of these jobs worked out. On the other hand, Jeff thought that a survival job like this would be depressing anyway and not really help in his overall job search.

12   Overcoming Employer Biases That Can Keep You from Getting a Job

"Seek and ye shall find, ask and ye shall receive, knock and it will be open to you."
—St. Matthew, Author of the First Gospel

There are many things that can hold you back in your job search that would seem to have little to do with your ability to do the job in question. These hindrances fall under the general category of employer biases. Employers may have biases against hiring candidates who have been let go by another employer; who have been out of work too long; who want to change careers; or who have had too many jobs. They may even have unstated (and illegal) biases against hiring older people, women, or minorities. As a job candidate, all you can do is face these kinds of employer biases head on and deal with them as positively as you can. The best solution is to keep knocking on lots of doors, presenting yourself to as many potential employers as possible, and pressing for the right door to open with a good job opportunity.

Let's go through some of the more common employer biases:

Been Fired or Laid Off

Yes, you can find yourself being discriminated against because you were fired or laid off. It can wind up being a blessing in disguise, but it is a big red flag of liability to most employers. The difference between being fired and being laid off is significant. You are going to have to overcome the stigma of being fired. So, you are much better off if you can communicate the idea that you were laid off rather than fired.

> If you were fired, it isn't a bad idea to write a letter to the president of the company thanking him or her for the time that you were there and explaining how much you appreciate the company and all you learned. It is not a bad idea to write letters to some of the people in the organization whom you might have felt close to—thanking them for their support and communicating how much you appreciate having worked with them and how much you appreciated their support. You should take these letters to interviews and use them at an appropriate time if the question of your being fired comes up. If your ex-boss is willing to give you an even halfway decent reference, make sure it corroborates your story as to why he or she had to let you go.

Hopefully, if you were in a position of potentially being fired, you got your most recent organization to lay you off rather than fire you. Most companies, rather than create a picture of an adversarial bad employee, would rather lay you off than fire you. Unless you were fired for a very serious cause, such as embezzlement or sexually harassing a coworker, most organizations will be amenable to stating that you were laid off.

There are some situations where a prospective employer is going to more easily understand you being let go or fired. A total change in management, the buyout of a company, or a large downsizing are all acceptable reasons for someone to lose a job. And if your ex-boss gives you a good recommendation, you're in good shape.

What to Say

As I've mentioned before, avoid true confessions and trying to justify what happened from your point of view. You will never win a job that way. In fact, how you present the whole situation of being fired is more important than what you say. You need to practice your presentation over and over again so that you can disassociate yourself emotionally from the actual firing.

Be humble about being fired; it also doesn't hurt to take on some of the responsibility. Saying something like, "You know, looking back on it, I would've done a little better about getting those reports to my boss in a more timely fashion," or "Looking back on it, I realized how much pressure my department was under to perform faster than we did."

Remember that you can overcome just about every unfortunate situation regarding why you left your last job if you can establish enough *value* for being hired. In other words, if the benefits of hiring you outweigh the liabilities and risk in hiring you, how you got there won't matter.

Out of Work for Six Months or More

I know you: You were laid off or fired, or you quit your job a while ago—a lot longer time ago than you want to admit. You are really hurt and surprised at having to look for a job and you thought you would take a little time off to get over the immediate emotional strain. Besides, you really hadn't taken much time off over the years, so . . .

It was summertime (or spring, or winter, or the holidays) and you really hadn't spent much time with your kids or your spouse in a while, or you hadn't visited back home (your family, your cousins, your old friends), so you thought you'd take a little time off. . . . You had some savings and some money in your 401(k) so, you thought, "We can live on that for a while." . . . The house needed painting, and once you started painting you thought, "This would be a great time to build onto the house." . . . You lost your job in September or October, and decided that since "nobody does any hiring around the holidays," you'd just take some time off and wait until after the first of the year . . . You had a friend who had a friend who had a friend who thought there might come an opening in their company in two or three months and you might just be the perfect fit, so you waited . . . and waited . . . and waited, but the job never came about. . . . Since the kids are only little once, you decided to stay home with them so you could really create a great bond with them, and one month led to another and that was six months ago. . . . You always wanted to take time off and see America, so you did.

The emotional and mental spiral downward began with the best of intentions!

The problem you have created is at least two-fold. The first problem is that you now must convince a prospective employer that you are *not* a risk! A prospective employer is going to look at what you have done—or should I say, what you haven't done—for the past six, nine, or whatever months. The prospective employer is going to think, "If this person can afford to be out of work for the past six months, how do I know that if I hire him, that three to four months into the job he just may decide to take another sabbatical and leave. I don't think I can afford that!"

The second problem you've created for yourself is that the longer you postpone looking for a job and go unemployed, the harder it is and the longer it is going to take for you to be successful in finding a new job. This is because the mental and emotional spiral downward often creates mild to severe depression. And, when people are depressed, they don't interview very well. The longer you go without making a plan to find a job and executing that plan, the harder it is to do!

I don't care what any professional or career counselor or psychologist or psychiatrist—or your mother or your spouse—might tell you, taking any extended period of time off to clear the cobwebs from your head and emotionally get used to the idea of looking for a job—by doing all the things mentioned previously—is nothing but ka-ka.

When people take an extended period of time to begin looking for a job after they have lost one, they begin to make all kinds of mental and emotional excuses as they spiral downward. They start saying things like, "Well, you know, I passed up a job better than that three or four months ago, so there's no reason for me to take that job." Or, "Well, I always thought that I could call my friends and I knew they would hire me."

A few weeks leads to a few months and then the person starts thinking, "What's really wrong with me?" Then the unemployment runs out and the savings run out and the 401(k) runs out, and the person begins to panic. And this panic may very well lead to depression. Then the person begins to think, "I'll never find a job"—even if he or she is not taking any action to look for a job. People in this state start telling themselves and their families that "the economy sucks" and "there are no jobs out there," and the whole thing becomes a self-fulfilling prophecy.

If you are reading this before you have hit that sixth-month wall of quasi-depression and confusion, and haven't gotten to that self-fulfilling prophecy of "there are just no jobs out there," don't keep doing things that are going to lead to postponing the activities necessary to look for a job. *Start today to work the process of finding a job!* Whatever you do, don't let this emotional and mental spiral downward happen.

If you find yourself mentally and emotionally mired in the "sixth-month syndrome," there is only one way to get out of it. And that is to take massive action by beginning to manage the process of finding a job. You cannot postpone it any longer. You have to start reading inspirational and motivational books, listening to inspirational and motivational tapes, and stop reading the newspaper and take *all* the actions I have recommended. Start at the beginning of this book and literally throw yourself into the job-finding process.

What to Say

You now need to figure out what you're going to say to a prospective employer when he or she asks you why you've been out of work so long. If in any way, shape, or form, you communicate the idea that you could afford to take the time off, so you did, you are going to give the employer the idea that you could take another six months off—and it won't bother you one bloody bit. But it will definitely bother him or her. You won't get hired. You are just too much of a risk.

So, you need to say something along this line: "I had no idea how difficult it was going to be to find a job. When I lost my last position, I took a few weeks off and then started to look around and interview fairly casually. I ended up pursuing a couple of opportunities that I waited on way too long. (*If you can be specific about names of companies and names of opportunities, and names of the people that you were talking to, it adds more credibility.*) Unfortunately, I hadn't changed jobs in several years and

> A popular approach for the past few years is for candidates to state on their résumés that they have been a consultant. Oh, God! Please, please, please don't do that unless you really truly have been consulting to organizations or people whom you can actually document. And I mean document with names, dates, types of projects, and so forth. Most hiring authorities with any brains at all, when they see the term *consultant* on a résumé, are absolutely positive that it just means a person has been out of work. So, if you are trying to cover up being out of work by saying that you are a consultant, you're outright lying, and very few people are going to appreciate it.

didn't know how difficult the process would be. I've been earnestly looking for a job by proactively going after interviews for the past two months. I am in the cycle with two organizations but I do not have any offers at this moment. Looking back on it, I've miscalculated how difficult the job market was. I thought it would be easier. I have to go to work. I need to feed my family.

I'm an excellent worker . . ." and then you start selling yourself in the way that I have recommended.

Admit that you miscalculated the market and communicate that you have been (for the past couple months) interviewing your butt off, that you can't afford not to work, and that you need to be hired, preferably by the person to whom you are speaking. Communicate that you are not a risk, that you can't afford to take off extended periods of time, and that you are a passionate and committed worker.

As with many of the other challenges in this chapter, if you create enough of a value for yourself in the eyes of a prospective employer, he or she really won't care how long it has taken for you to look for a job.

Note: If you *really* want to take a few days or a week to clear your head, immediately after you lose your job is the time to do it. But first make a plan for your job search. This plan will give you the emotional comfort that you are ready to go to work on going to work as soon as your short break is over.

You've Had Too Many Jobs

I discussed this issue to a certain extent in Chapter 11 when I addressed the question of, "Why have you had so many jobs?" This is as much of a concern about minimizing risk as anything else. One of the biggest fears that most employers have is to hire someone and then not have it work out—for whatever reason. It makes them look bad and no one wants to look bad. So, if you had two or three jobs in the last three or four years (it really doesn't matter in what profession it has been), there is going to be a concern that you've had too many jobs.

If you have had three jobs in three years, a prospective employer is going to assume (or be afraid of), that you will only stay on the job for one year. Suffice it to say, you will never win this argument.

What to Say

The key to answering this question successfully is not so much to offset the concern as it is to counterbalance and neutralize it. Since you know that you are going to get the question (if you don't, the interviewer is going to think it), you should bring up the question and provide the answer to it *before* the interviewer or hiring authority asks it. In fact, as you begin to make your presentation the way I suggested in Chapter 11, you should begin by saying something along the lines of: "Unfortunately, I know that I have to overcome the fact that I've had too many jobs in the past few years. I know that it appears to be somewhat of a risk, and I don't like it any better than a prospective employer would. However, I sure learned a lot. One of the very reasons that I should be hired by an organization like yours is that I can't afford to make a mistake and I plan on being in my next position at least five to seven years." Then go on and explain every job you had in the detail that I suggest.

If you have had a long stint of employment before the previous two or three short stints, it's a good idea to remind the interviewing or hiring authority how much you are looking for long-term employment. It is also a good idea to admit that one or two of the positions you had were mistakes. Say something along the lines of, "If I knew then what I know now, I probably wouldn't have made that decision."

You have to ask yourself, "How does my instability appear to a prospective employer, and if I were in his or her shoes, what would I think?" As I said before, whatever you say will be used against you. Remember to always reinforce the fact that you loved the previous jobs and appreciated all of the people—and you learned a heck of a lot.

The very best way to overcome any concerns about your previous employment or any challenging aspect of your candidacy is to prove the value of hiring you over anyone else whom the employer could interview. Along with this, you should have some really solid references that will substantiate your stability.

You Want to Change Careers

At least four or five times a week, our organization encounters well-educated, well-trained, well-experienced professionals who want to change their career. Their attitude is that since they have been even reasonably successful in one endeavor, they can automatically be successful in another. They look around and see people in other professions and have a tendency to think that, for one reason or another, it would be a better place for them. So, they want to change careers.

In the boom cycle when there are fewer people and more jobs, experienced people are hard to come by. Since companies have a difficult time finding experienced people in what they specifically do, they are willing to take as close to "like-kind" experience as they can get and train those people. That is why some people at different times appear to have an easier time changing careers than others. The opportunity to change careers was easier in the boom economy because hiring organizations did not have much choice. They had to hire people who didn't have any experience in what they did and train them. They could afford to hire people who weren't immediately productive, train them, and not be concerned about their immediate contribution.

In a more difficult economy, there are lots of very qualified people available on the market and companies are watching their bottom-line profits more carefully. When earnings are harder to come by, the whole concept changes. Hiring organizations need to find people with as much experience in what they do as they can get because those people need to be contributing almost immediately to the bottom line. Companies cannot afford to wait around for someone to catch on to what they do. Everyone must be able to pull his or her own weight immediately. This fact, coupled with the fact that there are many more experienced people available in the marketplace, allows a company to be very selective in its hiring and pretty much find exactly the kind of experience that would be best.

What this means to you is that just because you think you would like to change careers doesn't mean that it is going to be feasible to do. On top of all of this, you have to take into account the value you bring to a hiring organization when you have no track record in what they do. Why is an organization going to pay you the kind of money that you've been making doing one thing, or in one profession, to perform in a position or function that you have either absolutely no, or very little, experience doing?

Let me make it emphatically clear that changing careers is possible. But most people don't take into account everything that it entails. In the previous example, if a person were to start all over at the ground floor of a profession and work his or her way up, it is feasible. This usually means a drastic cut in earnings. Why would a company, on average, pay top dollar to a person whose experience and background doesn't fit exactly what they want done?

If a person has a father-in-law, brother-in-law, relative, or very close friend who is willing to pay what he or she has been making to do a job that he or she really doesn't know how to do, or has no track record in, it might work.

You might want to consider a career adjustment rather than a career change. If you can, try to find a profession or job that somehow relates to the kind of thing you've been doing, so that you can bring something to the party. This at least gives you some advantage. Write down all the functions and aspects of what you are currently doing and think about ways that you can apply those skills to something related to your profession.

There is always the option of owning your own business. This book is not about that approach, but it is a feasible option. There is a tremendous amount of entrepreneurial and franchise opportunities available in U.S. business. (Did you know that the industry that has created more millionaires from scratch in the United States is the dry cleaning business? It certainly isn't exotic and it has its problems, but it can be extremely lucrative.) Owning one's own business, especially a small business, in the United States is a lot more difficult than most people think. But, everything has its price and there are plenty of millionaires who got into the business that made them money because they had no other choice. It appears that success in owning your own business, in either a stand-alone or franchise opportunity, boils down to the same things that any other successful business does—no matter what the size, find a system that works and stick to it.

If you have *already changed careers* and are looking to get back into a profession in which you had previous experience before your most recent career change, you are experiencing the same difficulty that those people who want to change careers are experiencing.

Three years ago, I had a candidate who, after spending fifteen years selling software, bought a chain of retail dry cleaning stores. He was very successful and had the chance to sell the stores at a sizable profit. He really didn't like all the business problems he encountered in the dry cleaning business, so he wanted to get back into selling software. He had a hard time even getting interviews, let alone job offers. First, he didn't have any recent contacts or recent track record in the software business and second, all of the other candidates he was competing with did. Although he had a tremendous track record up until three years ago, there were too many other candidates out there, especially in this market: ones who aren't as great a risk. Prospective employers would say things like, "Well, Tony, if he really wanted to sell software, why did he get out of it?" Or, "Well, Tony, we can't run the risk of hiring this guy even if his track record was good, because, after a year or so, he may decide to do something else entrepreneurial. And the last thing we need is for someone to get into the job for a year or so and then leave."

The success that a person might have in returning to a profession or career that was interrupted by a completely different profession or career will depend on timing. If the economy is in a boom cycle and the ratio of candidates to job opportunities is low, then the hiring organization has to take the best candidate who is available, even if his or her experience might be two or three years old. But, if the economy is like it has been in recent years—where the ratio of qualified candidates to job opportunities is high—competition is very keen, so the hiring organization can take fewer risks.

How can you overcome the fact that you're changing or have changed careers? Knock on lots of doors until you find someone who will accept the risk!

Dealing with Discrimination

"If a man is called to be a street-sweeper, he should sweep streets even as Michelangelo painted, or Beethoven composed music, or Shakespeare wrote poetry. He should sweep streets so well that all the host of heaven and earth will pause to say; here lived a great street-sweeper who did his job well."
—MARTIN LUTHER KING, CIVIL RIGHTS LEADER

So, you think there is discrimination. The blunt truth is you're absolutely right. *All* hiring is discriminatory. The issue is that some things used to discriminate are legal and some are illegal. No employer is ever going to admit to the illegal ones. Any selection process for just about anything discriminates in favor of some qualities as opposed to others.

In the more than thirty years that I've been in the employment profession, I have seen discrimination drastically change. For the most part, it has been for the better, but the issues and types of discrimination have changed radically. Some of it has to do with the globalization of businesses in the United States, some of it has to do with the immigration policies of the United States, and some of it has to do with the United States still being a model of the world's land of opportunity for those who want to work.

When I first entered this profession, there was a lot more discrimination against women and minorities than there is today. We don't hear, "Don't send me a woman . . . or a black . . . or a Hispanic," anywhere near as much as we used to. We probably hear a little more age discrimination, in very subtle ways, than we hear about sex or race discrimination.

Discrimination, for all kinds of reasons, is always going to be with us. You're just as likely to be eliminated for lack of experience, or the wrong kind of experience, or salary considerations, or the kinds of things discussed previously in this chapter, as you are because of your race, religion, age, or gender. Just be aware that you might be discriminated against for all kinds of reasons. Move on!

If You're Over Fifty (or Forty or Sixty)

To start with, unfortunately, our society is youth-oriented. It is an attitude that we can do nothing about. This is all in spite of the fact that the majority of the working population is near fifty and we really know we are never going to be twenty-five again (who wants to be, anyhow). When it comes to hiring, there is an unconscious cultural bias.

The majority of employers in the United States don't really care about age. But they do end up being concerned about some of the *issues* people who are near fifty and older might bring with them. Here are some of the blunt, real issues that employers are concerned about:

"I'd be hiring someone old enough to be my father or mother." What this means is that hiring authorities are afraid that older candidates won't respect them, be subordinate to them, or want to work for them. The hiring authorities have enough to be concerned about without having someone appear to know more than they do.

"Older people are set in their ways." Of course, this is a myth. There is absolutely no truth to it. The fear here is that the new employee would be doing things his or her way instead of the company way.

"Anyone with twenty-five or thirty years of experience should be making much more money than we can pay and be further in their career. So, therefore, this person can't be very good." This, of course, is a relative statement. Some people advance, some don't, for all kinds of reasons. But the perception is out there. It is a terribly misguided theory, but it is prevalent nonetheless.

"Older people don't have the same passion, drive, and commitment as younger people. They are looking more toward retirement than they are to work." There is no way of disproving this. Some are; some aren't. But there are also thirty-year-olds looking toward retirement; they just don't talk about it, lest they look foolish.

"Older people don't have any energy." People have energy or they don't. People who have energy have it when they are fourteen, twenty-eight, or sixty-eight years old. People who don't have energy don't have it when they are fourteen, twenty-eight, or sixty-eight years old.

"We want people on the upswing of their career, not on the decline. We want them going up the ladder, not down." Well now, everyone cannot be climbing the same ladder. And older people get promoted the same as younger ones do. Since most promotions are based on performance—or should be—what is the difference?

"Older people are looking for security and a place to retire. We want aggressive risk takers who aren't afraid to fail." This is another ridiculous myth. Risk taking, like energy and passion, is either in a person's makeup or it isn't. It has nothing to do with age.

"An older person will be asking for too much money for our job. If they are older and haven't made more money than this, something is wrong with them." Earnings have nothing to do with age. Ask Bill Gates when he made his first billion. But the perception is that people should make more money the older they get.

"Older people have more illness than younger people and our insurance rates are already sky high." There is some validity to this comment. The older the workforce, the higher the insurance rates. Insurance programs are changing and

employers' options are becoming more flexible. However, this still presents a challenge for employers, especially the smaller ones.

"Our company culture is young. We party a lot together, and a fifty-year-old just wouldn't fit in here." We don't hear this one as much as we used to a few years ago. Why? Because the majority of managers are now near fifty. Ha? Being fifty years old (or older) looks pretty different when you're fifty years old or older!

Good News for "Older" Candidates

When a candidate over forty, forty-five, or fifty years of age gets refused (in his or her mind, "rejected"), there is a tendency to think it is because of his or her age. This person has no concept of how many job candidates the employer has, so he or she blames the rejection on age. But this person's thinking goes: "I can really do that job and there is no good reason I wasn't hired, except for my age." The vast majority of the time, age has absolutely nothing to do with getting hired or not. People (that is, companies) hire those they *like* and they *like* different people for different reasons.

The majority of the baby boomers are now in their late forties and early fifties. They are the largest generational population sector in the workplace. So, when the employment market got soft, it just so happened that there were more of them on the market than any other age group. There are just more people in that age range in the workforce. It's a numbers thing, not an age thing.

If you are in this age group, there is good news. You are among the majority of people in the workforce—the top of the baby boomer generation. That is good because most of the hiring authorities out there, who have risen to management positions, are in the same age bracket. Once people are forty-five to fifty years old themselves, they are no longer afraid of forty-five- or fifty- or sixty-year-olds.

These days, there is not as much bias about older job candidates as you might think. But you may be more sensitive to it because it is you, so you need to be prepared to face the issue.

The reality is that being older or "too experienced" is just another consideration for employers, like a candidate having had too many jobs, not the right kind of positions or experience, and so forth. The truth is that to a prospective employer the amount and quality of your experience are relative and subjective things. Your age isn't.

If you sell your age and experience the right way, it can be one of your best assets. But, it really has to be sold in the right way. Here are a few tips:

- Stress your longtime experience; don't try to hide from it.

- Use plenty of stories during your presentation to show that you've seen a lot of things in your work life, dealt successfully with most of them, and learned from the rest.

- Explain that you know what to expect from the job; you are not likely to be surprised by any aspect of it.

- Assure the interviewer that you want to work; you are not looking toward retirement.

- Where possible, mention things like your computer skills, to show that you are not a technophobe, or a sport or activity you enjoy, to show that you have energy and are not slowing down.

- Above all, emphasize how much value you would bring to the company and how much you would like to work for this employer.

If You Are a Woman

There is less discrimination against women than there used to be. However, it is still true that women, for the most part, have to work harder than their male counterparts. I am not here to justify why this is the case. But in the vast majority of companies in the United States, this is the case. Now, there are some professions where women are the majority, but if they compete in the normal realm of business in America, they simply have to work harder than men to prove themselves and to be recognized.

The cause of this inequality may be the stark reality that the majority of businesses in this country are run and managed by men.

If you are a woman and trying to raise a family, as well as work outside the home, you have to be a superstar to do both jobs well. Most employers are aware of the difficulty in performing both jobs. It is a choice that a woman has to make, but being a wife and mother and "earner" is a phenomenal challenge. On top of that, the underlying standard that women are measured by in the business world is more stringent. Being a mother and wife are two of the most difficult jobs there are, and when you combine those with business opportunities, most women need to be superhuman. Being a working, single mother is, maybe, even harder.

Having said all that, it appears to me that women have to perform better and have a better track record than men in competing for the same positions. I'm not saying this is right or making an apology for this, but that is the way things are. I've often thought that women perform better than most men in equal jobs simply because they know they have to compensate for the perceived inequities.

If you are a woman reentering the workforce after raising children, you are going to run into the same challenge that any candidate would, having left business for a number of years then needing to get a new job. This has nothing to do with you being a woman. The same would be true for any man if he were out of the business environment for a number of years. What it means is that you are, to a certain extent, going to have to start over in your career. Just be ready for it.

One nice thing about having raised children is that you can use it as a *selling point* for your candidacy. "Well, all of my children are raised (or just about raised) and they don't need me home anymore. I don't have to attend to them when they're sick; they get themselves to school (or they are out of the house), so I am free to focus on my career and my job." And, frankly, anyone who has raised children knows how complicated it is just to get your child to sixteen or eighteen years old.

If you are a woman of child-bearing age and you are asked if you have children, or if you intend to have children, or your ability to work or travel because of children in an interviewing situation, (which, of course, is illegal), you probably won't get very far by being indignant and informing the interviewer that his or her question is illegal. You have to decide how you are going to answer these questions before they are even asked.

Many female candidates we have worked with over the years simply make it clear in the interview, before they are asked, that they have small children. They clarify that they have excellent child care and it hasn't inhibited them from performing well on the job. Many women have felt that it is better to offer this "answer" before the question is asked—to keep the prospective employer from wondering about their ability to be at work every day. They say something along the lines of, "You need to know that I have a small child who is _____ years old. But we have excellent child care and even when they are ill, I've not had to miss work." It's even better when the candidate can say, "I do have two small children, but my mother (that is, a relative who cares more than a hired child care giver) takes care of the children and I've never had difficulty with them interfering with my work—even when they are ill." This comment keeps a prospective employer from having to wonder about that particular issue.

Some women don't feel comfortable telling a prospective employer that they have small children. It is their prerogative not to do so. But, if you don't feel comfortable in offering it to a prospective employer, you'd better be ready to suffer the consequences of the employer not being sure, and therefore not wanting to run the risk of hiring you because you may have small children.

You have to decide how you're going to handle this situation. But remember, the employer's concern isn't that you have small children, the concern is that you are going to be absent from work a lot because of small children. So that is the concern you have to address.

If You Are a Minority

If you are a minority of any sort, you're already familiar with the inherent prejudice and bias that many people have for others who are significantly different from them. Whether you're black, yellow, or brown or any other kind of minority, looking for a job has this one added difficulty. I have observed that this prejudice toward American-born minorities isn't anywhere near as great as it used to be, but there is no denying that it still lingers on in some quarters. I'm still of the opinion that American-born minorities have to be just a little bit better in performance and previous employment than the average white guy (if there is such a person). Again, it does absolutely no good to complain about the truth of this fact. Again, I say the best way to overcome discrimination is to knock on lots of doors until the right one opens.

In some instances, being a minority can be an advantage. In fact, many companies consider it a tremendous bonus if they get an excellent candidate who is also a minority. However, interviewing and getting hired are still going to be a challenge. You are going to have to prove that you are a better candidate.

When you interview, you need to be sure that you sell yourself extremely well. You are going to have to practice your interviewing techniques and perform them better than most of the average candidates the employer is going to interview. If you stress your strengths, skills, and experience, most companies will be willing to give you a shot—at least to go further in the interviewing process.

In no way do I want to belittle the effects of racial discrimination, but I do feel strongly that in this day and age, most reputable companies want to hire the best candidate, regardless of race.

Jeff and Amy's Experience

Jeff and Amy didn't feel that much of this chapter pertained to their experiences. As I've said, Jeff was very good at interviews when he got them. He was intelligent, outgoing, and friendly, and sold himself well when he got into the actual interviewing process. He had little trouble explaining his job history to interviewers.

Yes, Jeff had been let go from his job developing software, but this wasn't an uncommon occurrence in the industry, so he could simply weave it into his overall presentation. The fact that he had been out of work for more than eighteen months also didn't present that much of a drawback. Again, his industry had undergone great upheaval, so stories like Jeff's were not that unusual. He had clearly not been relaxing. He had moved from Colorado to Texas during his job search, so, if anything his story became a bit more compelling as he told it.

13 · Looking for a Job When You Have a Job

"The sky does not make dead-end streets for people." ("When God closes one door, He opens another.")

—CHINESE PROVERB

First of all, let me dispel the myth that you are a better candidate, in the eyes of a prospective employer, if you are currently employed. Although most surveys will tell you that a currently employed candidate is supposedly a better one, it just doesn't work out that way from a practical point of view. The blunt truth is that 99 percent of the hiring authorities with pain in 99 percent of the companies in the United States don't really care if the person who relieves their pain is presently employed or not.

In fact, there are some kinds of positions where being employed—and therefore not immediately available to start a new job—might be a deterrent. Many hiring authorities believe that they should interview for and fill a position at the very last moment of desperation. Most organizations and hiring authorities will rarely admit this, because they want to appear as though they plan and execute on hiring people well in advance of the need, with forethought and exceptional business acumen. Ka-ka.

So, you aren't a better candidate because you are employed. You may be harder to hire, and you may not have the urgency to take an offer because you are employed, but you aren't intrinsically a better candidate just because you have a job. (Conversely, you are not less of a candidate because you are unemployed.)

The simple economic and psychological comfort in having a job alleviates most of the emotional and psychological stress that is associated with finding

225

a job. At least most people feel that way in the beginning of their job search. There are, however, a whole different set of emotional and psychological challenges that come with looking for a job while you have one. And those should not be underestimated.

I would hardly recommend that an individual quit a job in order to look for one, unless there were extenuating circumstances, like following a spouse who is relocating or some other odd situation of that type. However, you will find that looking for a job, while you have one, is a lot harder than you think. An employed individual who is looking for another job has the added difficulty of not having the same amount of time to devote to a job search. In most instances, it's going to take at least twice as long, if not longer, to find a job. In fact, you will find that if you are employed, *looking for a job is like having a second job*. It's really, really hard to do.

Why Do You Want to Change Jobs?

The first issue you have to come to grips with when you have a job and you think you need to look for a new one is the great question of "why?" People leave a job for very personal reasons in the same way that they take a job for very personal reasons. Over the years, psychologists and business analysts have concluded that the top five reasons why people leave their jobs are:

1. **Job Content**—People really don't like the majority of what they spend their time doing in a particular job.

2. **Level of Responsibility**—People feel like that they can do more and want to experience more self-fulfillment and personal growth in what they do.

3. **Company Culture**—People don't feel compatible with the personality of the company. They disagree with the company philosophy and approach to doing business.

4. **Dissatisfaction with Colleagues**—People discover personality differences or "chemistry" differences between them and the people that they either work for or with.

5. **Compensation**—(Notice that this is the fifth reason.) People don't feel like they're compensated fairly for either what they are doing or for what they are asked to do.

After these top five, there are numerous other reasons for why people want to leave the job and, in relative order, they are:

- Lack of recognition
- Lack of teamwork
- Lack of support
- Lack of control
- Feeling isolated
- Lack of autonomy
- No compelling future

- Lack of feeling empowered
- Poor working conditions
- Lack of equity
- Poor management
- Unappreciative supervisors
- Stress

You need to analyze all these common reasons to be sure that you really want and need to leave the job you presently have.

On average, unless an individual has *at least three or four urgent, uncontrollable reasons* for leaving a job, the job search itself becomes too emotionally, mentally, and physically difficult; and eventually the candidate chooses to stay where he or she is.

The reason I bring this up is that often people want to change jobs on the whim of the moment. Abrupt changes in management, changes in pay scales, benefits, acquisitions, and so forth will cause employees to panic and begin looking for a job. They find out that looking for a job takes a tremendous amount of emotional, psychological, and physical strain; and, after a short-lived effort to change jobs, they decide to stay where they are. The immediate issue goes away or at least subsides.

So, carefully analyze the reasons you want to change jobs and make sure that these reasons will motivate you for the possibly long ordeal. Make sure, by the way, that the reasons you are looking to change jobs are *your* reasons and not someone else's.

The longer a person has been at a company, unless he or she is being forced out by downsizing, the company is changing hands, and so forth, the harder it is for the person to emotionally get used to the idea of changing jobs. When a person has been at a company for a lengthy period of time, he or she feels strong emotional ties to the company. The person feels a part of a family. And in spite of all the obvious, blatant proof in front of them that they really need to change jobs, they don't really want to and they often will do everything they can to postpone or avoid doing so.

> We often interview candidates who haven't changed jobs in several years, hear that the market is picking up, or haven't had raises or bonuses in their present employment for a few years, and think they want to look around to see if they can find a better job. Often, their spouse or a relative tries to convince them that they deserve better or a friend of theirs has recently changed jobs and they think it might be a good idea to see what they can find. Their reasons are more de jour and fleeting. They don't do very well in the interviewing process. They just aren't motivated enough to invest the time and energy it takes to do it right, especially in this market. And, after a few attempts (usually unsuccessful) at interviewing, they simply decide to stay where they are.

If you are in a situation where you are being forced to look for a job when you have one, and you feel emotionally tied to the company, you need to take extra care to come to grips with the reality of having to change jobs. You will eventually get over the emotional strain that this initially causes. You just cannot afford to have it come out in an interview.

Keeping Your Job While Looking for One

Once you have decided to look for a job while keeping the one you have, the first step is to become emotionally and psychologically prepared. You need to start planning and developing the process steps that I recommend. On top of that, you need to keep your job.

Keeping your job while looking for one is a difficult thing to do. Once people have emotionally and mentally left a job, the sooner they physically leave, the better! The longer you stay unhappily married to a job that you know you are going to leave for all kinds of personal and business reasons, the harder it is to keep the job and perform even on a mediocre level. So, ironically enough, once you have decided to leave the job you've got, you have to focus on it even harder to maintain a reasonable level of performance.

You cannot afford under any circumstances, to have word get back to your current employer that you are looking for a job, or you run the risk of being fired. Under no circumstances should you ever inform anyone you work with that you are looking to leave your company. There is a tremendous emotional side of everyone who wants support through commiseration; so people complain about the company and their job together and in a weak moment, some admit they're looking to change jobs. Dumb and dumber! I can't tell you the number of people we run into over the years who took someone at work into their confidence, told them that they're looking for a job, and eventually got fired when the word got to management.

If you are discovered and your supervisors ask if you are looking for a job, you absolutely have to deny it! I have read a number of misguided authorities who are going to tell you not to lie and to sit down with your boss or bosses, explain why you are being forced, in your opinion, to look for a job, and try to work with them to rectify the situation. Ka-ka! Don't let anybody kid you. Once you've admitted you're looking for a job, you're a marked person. If you aren't fired immediately, management is simply going to keep you around long enough to replace you.

Most of the time, if you are approached and asked whether or not you are looking for a job, your supervisors aren't sure. If they were absolutely positive, they'd probably fire you on the spot. Most of the time, they are fishing about your interviewing. Even if they are fairly sure, they may ask you about it just to keep you in check. You are now a traitor, an enemy of the state, and no longer the wonderful, upstanding employee you were before they suspected you were looking to leave.

Get a separate, personal e-mail address that you use at home. Use common sense. Do not let anyone associated with your changing jobs—that is, recruiters, potential employers, and people who might help you find a job—ever e-mail you at work. This is, again, something that most everyone says they know, but you'd be surprised how many people, in the emotion of the moment, think, "Well, it won't matter, just this once."

Do not put your résumé on any job board. In spite of what they promise, these boards are not as secure as they claim. Sure, they have means of only releasing your name with your permission; but most of the people who work with you, and most of your immediate managers, could recognize your résumé without your name on it. There is no way of knowing where your résumé might wind up when you send it out into cyberspace.

Going on Interviews

Interviewing is going to be the greatest challenge you will experience if you are currently employed. It is going to be a lot harder to find time to interview, unless you are in outside sales; and even then, if you travel, it is difficult. If you are in an office environment, getting out to interview usually takes a minimum of two and a half to three hours. There is a limit to the number of doctor, dentist, and school meetings for your kids that you can have before someone catches on to your interviewing. So, you need to arrange interviews for very early in the morning, 6:45 A.M. or 7:00 A.M., or early evening 5:15 P.M., 5:30 P.M., or 6:00 P.M., or on Saturday.

One way to find time to interview is to find out how much accrued vacation you have coming to you and use that time to take off for interviews. Do not take off large blocks of time, like two or three days, or one week, thinking that you will be able to spend that time doing nothing but interviewing. Interviews generally don't come that quickly or that easily; you can't line them up at your discretion. On average, you're going to have one, maybe two interviews a week (if you're lucky) and you are not likely going to be able to easily lump them into one day.

If your company will allow it, you might want to take a couple of hours off here, or a couple hours off there, and have them count against the vacation time you've accrued. Or, depending on the kind of job you are looking for, you might be able to arrange interviews on one morning or one afternoon and take that morning or afternoon off. At least by doing this, you won't feel as guilty and pressed as when you try to squeeze an interview in at lunchtime—or if you're late for work because of an interview that goes over the time that you have allotted. Interviewing on your time is much better for you mentally and emotionally.

It is also a good idea to inform an interviewing or hiring authority that you are either on your lunch hour or you have a time constraint about getting back to work, if indeed that is the case. Most interviewing and hiring authorities really understand that an employed candidate has to get back to work.

Dressing for Interviews

It has become very hard to dress for work and dress for an interview in the same way. People used to dress the same way for work that they would dress for an interview: dark suits, white shirts, conservative ties for men and suits and white blouses for women. Since business casual has become the norm at work, it is very difficult to show up on the job in a dark suit, white shirt, and conservative tie. The first thing that someone will ask is: "Are you interviewing?" There are a couple of approaches you can take.

The first is what we always called the Superman routine. (For those of you old enough to remember this concept, you know what it means; if you're not old enough to remember it, ask one of your elders). You can have a suit in your car and, on the way to the interview, change (preferably not in a phone booth). Although this is a pain in the butt and most people hate the idea, it works!

Another idea I recommend more and more is that, if a person dresses business casual at work, they should have a nice sport coat for a man or a jacket for a woman in their car and wear it to the interview.

Upon arrival, be sure to say to the interviewing or hiring authority something like, "You will have to pardon my dress. I normally wear a conservative suit to an interview, but we're business casual in my organization and it is impossible for me to wear a suit at the office without broadcasting to everyone that I am interviewing. I hope you understand." Many of the people with whom you interview are going to be dressed in business casual. The ones who are not will understand your situation if you explain it in this manner. This seems like such a small thing, but it is really important.

Selling Yourself Aggressively in the Interview

The fact that you are currently employed is going to affect you most in this regard: You will be comparing the job that you presently have with an opportunity that you might consider. Now, a prospective employer certainly may have to take into consideration the fact that you're presently employed by giving you good business and economic reasons to leave your job, and accept the one that he or she might offer you. But, whatever you do, don't let the fact that you are presently employed *go to your head.*

You have to remember that you are competing in a difficult market with a lot of people who are very qualified. You may not feel that you have to sell yourself very hard, since you have a job and you might be making it a comparison, rather than having to find a job. However, a hiring authority doesn't know that and, what's more, doesn't care. A hiring authority only cares about what you want to the extent that he or she may get your services by employing you. Your goal is to get an offer. Whether or not you are employed should not have an effect on how aggressively and assertively you sell yourself in the interviewing situation.

The reason that you have to approach each interview this way is obvious: Your competition is approaching it this way. So, if you go to an interview with the idea of, "Well, I might be interested in changing and I might not. . . . I'll see if it's a better opportunity than the one I've got. . . . Maybe I will and maybe I won't. . . . After all, the job I got really isn't that bad" your competition is going to eat your lunch.

Giving Your Reasons for the Change

Make sure in your presentation that when you communicate why you are looking to change jobs, you relate your reasons for leaving to the five most prominent reasons people want to leave their jobs, as I've mentioned previously. When you don't have a job, it is obvious why you need one. However, when you presently have a job, the reasons you want to leave can eliminate you for consideration by an interviewing or hiring authority. If you tell a prospective employer that you are leaving your present position because, "Management is stupid. . . . Idiots are running my company. . . . I'm simply not making enough money. . . . My husband (or wife) doesn't think I make enough money. . . . I hate my job," you won't do well in the interview.

I think you've probably caught on by now to the kinds of reasons you might give for leaving your job. Here are a few short scripts:

- "I really love what I do and the company that I'm with has been really great to me. But I have outgrown the function of my job. For the past two years I have felt underemployed. I am capable of doing so much more and I am not challenged in the position at all."

- "I love my job and the people I work with. However, the company culture has been very stagnant for the last few years, and I am limited both personally and professionally. I could be there for very long time, but I'm not challenged and there are no opportunities beyond the job that I have."

- "I love the company that I work for and the people I work with. But, for the past couple of years I have outgrown the level of people I work with. Because there is very little challenge in the job, I'm not likely to grow beyond this particular job. I am compensated fairly for what I do, but other than merit raises which I have maxed out on, I'm not going to be able to earn more and provide for my family the way I want to."

If you can provide examples and stories that support any one of these scripts, use them. But after you have made any one of these statements and you've provided proof in the way of an example or a story, drop the issue and move on. Continue to sell yourself.

Being Too Picky in Arranging Interviews

When you are employed, it isn't easy to make time for interviews. In fact, after the initial excitement of deciding to change jobs wears off, (especially if you have to cram in a number of interviews that don't wind up being successful), interviewing becomes a real pain in the butt.

When this happens, there is a tendency to be overly selective about the kinds of opportunities you will interview for. You don't want to "waste your time" and go to the trouble of interviewing, especially when the first three or four haven't been successful; so you start to overanalyze what a job opportunity would be like before you interview. This is one of the biggest mistakes made by most employed job seekers.

Candidates who have jobs will often make a decision about a prospective interview based on how it "sounds" to them or how they feel about the interview, the job, or the company before they physically interview. You don't want to make this mistake. You want to go on any reasonable interview you can get. These jobs, companies and the opportunities are completely different when you experience them face-to-face, compared with how you are probably imagining them.

There is no real way to evaluate a company or an opportunity unless you interview face-to-face. Don't kid yourself into thinking that you can qualify an opportunity over the phone by just hearing about it or reading about it on the company's website.

It is also unfair to compare your present job with any potential job you may interview for until you actually get an offer. Now, you may decide after an initial interview that the potential opportunity for which you are interviewing is not as good as the job you presently have. If you are absolutely sure of this, then you should not continue that particular interviewing process.

> Since it's such a pain to interview on a face-to-face basis, candidates who are presently employed have a tendency to want to either interview or qualify an opportunity over the phone to save time and effort. Big mistake! Let me ask you, if you were single, would you rather talk to a date over the phone or would you prefer to physically go out with a date? So, why would you think interviewing or hiring authorities would be more interested in a person who talks to them over the phone than they would a person they could physically interview.

When people don't make the passionate commitment to the long, difficult ordeal of finding a job (when they have one), their job search sputters and eventually stops; until the pain of the job they presently have becomes greater than the pain of looking for a new one. And the longer the search sputters, starts and stops, the harder it is to perform well on the job that you now have—and looking for a job becomes more frustrating.

Contacting Competitors, Suppliers, or Customers

Some of your best opportunities might be with your competitors, suppliers, or customers. If you are unemployed and you have no job to lose, it doesn't matter when you interview with them. However, if you are presently employed, you might contact these people (if you think that they might have a job opportunity for you), very discreetly and carefully. Your biggest concern is that you may, for instance, talk to a competitor and have the fact that you're looking for a job get back to your employer.

In the case of a competitor, you may want to initially call a person one or two levels above the position that you might be interviewing for. You would tell the person that you are employed by one of their competitors, for instance, and you were thinking of a job change. You would like to speak to them confidentially about any opportunities they might have.

If you discover that there is interest, I recommend that you have one or two telephone conversations to establish your credibility, experience, and background and also to establish the interest level on the part of employer. I would not recommend sending your résumé. You should tell him or her that you will bring a résumé to the interview. Arrange the interview at a neutral site. Do not interview at the office of your competitor, supplier, or customer. If you are recognized by anyone, it will get back to your current employer in a heartbeat.

Being Recruited

When you get a call from a recruiter, one of your competitors, or any organization that is interested in speaking to you about a job (when you're happily employed), you are being recruited. Most people associate being recruited with hiring mid-, upper-middle-level, and upper management types of positions. The truth is that when there is pain, recruiting a good candidate can be valuable on any level. Our firm has recruited just about every kind of position you can imagine—from hourly welders, chemical compounders, and production people all the way up to presidents and executive vice presidents. Wherever there is pain for a particular type of employee with particularly narrow skills, there is a recruiting opportunity.

If you are being recruited by an organization or a third-party recruiter, there are few things you must keep in mind. First, and most important, if you decide to pursue a new job opportunity that you were called about, when you were not mentally and emotionally looking for a job, you better prepare yourself to interview and possibly change jobs. When an individual is not contemplating changing jobs, and they are relatively happy with the job they presently have, getting emotionally and mentally prepared to look for a job is a very big hurdle.

When being recruited for a particular job, before you go on an initial interview, you need to emotionally and mentally come to grips with the idea of changing jobs. Having been recruited, if you go to an interviewing situation without at least acting like you are interested in the new opportunity, you are not likely to get to first base with the job.

Second, don't let being recruited go to your head. Often, because a candidate really isn't looking for a job, he or she goes into the interviewing situation with all kinds of ridiculous demands on the possible new employer—ones that are totally out of line with reasonable requests. The attitude is, "Well, I'm not really looking for a job, but if I'm going to change, I really have to have a lot of very good reasons to do it—they are going to have to make it worth my while."

The problem with this thinking is that the candidate, (unless coached by a good recruiter), may come up with ridiculous demands that are so obviously out of line that he or she could very well not only not get the opportunity, but embarrass themselves and destroy any potential future opportunity with similar organizations. So, if you are being recruited and you decide to pursue the opportunity, be realistic about what you can expect in money, title, and responsibilities in order to change jobs. Interview as though you were interested in changing, get a reasonable offer, and then see if it works for you.

Conclusion

Looking for a job when you have a job is much harder than most people imagine. It is like having a second job that you have to perform over, under, and around your current job—while continuing to perform that job to the best of your ability. In addition, you must make sure that your current employer doesn't discover that you're looking for a new job.

Be sure that you are completely committed to the job search and the time and extra effort it will entail, or it's not worth pursuing. Start by closely examining your reasons for wanting to change jobs; make sure they are valid and make sure they are *your* reasons, not someone else's. Once you have decided to take the plunge, give as much energy and time as possible to the job search. You will be in competition with serious job candidates, so you must be equally serious. You can't simply play job search as a sideline to your existing job. You must arrange as many interviews as you can possibly handle and sell yourself as aggressively as if you have been out of a job for months.

14 · Be Careful with References

"Who says you can be defined by what people say about you?"
—ELEANOR ROOSEVELT, FORMER FIRST LADY,
LECTURER, AND WRITER

Providing references to potential employers is something that everyone takes for granted, yet few people really understand the true implications or possible pitfalls. References can be silent cancers that kill a great opportunity. At least once or twice a month, we have a placement that looks like it is in the final stages, but it is sabotaged by a bad reference. A reference doesn't even have to be out-and-out bad to cause problems—hiring authorities will perceive a reference as poor because it is neutral, uninformative, or downright unhelpful.

If you are the kind of candidate who has excellent references from everyone you have ever worked for or with, you probably don't need to read this chapter. It may not hurt to read it because some of the logistical ideas are of value, but you may not need much help. At least, you don't think you do. But, one of the most shocking surprises you can ever have is the experience of assuming that all your references are excellent, only to find out that one or more of them cost you a job opportunity. I would estimate that at least 20 to 25 percent of the job-seeking candidates out there have at least one reference challenge in their background—and they have absolutely no idea that it is there.

This may come as a surprise to most readers, but (except in instances of disclosing acts of violence or acts of financial mismanagement) companies are not legally required to provide any kind of references about previous employees. Companies may be subject to a charge of defamation by giving a reference that could be construed as bad; and they have absolutely nothing to gain by giving any kind of a reference, good or bad. So, any kind of reference an organization will provide goes beyond what they *have* to do.

Companies will usually verify dates of employment, earnings, and confirm if a person is eligible for rehire in the eyes of the company (but there is nothing that states they have to do any of this). Many companies will not even respond to references that are solicited over the telephone; they require a written request for references and only respond to those requests in writing. Most prospective employers are going to ask you for specific references from the most recent jobs you have had. Even in situations where you know that a previous employer is not going to provide an adequate reference, you are going to be forced to find someone within the company who can speak of your performance, even if it's against the policies of the company. This poses a tremendous difficulty for many candidates.

Don't Take Them for Granted

Most employers will ask you to give them three or four people as references and specify the relationship you had with those people. Some employers are going to ask you for specific people, like previous supervisors, customers, or maybe peers. Be sure that you're prepared to provide these different kinds of references when asked.

As you begin your job search, it is a good idea to think about who you might give as a reference in just about any interviewing process. I would recommend calling those people to let them know that you are actively looking for a position, and ask their permission to use them as a reference. It is very rare, but I have seen situations where the people who candidates thought would be references for them refused to do it. After they give you permission, inform them that you will let them know who might be checking your reference, what kind of position it is, and exactly what in your background they should emphasize when the reference is checked.

When to Provide References

Most potential employers are going to ask you to give them permission to check references. Some ask to do it with a form to sign. Others simply ask it verbally from you before they make an offer. I've encountered a number of companies over the years that ask for references before they even interview the candidate. My advice is to provide your references when you are asked to, not before, no matter how proud you are of them. Employers have their preferred way of asking for and handling references, so you're not going to gain any advantage by handing them in early.

I also have known candidates to put references on their résumés. I don't recommend doing this. You don't want your references contacted unless you are a serious candidate for the opportunity and you are close to getting an offer. I've known situations where a prospective employer used the references on a person's résumé to find other candidates (ones that the candidate provided in the résumé), so that they could have, in essence, more competition for the job. There are few things that will make you feel as stupid as finding out that one of your references got the job for which you were interviewing, simply because you provided the person's name and their number. Betcha never thought that would happen!

Reference Letters

It certainly doesn't hurt to have letters of reference from previous employers that you can use in the interviewing process. These are usually very broad statements regarding your work, but they certainly can't be denied. A hiring authority may likely want to speak personally to the person who wrote the letter, but having a letter certainly can't hurt. Having three or four reference letters ready at the time references are requested is pretty powerful.

Treacherous References

Bad, poor, and mediocre references occur all the time—far more often than you probably realize. Let's discuss situations where references can jeopardize your candidacy and give you solutions for each situation.

When a Blatantly Bad Reference Is Given

Few people will admit they might get a bad or poor reference from a previous employer. It happens so often that I need to address it in detail. Remember that 97 percent of the companies in the United States are run by people who are involved in businesses they know well, but these people are not really people-oriented. The owners and managers of many of these organizations simply don't realize the liability they might incur for giving a bad reference.

If you have been fired by a company, the best that you can hope for is to convince them to provide a neutral reference when they are contacted. A neutral reference is simply the verification of dates of employment, earnings, and the question of being rehired.

There are professional organizations that will actually check a reference for you. I've known candidates who had friends do it or a previous manager whom they could trust. If you suspect that you are going to get a bad reference from anyone in the company, the most effective way to deal with it is not to get mad or angry. The first thing to do is to call the person you think might give a bad reference and discuss the reference that he or she might give. Go over your strengths and weaknesses and ask for the person's suggestions. Most of the time, people will soften and at least provide a neutral reference. Ask the person if he or she would be willing to give you a positive reference in certain situations; tell the person that you will call and inform him or her about who will be calling and what might be asked.

> When you think you might get a poor reference from a previous employer, it is advisable to mention your concern to the prospective employer. Say something like, "You know, I really appreciated all of the things that I learned at _____ company. The people were wonderful and I really loved the job. I may not get a particularly good reference from these people because _____ " and then proceed to explain why you think you may not get a particularly good reference in a calm, reasonable, forthright, unemotional, businesslike tone. Explain what happened in as positive a light as you can make it, even to the point of admitting mistakes that you might have made. Make sure all of the issues on your part are as much business issues as you can make them. If there are personality clashes, or any kind of personal issues, you need to present them in as positive a light as you can in the same manner.

If you are certain someone is giving you a bad reference and you cannot talk to him or her, write a letter to this person explaining that you understand he or she has been giving you a bad reference and you would like it to stop. Send the same kind of letter to the president of the company. Do not threaten. You're trying to get, at least, a neutral job reference. You do not want to threaten legal action unless you have absolutely no other choice. Most of the time, an organization in this situation will get the message loud and clear, and start providing neutral information.

If you know that you are going to get a poor reference, even if it is neutralized, especially for the last position you had, it is advisable to line up a number of positive informal references at the organization from which you were fired. To do this, ask a number of peers or supervisors if you can get them to talk off the record to a prospective employer about your work habits. So, the party line of the company might be a poor or, at best, a neutral reference, but it is offset by three or four people at that company who will say very positive things about you.

Another way to counterbalance a bad reference at one particular organization is to provide a number of other glowing references from previous organizations that you've worked for.

A third way of counterbalancing a potentially poor reference is to have letters of reference from some of the customers for whom you have done a good job. It is not uncommon for salespeople, when interviewing, to be asked for customer references. If you are an accountant and you were the interface between your firm and an external auditing or external accounting firm, you might find one of those people with whom you interfaced to write you a letter of reference. No matter what position you were in with the company, think of whether there were any external organizations you worked with where you built rapport with individuals.

When Silence Is Interpreted as a Bad Reference

This is a situation where a reference is called, usually a previous employer, and he or she refuses to answer any questions at all. He or she ignores the phone calls, refuses to talk with the potential hiring authority, and sends the person checking the reference to the HR department, if the company has one. This kind of response does not normally come from someone who the candidate has asked to give a reference. It's usually a supervisor or manager whom the candidate has worked for whose name the candidate had to provide during the interviewing process. I've had previous managers or supervisors of my candidates, when contacted about a job reference, simply state, "I'm just not going to discuss it."

When an ex-manager or ex-supervisor will not discuss anything about you as a previous employee, it throws up all kinds of red flags to a prospective employer. Unfortunately, people will generally assume a dreadfully bad reference in a situation like this. The silence is then interpreted as a negative reference.

You want to offset this kind of poor reference in the same way that you offset a bad reference. Get a plethora of positive references from peers you worked with, customers, or previous employers. If you know silence is going to be the response, you need to forewarn the interviewing, hiring, or reference-checking authorities that they're not going to get any reply from anyone, even when they ask.

When a Bad Reference Is Implied but Not Specified

This is where the person giving a reference only answers the minimal questions but answers them in such an emphatic, disdainful manner that it communicates nothing but a bad reference. For instance, the person inquiring about a reference asks, "Would this previous employee be considered for rehire?" And the answer comes across something like, "Are you kidding me! Absolutely, unequivocally, undeniably, under no circumstances, over my dead body, not in this lifetime. *No!*" And it is said with the most animated, terse, hateful tone imaginable. True, all the person giving the reference did was answer the question, but the way he or she answered it communicates a very bad reference.

> A prospective employer is going to assume that an inability to find some of your previous employment references is an implied bad reference. When that hiring authority can't find anybody from that particular company, he or she tells the candidate to come up with some references from that organization. When the candidate cannot do it, the hiring process is stalled—if not killed outright. The lesson here is to keep track of previous managers from every company for which you have worked in the past eight to ten years.

There is not much you can do about this type of negative response to a simple question. It just happens. But, again, if you have some reason to suspect that this will happen, you can mention your concern to the hiring authority.

When a Reference Is Given by a Poorly Informed Source

This occurs when the candidate neglects to brief the person giving the reference on exactly what kind of position the reference check is for. It is important for you to call your references that will be checked and inform them what company will be checking the reference, who will be checking the reference, what kind of job you are being considered for, and, most important, what aspects of your history pertain to the job being pursued.

Recently I had an employer check a reference of one of my candidates. My candidate was in the final throes of getting an offer from a company that sold small-ticket products to mid-market organizations (that is, $500 million companies and under, which required a high number of cold calls to generate a high number of small transactions). He was an excellent candidate and the opportunity was outstanding. It looked like a great match.

When the hiring authority got one of my candidate's references on the phone, the reference started telling the hiring authority how wonderful my candidate was on large big-ticket sales, how wonderful he was at schmoozing with large, national accounts, how great he was at going after large deals, along with mentioning that he had never seen the candidate make a lot of cold calls or generate a high number of transactions. End of reference. End of being considered for the job.

All my candidate would have had to do was talk to his reference and explain to him the nature of the position for which he was being considered.

Backdoor References

There is nothing more treacherous than backdoor references. These are people who are known by a prospective employer who know people who know people who know you. And, supposedly, these people know something about your personal and professional capabilities. For the most part, backdoor references will hurt you more than they will help you.

Usually these backdoor references are so far removed from knowing the candidate that their opinions are not valid. I guess that the reason most of these kinds of references are negative is this simple fact: If I imply that you should not hire someone, based on a negative reference that I give—and you don't hire that person—you will never know if I'm right or wrong. So the safest thing for a distant, backdoor-reference giver to do is to give a less-than-positive reference—even if they don't know what they're talking about—because, if you're not hired, they're right and you're never going to know the difference.

If you find out that a hiring authority is going to try to check backdoor references of people who may or may not know you, you need to be on your guard. One way of overcoming this problem is to provide a number of written references, as well as an extensive list of people for whom you have actually worked, trusting that the hiring authority will focus on them rather than trying to find backdoor references elsewhere.

Reference from Your Current Employer After You Are Hired

Many people think that if they fudge on the dates of employment in their most recent job, they will not be discovered. In other words, a person will put a date of employment, for instance, of "April 2001 to Present" when they really recently left the job, but want to appear currently employed. Candidates often fudge on their current earnings, too, thinking it won't be checked since they are employed.

I really don't have a problem with using "to present" regarding employment dates. Of course, if you left your most recent position nine months ago and you are still putting this phrase on your résumé, you're going to run into big problems. But if it was in the past two or three months, you can probably get away with it, if you inform the prospective employer, during the interview process, of when you departed. However, embellishing your earnings will cause you a problem, even after you've been hired.

Many companies will hire you conditionally with the understanding that they may change their mind after they check the reference of your present employer, even once you have gone to work for them. You would be amazed what these companies find out in checking such a reference. So, if you are lying about anything regarding your present employment, thinking that no one will ever check the reference because you are currently employed, you're likely to get caught. The bigger the lie, the bigger the problem it will cause.

General Guidelines on References

Here are several helpful thoughts about references:

Whom to Ask

A prospective employer is going to be interested in references from people who can tell him or her about your work and your ability to perform on a job.

Personal references are nice, but most employers don't really care that much about them. They want to talk with people you've worked with, whether those people really like you or not. In fact, if you provide too many personal references rather than professional ones, you appear to be covering up the professional ones.

Try to find these references before you are asked for them, because there is nothing more frustrating than spending two or three days scrambling around trying to find references when a job offer hinges on it. So, locate those people before you need them and know where they are.

Make a list of your references. Start with the people whom you are confident will give you a positive reference. Obviously, people you were friendly with and worked well with are better than those you didn't really get along with or with whom you had work-related problems. Choose people with titles as far up the food chain as you can, but you want to use people who actually knew and worked with you. (The president of your former company, whom you met once in five years, may look good as a name and title on the page, but he or she is unlikely to have much of substance to say about you, if anything.) In addition, you should list people who held a specific position that you might be asked about, such as your immediate supervisor or team leader.

How to Ask

Asking someone to be a reference for you is a fairly simple thing to do. You just want be sure that you don't communicate the idea that you are going to be burdening someone. Giving a reference for someone can get old really fast if it is necessary to do more than four or five times. After all, you are asking someone to do something out of the kindness of his or her heart without any compensation.

Here's a basic script of what you should say:

> "_____(name)_____ this is _____(your name)_____. I am in the process of changing jobs and I would like to use you as a reference. Please keep this very confidential, but I have to change positions (or, I lost my job). (Then explain in a brief manner why you are looking to change or why you lost your last position. Make sure that they are the _exact same reasons_ that you are giving to a prospective employer, so that you and

your references are consistent with what you say, and make the reasons as positive as possible.) I would like to ask for your help.

"I will not take advantage of your kindness and your time. I will only have people call you when I am a serious contender for an opportunity. I will call you before each prospective employer speaks to you and brief you regarding the kind of position and the kind of opportunity I am applying for, so that you can be prepared. Would that be all right?"

Most reasonable people are willing to help you. Assure them that you will inform them about each prospective employer before that employer calls them. You will want to prepare them for the specific opportunity that you might be applying for. As I mentioned above, a poorly informed reference can be a bad reference.

Customizing Your References

This is a simple concept, but most people don't think to take advantage of it. It is the idea of providing different kinds of references to different employers depending on the type of position you are seeking.

Not only would you consider providing different people for references in different positions, but you definitely should call those people and prepare them for giving a reference. It is important that when you prepare a reference, you clearly explain to the reference *exactly* what kind of job you are applying for; the company you are applying to; the person who is going to actually be checking the reference (such as the hiring authority or the HR department); what kinds of questions they may ask; and most important, what kinds of specific attributes your reference might emphasize to the prospective employer, or what kinds of issues the prospective employer might have concerning your candidacy that the reference might be able to address.

You want to set the stage for the prospective employer to not only get a specific work reference but also become more convinced of your ability to do a specific job.

An example would be something like this:

"_____ this is _____. I am a finalist for a job as an assistant controller for _____ company. The comptroller of _____ company is going to give you a call to check my employment reference with you. I would like to know your availability over the next few days and ask if it would be convenient for this person to give you a call?

"They are particularly interested in someone who has had supervisory experience because there are three accountants who are going to be responsible to this person. I would appreciate it if you could relate to them the supervisory skills you observed in me. Two of the people that this person is going to oversee are going to need to be released and two new ones hired. I would like you to pass on to the hiring authority, Mr. or Ms. _____, your knowledge of my ability to let people go, as we did when I worked with you, as well as my ability to successfully hire good employees.

"One of the important aspects of the job is to be able to supervise and be responsible for the filing of SEC reports. The one concern that Mr. or Ms. _____ might have about my candidacy is that I was involved in filing the SEC reports only once, when I worked for you. I would appreciate it if you can emphasize when he or she calls, the kind of contribution I made in supervising the filing of those reports for _____ company, when I worked for you. Please remind him or her of how independently we worked and how unsupervised I was.

"The opportunity is a very good one for me. (*Then you might want to describe the job in as much detail as necessary*). I really want the position. Anything you can do to help me would be appreciated.

"Does this all make sense to you and might you have any questions?"

In this scenario, the reference would not only report on the candidate's work ethic but also address the candidate's specific ability to supervise the filing of an SEC report. This doesn't sound like a really big deal, but people are often hired or not hired for relatively small, minute issues.

If You Burned Some Bridges

Hardly anyone will ever admit to having burned bridges when they leave a job, but it probably happens at least 25 to 30 percent of the time. Few employees or managers would ever want to admit to the embarrassing things that they did as they were going out the door.

Burning bridges can occur in a couple of different fashions. The first can be an overt, obvious action like a yelling or screaming match with the supervisor or someone in authority in the company. It can be a relatively passive activity, like just plain not showing up for work. Both types of burning bridges are usually cases of being very emotional at the moment and being so embarrassed afterward that a person doesn't really know how to rectify the mess he or she made.

When this ex-employee later needs a reference from that organization, he or she is really in a predicament. The only thing you can do when this situation has happened is call your former supervisor, or the person you are going to give as a reference, and ask for forgiveness. Explain to that person that it was a terribly emotional time in your life for many different reasons, and that if you had it to do over again, you wouldn't have done what you did. You would like this person to be a reference for you, speaking of your work habits, the quality of work that you've done, and so forth. Now, unless you physically threatened someone, most people are willing to go out of their way to forgive. Why? Because they want forgiveness from other people themselves.

I would then recommend that you describe the kind of position for which you are applying and handle the call just like you would when you customize a reference. I have known candidates, who, when they can't get their previous employer on the phone, write a letter or e-mail the individual. You might not get a phenomenally glowing reference, but if you can neutralize a blatantly negative one, you're better off.

Overworking References

You need to be careful not to overwork your references. People don't mind being a reference two or three times. When it gets to be more than three or four times, they may become irritated at having to do it so many times. A bit exasperated, they will put off calling the prospective employer back or be hard to reach. It isn't so much that they won't do it; it's just they feel taken advantage of.

There are two ways to keep this from happening. First, have several different references you can use in different situations. Unless an organization that you are interviewing with asks for more, it is reasonable to give them two or three references. Coming up with two of your previous managers is reasonable.

The second way to deal with the reference that you really need is to be sure that you call the reference *every time* a prospective employer is going to call the person. The personal touch each time a reference is going to be used makes the whole experience more palatable. Once you are employed, if you feel like you have overused a reference or two, you may want to send the individual a gracious thank you note, along with a gift certificate to dinner or tickets to a play or a movie.

Key point: *References are crucial to your successful job search. Prepare them and use them wisely.*

Credit Checks, Criminal/Arrest Records

All of these practices have become more prevalent in the hiring process than they ever used to be. It is much harder to get real personal references so companies now rely more on objective reports like credit and lawsuit reports, as well as criminal reports. "Bruised" credit, or a very poor credit report, will disqualify a candidate from being hired in certain businesses. Arrest records are extremely difficult to overcome in a hiring situation; although I have seen companies discover DWIs on a candidate's record and still hire the person.

Credit checks are a bigger problem than most people will admit. People with a poor credit report will rarely admit to it until it is checked. If your credit has been badly bruised, or you have a poor credit rating because of being out of work for a long time, you should share that fact with a prospective employer before the credit check is done. You can check your own credit reports to see what the results are through the credit bureaus themselves. If there is a problem with your credit report that the company may not like but can tolerate, at least your telling the hiring authority softens the blow.

I recommend the same procedure regarding an arrest record. Different companies may respond to different issues different ways.

•   •   •

Jeff and Amy didn't need any of the advice in this chapter because Jeff's previous employment references were impeccable.

15 Stay Focused on the Process Even When You Reach "The Finals"

"Always make progress . . . examine yourself constantly . . . let your present state always leave you dissatisfied, if you want to become what you are not yet . . . you must always look for more, walk onward, make progress."
—St. Augustine, Philosopher and Theologian

So now you've reached the finals. You've been through numbers of interviews and you've gotten to third base with a couple different opportunities. The end is near! Wrong! As with many of the parts of the process, the final activities—getting from third base to home plate—are just another series of events that you are going to manage. Like St. Augustine says, keep making progress. You have nothing until you have a job offer.

One of the biggest challenges that you have in all of this job-finding process is to unemotionally, objectively, and mindfully manage the process of finding a job from one step to the next step.

Most people get to the finals with one—or at most, two—job opportunities and they quit working the process. They think that when they get to third base, it's just a matter of time before they get to home plate. Big mistake! You cannot afford to count on anything regarding a job opportunity until you actually have an offer and start date. Even then, I would not recommend that you shut down all the other opportunities that you might have at various stages of the process.

So what do you do when you reach the finals? Exactly the same thing you did to get to there. Keep working the process. Find the employer's pain, sell yourself as hard as you can, get a commitment from a hiring authority, go to the next interview, do the same thing, go to the next interview, get a commitment, and try to get an offer. The goal of the process is to get an offer—one, two, or as many as you can.

Don't become overly excited, don't get down in the dumps—just keep working the process. Every event in the job-seeking process is just that, an event. Some events will be more beneficial than others. The key to the whole situation is to understand that all events are positive, some are more beneficial positive events and some are less beneficial positive events. But all events are just steps along the way to a positive outcome. If you are juggling enough opportunities in the job-seeking process, you don't have to worry about landing on a more positive event. It's a numbers game.

Handling the Less-Than-Beneficial Positive Events

These are the events that in one way or another do not get you a job offer. You are going to experience a much greater number of these events than you are going to experience getting job offers. And as you go through each one of them, *you need to assess what you could have done better.*

Make notes about each opportunity you pursue. Follow those notes up with a phone call ten days or so after you last had contact with a hiring authority. You will be amazed at the number of opportunities that present themselves to people simply because they were persistent in calling. Oftentimes, a hiring authority zones in on one or two particular candidates, but drags his or her process on so long that the primary candidates are lost and the process must start all over. And when the hiring authority needs to start over again, you want to be the one who is available at that time.

If you do not hear from a hiring authority after you call several times, you need to call or write and ask his or her input as to why you weren't pursued. If you can get the person on the phone, something like the following script works well:

> "Mr. or Ms. _____, I really appreciated the interview that we had the other day. Since I did not hear from you at the time that you said you would get back to me, and I called a number of times, I'm assuming that I'm no longer a candidate. I would like to ask your help.

Could you please tell me where I might have gone wrong in the interview, what I might have been able to do better and, constructively, tell me why I was not considered beyond the initial interview?"

Don't expect a call back or an e-mail from every initial interview that you follow up like this. If you do not hear from the hiring authority after you've gone to this effort, put this person on the same rotation to call ten days later to remind him or her that you are still available. Remember to keep your cool. Never sound irritated or mad. Do not take it personally!

If you are eliminated as a candidate after a second or third interview, the hiring authority will usually communicate directly with you as to why. If he or she does not, it is a good idea to call—or, as a last resort, write—and ask what happened. Again, remember to keep your cool. You will be amazed at the number of times that the reasons for not being hired have nothing to do with you.

Most people, even hiring authorities, think they are going to interview and hire someone within a two- to three-week period. But the average hiring cycle (even when there is pain) is nearly ninety days. Many things can happen in ninety days. Primary candidates can take a different job or turn an offer down. So keep calling and keep yourself on the mind of a hiring authority.

My experience has been that if you make it to a second or third interview with any organization, you are probably qualified to do the job. When a company hires someone else, it is not necessarily based on that person's ability do the job, but for other kinds of reasons that are intangible. If you have gone beyond the second or third interview, you may still very well be a viable candidate—even though the company is pursuing someone else. So, for goodness sake, unless you have found a job, keep pursuing this opportunity at least four or five weeks after the new employee has reported to the job.

If you get to the second and third level of the interviewing process and are not hired, it is always a good idea to call and talk to the hiring authority. Let this person know that you were very interested in his or her opportunity and company, and say that you would like to be considered for any other opportunities that may arise. Tell the hiring authority that you really appreciated him or her and the company and you would like for him or her to keep your résumé or pass it on to any other hiring authority, in or out of the company. You will also want to ask permission to call the person from time to time and ask his or her advice about other opportunities that you may come across. The idea here is to make this hiring authority your friend and mentor.

You would be surprised how often people are hired this way. If they made it that far into the interviewing process, they were obviously well thought of by the hiring authority. Making that authority your friend and calling this person every once in awhile to keep your name in front of him or her, especially if you haven't found a job yet, is a great idea.

I cannot keep this disappointment from happening. In fact, this kind of disappointment is just part of my profession. But, if you work this system like I have taught you, you will have so many other opportunities that may be equally good, that your disappointment will be short-lived.

Handling the More Beneficial Positive Events

These are all the events that culminated in getting a job offer. Getting a job offer is the most important thing you can do in the job search. You can't accept an offer that you don't have. I must warn you that there are going to be times when you are going to expect an offer and it won't come. In fact, from time to time you are going to hear momentary lies like, "We really want to hire you. We will get back to you in a day or so." Whatever you do, don't celebrate anything at that point. Don't do anything until you have an offer in your hand.

Qualifying Your Job Opportunities

Most people who write books about finding jobs talk about qualifying your opportunities before you really get to the end of the interviewing process. I don't agree with that concept at all! The reason is very simple: almost everything about a job opportunity can change between the initial search for a candidate and the final offer and acceptance. If there is one thing that I have learned in thirty-one years, it is that what companies normally start out looking for in an employee from the top to the bottom of the organization—the titles that they will give, the duties and responsibilities that are associated with a particular job, and, probably most important, the money that they're willing to pay for it—can change anywhere from a small amount to a drastic amount from the beginning of the job search to the filling of the position.

I've experienced candidates getting starting salaries as much as $50,000 a year more than what a company originally wanted to pay. They accomplished this simply because they did not qualify themselves out of the opportunity in the initial part of the interviewing process—and they proved value to warrant a larger starting salary. So often, candidates start qualifying opportunities before they establish their value to a prospective employer.

Sell, sell, sell yourself and communicate what you can do for a company to the point that you are the one the organization wants to hire. Then you can talk about what the company can do for you.

The Time to Qualify

Once you are told that you are the person a company would like to hire and they want to make you an offer, it is your turn to start asking questions and qualify the opportunity. Up until now, your interviewing process has pretty much been a one-way street.

These particular qualifying questions are not, in my opinion, the same things that you might negotiate. We will get to negotiations in a moment. Negotiations center on the things that have inherent flexibility, such as benefits, title, base pay, bonuses, commissions, and so forth. Things like the working environment, employees, peers, subordinates and superiors, customers, market space, and so forth are not negotiable 99 percent of the time. They are real factors and part of the job opportunity that exists, regardless of who takes the job. But now, since you are the finalist, if you have any questions about the opportunity—and I mean down to the minute detail—is the time to get them clarified.

How to Qualify the Opportunity

Keep it simple. Once you are told that you are the candidate the company would like to hire, explain that you would like to have a meeting with the hiring authority and get as much clarification about all the questions you might have before you start negotiating.

Now, when you meet with the hiring authority, he or she may think that you're ready to accept the job, or at least start talking about specifics such as title, money, and so on. However, you may say something along the lines of, "Mr. or Ms. (*hiring authority*), I'm really excited about this opportunity. However, I have a number of questions about things that I would like to investigate. So, before we get down to the nitty-gritty, I'd like to find out . . ." You are prepared with a list of questions about the opportunity that you are either unclear on or haven't had a chance to ask before.

It is likely that a hiring authority will have covered or explained many of the issues that you might ask about in the interviewing process. However, now is the time to get clarification. Do not hesitate to get detailed in your investigation. And do not hesitate to ask for an audience with anyone whom you feel can answer your questions. It is not out of line for you to ask to talk to peers or subordinates or even other managers in the organization. You have to be sure that you have a clear understanding of everything as much as you can before you *consider* accepting the job.

Try to talk to someone who works for the company and has nothing to do with the job for which you are interviewing. Tell the person that you are thinking about going to work for the company and would like his or her candid opinion. Try to find people who have worked for the company before but are no longer there. Take their opinion with a grain of salt, but nonetheless, try to get it. If possible, get the opinions of customers or suppliers of the company with which you are interviewing.

> There are always going to be problems and challenges with any job. Why do you think we call it *work*? In fact, if there weren't a lot of challenges and problems in a job, neither you, nor anybody else, would be needed. We're all hired to solve problems and challenges. The issue in this part of the interviewing process is to be sure that you are as clear as you can be as to exactly what the problems and challenges are in the job that you are going to accept. Your goal, in this part of the investigation, is to figure out where those surprises might come from. That's all. It really isn't a matter of *if*. It is a matter of how you're going to handle them *when* they arise.

This due diligence may take one or two more meetings with a hiring authority or other people. Do not string it out for more than one or two days at the most. If you come across as hesitant about the opportunity, it's just too easy for a hiring authority to move on to the second candidate. Be interested and proactive, but do it quickly. The purpose is not to overanalyze; it's to have a clear idea of what you know and what you don't know.

Don't be surprised if you find out information that will cause you to stop the interviewing process and, in essence, turn the opportunity down. I cannot tell you the number of things I have seen candidates discover once they got to the altar but before they said, "I do." I've had candidates find out things such as the hiring authority is an alcoholic; there have been four people in "your" job over the past twelve months; the hiring authority is being sued for sexual harassment; the owner of the company is going through a terrible divorce that was going to jeopardize the company; and all kinds of other drastic issues that nobody wanted to talk about in the hiring process.

Before accepting any job offer, you must ask yourself, "Do I understand clearly everything I need know about this job?" There should be no loose ends or unanswered questions. Sit down and write out everything you think you know about the job that you gathered in the interviewing process. Write down all the questions that are not clear to you. Then start asking.

How to Evaluate an Offer

It's hard for me to recommend to you exactly how to evaluate an offer. A large part of an individual's decision to take a job is *emotional.* No matter how objectively all of us try to evaluate things, no matter what kind of formulas we can come up with, the primary difference between an individual taking a job and not taking a job comes down to how they feel about it. Emotions rule most decisions.

There can be, however, reasonable questions that can be asked to go along with or, in some cases, offset a purely emotional decision. I'm not particularly wild about purely emotional job and career decisions. There has to be some logic, common sense, and reason to the decision. After those kinds of evaluations have been done, the "feel" for the opportunity will help make the decision more clear. So, over the years I developed a ten-question formula to help people decide if an opportunity was good for them. These are simple questions with simple yes or no answers:

1. Do I like the nature of the work that I will have to perform?

   Yes   No

2. Can I do the job? Is there a good balance of risk/challenge to the job?

   Yes   No

3. Am I well aware of the company's stability or position stability?

        Yes   No

4. Is the chemistry of the people appropriate?

        Yes   No

5. Is the compensation program fair, reasonable, and commensurate with the job?

        Yes   No

6. Is the opportunity for growth in keeping with my personal goals?

        Yes   No

7. Is the location or territory appropriate?

        Yes   No

8. Is the philosophy of doing business compatible with my personal philosophy?

        Yes   No

9. Does this opportunity build on my previous experience?

        Yes   No

10. Is it likely that this experience would have carryover for my future goals?

        Yes   No

My rule of thumb is this: If you can answer "yes" to eight of the ten questions, that's about as good as you're going to get. If you can answer "yes" to five to seven of the questions, the opportunity may very well be a reasonable one, but you need to think about what kind of compromises you may have to make. If you answered "yes" to less than five of the questions, the opportunity is probably a questionable one.

Now, this is about as simple and logical as it can get. The purpose of this approach is to make you think. It is mostly a quantitative exercise and does not take into account the qualitative aspects of how you feel about the entire situation. There is no way to speculate about that for anyone. But I will tell you that if you only have, say, six yes answers to this exercise, and you don't feel emotionally attracted and strong about the opportunity, you should not take the job because you probably won't be very successful. If you have a total of five yes answers to the survey but you feel tremendously passionate, enthusiastic, and have a "failure is not an option" attitude toward the opportunity, you may well be able to make it a good one.

The purpose of these questions is to help you think out on paper (or aloud, with your coach) all aspects of the opportunity. The final decision will be an emotionally driven one, but at least you will have a reasonably logical assessment of the job opportunity's compatibility.

These questions do not take into account things such as how long you've been out of work and how many other opportunities you may have available to you. If you have been out of work for six months, and this is the only offer that you have received, the number of yes answers may not even matter.

Another way to evaluate an offer is the Ben Franklin approach, which means to simply write down the pros and cons, and analyze them. If you have ten or twelve reasons as to why you ought to accept the job and only two or three reasons as to why you shouldn't, the decision is fairly obvious. The idea is to make you think about all aspects of the position. The T format for this "Ben Franklin" approach simply looks like this:

Cons	Pros

Forcing yourself to write out the pros and cons so that you can see all the issues is also a great catharsis. Having your coach helping you out with this exercise is certainly of value. Talking it out with your coach is also of value. Hearing yourself talk about an opportunity and what you think and feel about it will also give you a great perspective.

In the final analysis, I have always stated that if you can get 70 to 75 percent of what you would ideally like in an opportunity, it is about as good as you are going to do. Now, again, this depends on situations to which I am not privy.

At the end of the game, there is always a risk in taking a new job. Do the best you can to analyze all the factors that are involved. Then, follow your gut!

Getting an Offer You Don't Want

If you get an offer that you just don't think you are going to take, it may not hurt to hear the offer out in total. There is a chance that you may have misunderstood many things regarding the job, title, money, or benefits. Again, you have nothing to consider until you have an offer.

If you are certain that you are not going to accept the job, it is best to tell the prospective employer within a reasonably short period of time. Also, I recommend calling the hiring authority to tell the person how much you appreciate the offer, but at this time you are not in a position to accept it.

Always try to leave the door open. If you turn down an opportunity, do it with grace and style. Whatever you do, do not burn bridges by being aloof, condescending, or egotistical. Be very graceful and recognize that you may need an offer from this organization somewhere down the line. I cannot tell you the number of times that I have tried to present a qualified candidate to a good opportunity with a firm that in the past tried to pursue the candidate and he or she had been so rude in dealing with the company that it's staff wouldn't consider giving the candidate the time of day. People don't forget when other people are rude to them or treat them in a condescending manner.

If you really want to keep the door open for the future, try this: After you turn down the offer, send the hiring authority a nice note thanking the person for his or her time and effort along with a $10 gift certificate to Starbucks or some place like it, maybe a book on the hobby you have in common, like golf or cooking—any small gift that the person will remember you by. This gesture alleviates the irritation that the hiring authority might have over your not taking the job, it keeps the door open for future opportunities, and, above all, it reinforces the personal relationship that you might have established with the hiring authority.

Getting an Offer You Might Take

Begin by knowing everything there is to know about the opportunity. Get the offer and evaluate it. If you are fortunate enough to be able to compare one offer with another, do it quickly. Another bit of advice is *never compare an offer in hand with one that you might get in the near future.* A bird in the hand is always more valuable than one in the bush.

Now, if you have a job offer in hand, it is advisable to call any other organizations that you might be considering and tell them you have an offer, and you would like to hear from them by a certain time. You need to put a time limit on this. You don't have much choice, but you might ask the company that has actually given you an offer if you could have a day or so to think about it. However, most organizations won't go beyond a day or so in granting you that time. This is due to fear of losing other candidates who might be viable if you turn the offer down.

By the way, if you are going to discuss other offers with the hiring authority, in order to negotiate and compare, only do it with offers you actually have. And don't hesitate to tell the hiring authority who those offers are with. Most hiring authorities don't believe you when you talk about the proverbial other opportunities, unless they are real. They consider it to be a bluff.

> Things can get really sticky in these offer-and-acceptance situations. A few years ago, I had a candidate (unbeknownst to me) who accepted three offers on a Friday and agreed to start all three jobs on the following Monday. One of the offers that he got was from a company to which I represented him. Another was with a company that I did not represent him to, but I found out on that very Friday that he had interviewed with the company and had accepted their offer. Then I found out, after confronting him that he had accepted yet a third offer.
>
> When I confronted him, he laughed and told me to cool my jets. He claimed that all three opportunities were very good and that he wanted the weekend to think about all of them; and then he was going to show up to work on Monday morning at the job that he thought was best. I really couldn't believe that this guy was doing that, but there really wasn't much I could do. He ended up reporting to work at the company that I had referred him to (a more beneficial positive event). He called the other two that Monday morning and told them that he had taken another job. (Not very nice!)

Getting an Offer You Would Like to Accept

This is really easy to do. Once you get the offer, tell the hiring authority that you would like to come in and personally discuss the offer face-to-face. The only word of caution I might give you in this situation is to not shut down the interviewing process with any other organization until you are sure of the offer and have it in hand. Even then, I would be sure to try to keep my options open just in case things fall through.

I don't want to jinx anything, but I have experienced numerous instances of candidates being told that they were going to get an offer and the job never actually materialized. So, when an organization tells you that it would like to make an offer, set a face-to-face meeting to go over the details of the offer and negotiate, if you are going to, but don't tell any other organization that you are in the process or that you are going to accept an offer with someone else.

Negotiating

In general, your ability to negotiate an offer depends on the economy and your individual situation. In the late 1990s, it was common, especially for high-tech types of candidates, to be able to look for a job, collect several offers, and literally go to work for the highest bidder. When competition for candidates was very keen, all kinds of things could be negotiated in an offer situation. Much has changed since that time, so you probably won't be selling your services to the highest bidder.

You can get a good sense of the latitude and leverage that you might have in the offering stage by simply paying attention to what you are hearing during the interviewing process. For example, if there are few people in your profession and they are always in high demand—as in the healthcare professions—the numbers of opportunities that you are going to have available to you, and your ability to leverage offers, is greater. If, on the other hand, you are in the telecommunications industry and you can even find an interview, let alone get a job offer, your choices and leverage are still not very great.

I would never recommend negotiating an offer over the telephone or through e-mail. The only exception to this might be when distance is in issue. Now, the final offer can be discussed and confirmed over the telephone or by e-mail, but if there is going to be any kind of negotiation over specific aspects of the offer, those are always best done face-to-face.

Negotiating an offer, and how it is extended, is done in many different ways by many different organizations, so I can't cover them here. Some companies send offer letters through their corporate office, sometimes from far away. If any negotiation is to be done, it needs to be done before the offer is put into writing. Some companies provide an offer letter; and, once that offer letter is in the candidate's hands, the candidate negotiates with the hiring authority. To avoid problems, the candidate—once it is understood that he or she is going to get an offer—should ask the hiring authority how the company would like to proceed with negotiations. Some companies will make it very clear that there is no negotiation at all in the offer that they will make. Some companies accept the idea that everything is negotiable. Since there is no way of knowing where a company falls between these two poles, you should simply ask for a face-to-face meeting to discuss the offer before it is formally given.

Once you ask for the face-to-face meeting, you should write down every issue that might be covered in the offer discussion. By the way, I do not recommend negotiating an offer with anyone other than the hiring authority. If the HR department insists on making the offer, you have to insist that you need to have a conversation with the hiring authority before you entertain a formal offer. It would be a bad sign if a hiring authority will not discuss a job offer with you before a formal offer is made. In other words, you want to negotiate with the person who has the greatest pain.

By the time you get to the final stages of an offer, you pretty much know what the parameters of the job opportunity are. It is a good idea, at this offer discussion meeting, to cover each one of these issues to make sure you understand everything that has been discussed and that you and the hiring authority are reading from the same page. Leave absolutely nothing to chance.

The most important issue in your negotiating is for you to know as much as you can about the hiring authority's pain level. You will clearly understand the strength of your negotiating position if you understand as many aspects as possible of what the hiring authority sees and what he or she is experiencing. If you can, you need to find out how many candidates the employer has on the final list. You need to know how long the hiring authority has been looking and whether there are any dates of impending doom—that is, a time when there absolutely must be someone in the job. Has there been a vacancy in the job for a long period of time? Is someone being promoted out of the job within a short period of time? Is there pressure to hire someone, and who is bringing that pressure on? How long has the interviewing process taken?

Step back and put yourself in the shoes of the hiring authority. Try to objectively analyze all the things that have gone on in the interviewing process. Answer this question, "If I were the hiring authority, interviewing me, at this point in the hiring process, how badly do I need and want me?" If your answer is "desperately," then you have a lot of leverage. If your answer is "Nice to have, but no worries and no big deal. If I hire, I hire; if I don't, I don't," then you don't have very much leverage at all.

Some Thoughts on Negotiations

The first rule in negotiation is to "never be afraid to walk away." That is a hard concept to understand and difficult to do, especially if you really need a job and this is the only offer you have received in some time. But, the hiring authority doesn't know that—and remember, most of negotiating is knowing how to act.

If you sense that the hiring authority is adversarial in the offer discussion meeting, you're off to a poor start. You may not be able to do anything about this, but, I assure you, if the relationship in this conversation doesn't have a "we're all in this together; let's see if we can work it out," tone or attitude to it, you're off to a rocky start and it's not likely to get any better. Most of the time, when a hiring authority comes across in an adversarial way, it's because he or she is scared.

It doesn't hurt to start out the conversation by saying something along the lines of: "Mr. or Ms. *(hiring authority)*, I'm really excited about accepting this job and going to work for you and your company. I want you to know I really want this job and I'd like to see it happen for both of us."

This kind of statement lets the prospective employer know that you want the job and you want to try to work something out. Again, the fear of you rejecting them is lessened. (By the way, you still have the right to turn down an offer for whatever reason you wish.) Studies have shown that this kind of "let's all win together" attitude is the best negotiating statement a person can make.

Contrary to what many people might think, most employers are not interested in paying as little as they can get away with paying. Also, most candidates are smart enough to know that if they are grossly overpaid for the service that they render, their employer will catch on and they may be looking for a job, again. Most people are trying to work out as fair a deal as they can for themselves, as well as for the other person.

When you write down all your questions about the opportunity before you get into the final negotiations, you should write down some kind of salary range that you think is reasonable. If you've done your research on this job, you will already know what salary range the hiring authority has in mind. But, if you haven't, you should have some idea about the minimum amount of money that you will consider. If you have been out of work for the past three months or more, you might come up with one figure. If you are currently employed, but anxious to leave your job, you may come up with another one. If you are happily employed, you may come up with a different one. But, remember, compensation is just one aspect of a job. Don't let it be such a focus that you don't take into account other important aspects of the opportunity.

If you are asked about the salary requirement that you seek, answer by saying something along the lines of, "I'm more interested in the whole package—salary, benefits, the company, the future—than I am in one particular salary figure. I'd like to know what you and your company think is fair and to discuss money along with the other benefits of the job. Then I will know what I can and cannot do."

Make sure that you know all the aspects of a job offer before you start negotiating. Here is an elementary list of things that you may want to consider when you look at the total compensation:

- Salary/commissions
- Bonuses
- Salary reviews
- 401(k) investment plans
- Car and insurance
- Car allowance
- Business expenses
- Title
- Insurance plans (both health and life)
- Overtime pay
- Sick leave
- Pension plans
- Educational reimbursement
- Children's college tuition plans
- Day care programs

- Ability to work from home a designated percentage of the time

- Membership to a buying club

- Performance bonuses

- Flextime

- Vacation

- Paid personal days off

- Health club/country club

- Vision/dental/family insurance

- Real-estate assistance

- Custom-designed bonus program

- Stock options

- Stock purchase plan

- Sabbaticals

- Disability insurance (both short and long term)

- Separation package

- Sales territory realignment

There can be all kinds of other benefits that a company might be able to provide. I have seen benefits such as the personal use of a corporate jet; a deer blind or duck blind lease; entry fees to golf tournaments; ski lodge participation; vacation condo usage; and partial sponsorship for a race car. I once had a candidate, before accepting the job, negotiate time off (with pay, I might add) to train for the World Iron Man contest in Hawaii that he had entered a year in advance.

With healthcare costs rising as they are, you need to be sure about the deductibles, co-pays, and limitations of the insurance program that might be offered. Healthcare and insurance costs have been some of the biggest challenges for 97 percent of the companies in the United States—the ones with fewer than a hundred people. You just need to be sure of exactly what those benefits are, especially in the case of insurance.

Candidates often jump the gun and start negotiating money before they hear the whole offer. It is not a good idea to pick out one or two issues about an offer until you have heard and completely understand all of the compensation, benefits program, and any other aspects of an offer. So, even during the face-to-face meeting with a hiring authority, write down all the details of the offer. Most offer letters do not include any of the benefits that I've just mentioned.

As you go through each item in an offer, it never hurts to ask the simple question, "Is that the best that you can do?" Some things such as life insurance or health insurance benefits are cast in stone. However, things like base salaries, salary reviews, commissions, and so forth may have a great variable—that may not be known to you. Pausing and asking, "Is that the best you can do?" is a nonthreatening way of asking for more.

> Remember to relax during the whole process of negotiation. Being too intense communicates fear. Being too casual communicates flippancy. If you practice the negotiation process with a good coach, you will be relaxed in your conversations.

Practice, practice, practice negotiation situations. Just like so many other things that I have presented to you in this book, you need to role-play negotiation sessions with your coach.

Accepting an Offer

Once you have received an offer, negotiated every aspect of the offer that you need to, and have a clear understanding that the opportunity is reasonable, you can either come to an agreement at that meeting or explain to the hiring authority that you would like to think it over and/or discuss it with your spouse. Do not postpone letting the hiring authority know your decision for more than one day. When a candidate asks for more than a day to inform the employer, this will usually result in one of two conclusions: the candidate is not very decisive or the candidate is going to use the offer to leverage another opportunity. I've known hiring authorities to rescind an offer on the spot if candidates didn't appear decisive in their acceptance.

Until a candidate has accepted an offer, most hiring authorities feel absolutely no moral obligation to that candidate. Hiring authorities, just like anyone else, want to avoid the fear of loss. It is not uncommon for an employer to make an offer, be told by the candidate that he or she will let them know in a few days, then the employer gets scared that he or she may be left in a lurch, so the job is offered to the next candidate—without even telling the first candidate.

An Excellent Example of Negotiating

I recently placed a regional sales manager with one of the East Coast companies that I work with. He did an excellent job of negotiating a good opportunity into an outstanding one. Because of his negotiation skills, he got the company that I placed him with to raise its initial salary offering by $50,000 (it went from $125,000 to $175,000). On top of that, he got the company to increase by $100,000 the amount of money he would earn if he and his team exceeded their yearly quota. He increased the original commission plan as well as negotiated a six-month termination package. (Which is virtually unheard of these days.) I asked him to comment about the whole process. Here are a few of his thoughts:

> "Knowledge is power. I knew in exact detail everything that the job entailed, what the company had done up until now (in the region), and what they needed. The more I knew about the opportunity, the more I was able to communicate exactly what I could do for them better than what they have before or what they could see or find in other candidates. Early on in the process, I knew that it was my job to convince the company that I was absolutely the best candidate it could hire. Fortunately, I was already employed in a very good job and I had to explain to them that not only could I do a better job than any other candidate they could find but they had to make it worthwhile for me to leave a reasonable job.
>
> "I never would use the term *leverage*, but I knew that it was my job to come up with my unique attributes that made me different from anyone else. I was nice, logical, reasonable, and I walked them through all of what I could do for them that they didn't have already. Even though they were 'coming' after me, I kept selling myself to them, constantly reinforcing what a good job I could do. I did my homework. I not only talked with just about every senior manager in the company but I also talked to the other regional managers around the country who would be my peers. The whole thing had to be a win/win situation for both of us. If I forced them to do something that wasn't good

for all of us in the long run, they would eventually catch on and the relationship would be a poor one.

"Once I convinced them that I would 'invest' in them by performing better than anyone else could, I communicated that they had to 'invest' in me. I put myself in their shoes and asked them to put themselves in my shoes. I had a good job and they had to show me reasons why I should leave my 'good' job and take their 'better' job. I essentially told them what they would have to do in order to make the job so much better that I couldn't refuse it. They agreed and we both won. It is really that simple."

Getting It in Writing

Contrary to what people may think, a signed written offer, except in very rare instances, is not a legally binding implied contract. Candidates often think that because they have a written and signed offer, signed and accepted by them, that they have some sort of legal document that protects them if they show up for work and the job has been eliminated before they even begin. There is nothing that protects the candidate from that scenario. According to our labor law attorney, most states are employment-at-will states, which means that the employer or the candidate can terminate the employment relationship at any time for just about any reason, except for illegal ones like race or age discrimination. I'm not an attorney and don't want to interpret law. But I do know unless there is a clear or implied long-term promise of employment—as well as hefty damages that can be proven—if a candidate accepts a job, even if the offer is spelled out in writing, he or she has practically no legal recourse if the job doesn't materialize.

However, there are two major reasons you want to get a written offer with as much detail as possible. The first reason is that at least 30 percent of the time, the written offer you received will be somewhat different from all the things you talked about with the hiring authority. These usually are not malicious mistakes. Often these letters are standard letters that emanate from an HR department or simply an administrative person whose job it is to write offer letters, among other things. Sometimes things get lost in translation.

The biggest shock in this kind of situation is that often hiring authorities literally overpromise what the company will allow him or her to do in an offer situation. Now, nobody is ever going to admit to doing that, but it does happen more than you would think. An overzealous hiring authority convinces a candidate to come to work by promising things that the company won't allow such as special stock options, large signing bonuses, or a salary beyond the permissible limits. The hiring authority often waits until the candidate—who has emotionally already bought into the job and emotionally accepted the opportunity—receives the letter and then explains, "Oh, by the way, I wasn't able to get you _____, but I tried." This can cause a great deal of heartburn and pain for a candidate who thinks he or she is accepting a position with one set of terms and then is faced with another set when he or she receives the offer letter.

Along this same line, special arrangements that you might make with the hiring authority in order to take the job may completely change if crazy things happen—like the hiring authority leaves the company three or four weeks after you start. So, any kind of special arrangements that are made between you and the hiring authority should be reflected in the offer letter.

The second reason that you want to get an offer in writing is to be sure that your paychecks, when you start getting them, are what you agreed to, including benefits and benefits deductions. It is not uncommon for an earnings agreement, either verbal or actually written, to be "handled" by a number of different people on its way to getting put into the payroll system. These are normally just human errors, but the shock of something like this doesn't make the start of your new job any easier. You don't want any surprises, so have as much written down in the offer letter as is reasonable.

Setting a Start Date

"The path was worn and slippery. My foot slipped from under me, knocking the other out of the way, but I recovered and said to myself, 'It's a slip and not a fall.'"
—ABRAHAM LINCOLN, PRESIDENT WHO ISSUED THE
EMANCIPATION PROCLAMATION

Most people would think that this is an easy thing to do once you have accepted a job. But as I've mentioned before, it ain't over 'til your butt is in the chair—and even then it might not be over. You will want as little time to go by as possible between the time you accept the job and when you actually start the job. Why? Because strange things can happen.

Once you've accepted the offer, you should try to get to the new job as soon as possible. It is rare to have something happen to the job between the time of accepting the offer and actually starting the job, but it can and does happen. I have seen companies sold, head counts frozen, changes in management, and all kinds of other things that may alter the status of the situation just before the candidate shows up for work at the new job.

Personally, I always get a little nervous when the starting date for a candidate is further out than two weeks. If there are extenuating circumstances and a starting date has to be set beyond a two-week period of time (I have seen them as much as ninety days), you need to take precautions to be sure that you stay on the mind of the hiring authority. I recommend that if the starting date is more than two weeks away, you should call the hiring authority; take the hiring authority to lunch during that period of time; or take some other action that will keep your interest on the forefront of the hiring authority's mind.

Jeff and Amy's Reaction to This Chapter

Boy! This chapter was tremendously indicative of many things that happened to Jeff and Amy, even after Jeff had become one of my candidates.

Jeff admits throughout this whole book that he had a terribly difficult time in getting emotionally wrapped up in just about every event that took place in his job search. His highs were tremendously high when he thought he was close to an opportunity and his lows were tremendously low when things were not going very well. Jeff acknowledges that he knew he should have accepted every event that took place in an objective, detached manner.

Jeff and Amy had one story from his past that he found particularly appropriate to this chapter. At one time, Jeff worked for the Olympic Committee in Colorado. When the Olympics were close to over, he looked for a job and immediately found one with a major software developer. As soon as Jeff received the verbal offer from the company, he quit his job at the Olympic Committee. Unfortunately, between the time he was offered the job and the time the offer letter was to show up, the software company instituted a hiring freeze. The result was that Jeff was out of luck.

Even though the job fell through, within four weeks, Jeff had a job with a valuation software developer. (Those were very different times, as Jeff discovered to his dismay during his long job search that led him eventually to the *Dr. Phil* show and my help in finding quality work.) However, the point of Jeff's earlier experience is clear: Even when you have an offer, don't stop working the process.

16 : Handling Your Transition Smoothly and Confidently

If you were unemployed and have recently found a job, resigning is not a crucial issue to you. However, if you are currently employed, and especially if you have been for a fairly long period of time (five years or more by today's standards), leaving your job may be harder than you think. You should be prepared for your own trepidation. Even if your resignation ought to be an easy thing to do, it is still emotionally charged and doing it the right way makes a really big difference.

Whether you think resigning is going to be emotionally easy on both you and your employer, or not, you need to be prepared to do it the right way so that you don't burn any bridges on the way out.

I've had candidates resign by e-mail. I've known people to just not show up for their job and, three or four days later, call their superior to tell them that they are resigning. In other cases, they simply did not show but never called; after a number of days, it was just assumed that they had left the company. None of these are the right way to do things.

People will often resort to this type of final exit simply because they are nervous, scared, and just don't want to face up to the task of gracefully resigning. Most people mentally and emotionally leave the job a long time before they actually physically leave. They are so mentally and emotionally spent and so sick of the whole thing that they just want to leave as fast as possible.

Where this sort of thing comes back to haunt them is in a reference check. It is common for a previous manager, even though he or she knows better, to tell someone who is checking a reference in a situation like this to say something along the lines of, "Well, when he or she left here, it was a real mess." A poor reference is implied simply by communicating a veiled aura of negativity surrounding the previous employee's departure from a company.

272

There are some people who will have a more difficult time than others in resigning. If you fall into any of the following categories that I'm going to mention, be prepared for the process to be a little more difficult than you thought. The kinds of people who have the most difficult time in resigning are:

- **First-Time Job Changers.** You feel guilty about leaving the company that gave you your first chance.

- **Longtime Employees.** You feel like you have grown up with the company; it's hard to say good-bye.

- **Those Who Hint About Leaving All the Time.** You have repeatedly threatened to leave before and now you really are!

- **Single-Reason Leavers.** You may be reluctant to tell the single reason for your wanting to leave or you may be afraid your reason sounds insignificant to others, although it is important to you.

- **Multifaceted/Multitask Person.** You're the kind of person who has significant influence in the company; you feel like you are letting everybody down by leaving.

- **Family Member.** You are either immediately or closely related to the people who own or manage the company.

How to Resign

Always resign with a written letter. Be resolute and firm in your commitment to resign. You cannot afford a weak or ambivalent attitude.

Sample Resignation Letter

Date _____

Dear (direct supervisor's name):
My resignation from the position of (current title) is effective as of today.

I really appreciate and will always remember my experience in working with you and (<u>your company</u>). Thank you for what you've taught me over the (<u>a period of time</u>) and for the many contributions that you have made to my personal and professional development. I truly hope that we can stay in touch from time to time in the years ahead.

I will always have positive memories about the professionalism at (<u>your company</u>).

The status of my work is up-to-date and I will turn it over to whomever you designate.

Sincerely,
(Your name)

That's it! Do not make the letter more complicated than this. Do not teach, preach, cajole, or elaborate as to why you're leaving. Many people want to set 'em straight . . . tell them where they went wrong . . . tell them where they can get off . . . explain to them why they have a stupid company . . . what they ought to do to fix the company and so forth in a resignation letter. You're wasting your breath.

Be relaxed and easy. Don't be nervous. Take a deep breath. Play a movie in your mind that it's going to go very smoothly. Practice the scenario in a role-play with your coach. You want to be aggressive and prepared. Then execute. Do not make an appointment to resign. Simply go to your supervisor during a regular, workday moment and say, "May I speak with you a moment?"

You should only resign to one person. Do not convene a group or committee. Doing so creates a one-against-many situation and the emotional odds are against you. Resign with your direct supervisor. Try to do it in person, unless your supervisor is in a distant city and you must do it by phone.

If you have to resign from a distance, have a telephone conversation before you either send or e-mail the letter. If you think that there is going to be a negative emotional response to your leaving, you want to communicate person-to-person.

Begin by thanking your boss for all the opportunities that he or she, and the company, have given you. Even if you hate the person, the job, and the company, it is hard for a person to have an acrimonious conversation when you are thanking him or her. Be sure to include in your opening statement that you have already accepted another position and that you are going to be leaving the company. Something like this:

> "Mr. or Ms. _____, I have accepted another employment opportunity and I want to give notice today. I'd like to thank you for making a real contribution to my career development. I would like to do everything possible during the next (*time frame*) to make my transition out of your department and the company a smooth one.
>
> "What is the easiest way for us to make this transition?"

If the boss tries to engage you in conversation about the new job, or the offer, or says, "How could you do this to me or us," or even hints at a counteroffer, preempt his or her comments by saying (script):

> "(Name) I think you know I really respect our relationship a lot and I know that this comes as a surprise to you. However, I would really appreciate if you would not try to make the process of my resignation any more difficult than it has to be.
>
> "I have accepted another opportunity, and I appreciate all that you've done but I am resolute about leaving. I have made my decision. I ask for your understanding. Now, what is the easiest way to make this transition?"

You might also add:

> "I have taken the liberty of writing up all of the projects I am working on and their current status. If you could take a moment with me to review them in the next day or so, I'd be happy to do anything I can to complete them or hand them in over during the next (*time frame*)."

Do not go into resigning by stating that you are "thinking about taking another position," or that you are "thinking about changing jobs," or anything that is wishy-washy and spineless. You must go in with the decisive, factual, "I have taken another job" statement. This has to be an absolute fact, not a whim.

Be prepared to preempt a counteroffer. I will discuss counteroffers in a few moments, but even entertaining the idea of a counteroffer is suicide. If you go on and on about how difficult a decision it was or how hard you thought about it, or how you talked it over with your spouse, you not only compromise your position, but you appear weak and pitiful.

Offer two weeks' notice. Even if you know that the company will want you to leave immediately, you still want to be courteous and offer two weeks. *Do not offer more than two weeks!* It is not good for you or your company. You have mentally and emotionally left a long time ago. You're gone—so physically leave as soon as you can.

> If you really want to leave the organization with grace and style, try this: At the end of the last day of your employment, when most everyone is gone, leave a small gift on the desks of the people whom you were closest to in the organization. A small box of candy, a card, gift certificates to Starbucks, an appreciative note, or a small, framed motivational quote can be left. No matter what your relationship with those people was, they will think highly of you, and who knows when you will run into them again?

It is best not to gloat about your new job or your new company. It isn't good to brag about the opportunity for which you are leaving. There is a tendency to be proud of your new job and run off at the mouth about the new opportunity, as though to say, "Wow, look at me, guess what I've got!" Simply remember that you are resigning, not competing.

Stay away from lecturing or trying to instruct the company on how they ought to change things in the future so people like you wouldn't leave. It will only insult them.

It is advisable not to discuss your new job, your new company, or all the reasons that you are leaving with any of your peers, subordinates, or anyone else in the company. Your leaving should not be a topic of conversation with you or with anyone else. Even if your parting is amiable, once you quit, the relationship with everyone is strained. Make it simple and easy for everybody.

Counteroffers Rarely Work Out

I don't think that I would say counteroffers are a disaster 100 percent of the time. But I do figure that they don't work at least 98 percent of the time. A counteroffer is when the candidate goes in to resign and the company tries to buy him or her back. The employer tries to do things to patch up the relationship when the person goes in to resign. It hardly ever works out for the candidate.

I have seen hundreds of counteroffers over the years, where a candidate decides to stay with his or her current employer. However, I know very few who have ever lasted long at all. Most every candidate that I've ever known to receive and accept a counteroffer leaves the company within a four to six month period of time—either on their own volition or because they are fired. And most of the time, when this happens, it is an adversarial, acrimonious departure. Once a counteroffer is made and accepted, the whole relationship between the employer and the employee who was looking to leave has changed. The emotional strain that it creates results in a distressful, distrustful relationship that becomes irreparable.

More often than not, a candidate who goes to the trouble to go out and look for a job (and actually receives another offer) doesn't really think about a counteroffer. It usually comes as a little bit of a surprise. Don't let that happen!

Here are sixteen reasons why counteroffers rarely work:

1. If your company really recognized your worth, they would've given you the added income, advancement, title, whatever without the necessity of you, in effect, blackmailing your employer by finding another job and threatening to quit.

2. If you accept the counteroffer, you will usually be looked upon as a person who blackmailed management or the company into giving you what you wanted.

3. When the next salary reviews come around, you will already have received your raise and you will be bypassed.

4. The reason that you were made a counteroffer is because, at that moment, they needed you worse than you needed them.

5. In essence, you are firing your company. No one likes to be fired. So, the company is going to do what any fired person would do: hang on until it can rectify the situation—that is, replace you.

6. Good companies (well-managed companies) don't buy people back. The only kind of company that will buy you back is the kind of company that will take advantage of you somewhere down the line.

7. It is cheaper for a company to try to make you a counteroffer than it is to immediately replace you.

8. Money and title are temporary. If the major complaint about your job has to do with money, when the money changes, you'll only be temporarily content.

9. The momentary emotion of suddenly being made to feel special overrides the logical, common sense that forced you to go out and look for a job.

10. The trust relationship that you had with your employer is no longer there.

11. The fact that you can no longer be trusted affects everyone you work with. You held management's feet to the fire, you blackmailed them, and, what is worse, everyone in the company knows it.

12. You caught management with their pants down. Most likely, they had no idea this was coming. So, they're going to do whatever they can to keep you so that they can buy time and find a replacement.

13. Your supervisor and your company, at least for a while, are going to put their finger in the dike to keep you around simply because other people are going to have to take up your slack if you leave.

14. Your immediate supervisor is likely to say, "How could you do this now? It couldn't come at a worse time!" Your ego will be stroked and fed simply to buy time for your manager to recover by replacing you.

15. The world is motivated by self-interest. If your leaving makes your supervisor look bad, he or she is going to do anything reasonable to look good by keeping you.

16. The higher level position that you have, the more likely you are to be offered a counteroffer by more than one person in the organization. I've had candidates who, once they gave their resignation notice, were

literally escorted from manager to manager throughout the company to convince the candidate to stay.

Put your ego aside and follow good common sense. Tell the people making you a counteroffer that you really appreciate their offer, but that you have made up your mind and you are going to leave. *No matter how tempting it is, never accept a counteroffer.*

A New Job

Most people think that once they have started a new job, their job search is over. Even after thirty-one years of doing this, I am continually amazed at the strange things that can take place even after a person has started a new job.

The first bit of advice is for you to expect that the job is going to be quite a bit different than what you thought it was going to be when you were going through the interviewing process. Things are never the way they appear on the outside looking in.

The second suggestion is to spend the first few weeks or even months simply observing what goes on in the company. The higher the position that you may have, the more you want to quietly observe how the company is run. You really want to get a good idea of what is going on in the company before you start actively showing people what you can do for them.

The best way to find out what really goes on in an organization is to talk to the most senior level administrative personnel (we used to call them secretaries). These people know more about what is going on in the inner workings of the organization than anybody else. Now, these people may not be the decision makers in an organization, but they still know more of what is going on in a company than all the managers combined.

Get to know your supervisor's personality and style. Do this with all the people with whom you might interface. Remember that you are the new kid on the block and that you don't know the character or personality of the people, or the part, of the organization that you are working with.

Don't hesitate to ask lots and lots of questions regarding procedures and protocols. Nobody expects you to be intuitive about anything. It may not hurt to take notes about what you learn, especially regarding the unofficial procedures.

Recognize and avoid the negative people who exist within every organization. They can range from the people who always see the glass half empty to the people who are downright negative, gossipy, and in some cases, slanderous. Avoid them like the plague.

The most important thing you can do as a professional when beginning a new job is to be quiet and try not to draw attention to yourself until you really learn about the company and the personalities of the people from the inside. Too often, newly hired professionals try to make an immediate impact to show how good they are by drawing attention to themselves in a number of ways before they really know the so-called lay of the land.

No matter how good you might be, no matter how smart you are, no matter how much you might be able to contribute to the organization, you will have much more impact and be received with much more respect if you learn as much as you can about the organization and its personalities before you start having significant input. There is going to be plenty of time to prove yourself.

Jeff and Amy's New Start

Jeff and Amy really had no comments on this final chapter, except to say that Jeff is happy in his new position at Dell. Their long and arduous journey had many complications and setbacks, but reached a successful conclusion. Would they want to go through it again? No! Was it worth all the hardships along the way? No! But hopefully, their story will help others who find themselves in the same situation. By applying the ideas presented in this book, you, too, will be able to manage your job search and find the kind of quality job you want and deserve.

17 Tony's Top Ten Reasons Why People Have Trouble Finding a Job

In order to reinforce the ideas that I've presented throughout this book, I came up with my gut level top ten reasons why people have a hard time finding a job.

1. People don't make finding a job a "job" itself! They don't adopt a committed, passionate, "failure is not an option" attitude and recognize that finding a job is a numbers game. And I mean *numbers* all the way around. You must follow a tremendous number of avenues for seeking interviews, such as friends, relatives, previous employers, previous peers, competitors, and cold calling on the phone. When it comes to interviews themselves, it's all numbers: the more interviews you get, the better your chances of getting called back; the more times you're called back, the better your chances of landing a good job.

2. People don't develop a system of finding a job. The system should entail everything from goals and intentions that dictate planned activity to role-playing of interviews. Most people either decide to look for a job, or it is decided for them and they stumble around with no direction, intention, or goal. They don't develop a systematized strategy that will get them what they want.

3. People have an unrealistic idea about the market for their skills. There is a tendency for people to overinflate the value of their ability to find a job, based on a distorted view of the marketability of their skills. This can lead to frustration and disappointment when the job search takes longer than expected.

4. People don't acknowledge the psychological and emotional stress that changing jobs entails. By denying this reality, people operate out of fear of rejection. They confuse activity with productivity and focus on minor things that appear to be job-finding activities, but aren't the most fruitful activities.

5. People forget or don't realize that 97 percent of the businesses in the United States employ fewer than one hundred people. America is not run by big business. It is run by small groups of people who organize to provide goods and services. Although they might be professional companies and people, they are not professional "hirers" or professional people-oriented companies.

6. People don't recognize that face-to-face interviews are the only thing that matters. There are all kinds of things you can do to get face-to-face interviews, but you have to get them. Pulling out all the stops by doing anything you can to get in front of a hiring authority with pain (the need to hire someone) is the key.

7. People don't prepare well for interviews. Most people are not as confident in themselves or have too much self-esteem in the interviewing process simply because they are not as prepared as they should be. They don't prepare and practice presentations on themselves and with others as to why they ought to be hired.

8. People don't sell themselves in interviews. The vast majority of people going into an interviewing situation simply don't sell themselves very well. People neglect to do everything from dressing the proper way to focusing on what they can do for a prospective employer. And worst of all, they don't come right out and ask for the job.

9. People interview with the attitude of "What can you do for me?" Most people consider interviews a two-way street. They believe that the employer is just as responsible for selling them on the company and the job as they are for selling themselves to the employer. They don't realize that there is nothing to consider until you have an offer. If you give enough reasons to employers as to why they ought to hire you and what you can do for them, they will give you plenty of answers on what they can do for you.

10. People present very poor reasons as to why they are leaving their current employer (or why they left their last one) and why they want a different one. Most people present the reasons they are looking to leave their current job or the reasons that they left their last one from a selfish, "me centered" point of view. They badmouth and criticize their current or past employers and justify their own convictions, thinking that a prospective employer is going to identify with them. They're wrong!

• • • Epilogue

*"The purpose of this life is not prosperity as we know it, but
rather the maturing of the human soul."*
—ALEXANDER SOLZHENITSYN, RUSSIAN MATHEMATICIAN,
AUTHOR, AND PLAYWRIGHT

Goals are always elusive. We all have a tendency to set goals; once these goals
are achieved, we set others. It seems that the condition of striving for something better is a human condition. But what we become on the inside, how
much our spirit and soul grow in the process of attaining our goals, is where
we need to keep our focus.

If our soul and spirit don't expand to the same relative size as the physical,
social, mental, or emotional goals that we attain, then our lives become confused as we struggle with the mismatch of the inner and outer person.

So, you ask, "Well, Tony! What does this have to do with me getting a new
job?" What this has to do with your getting a new job is pretty simple. As you
are going through the emotional process of changing jobs—through the ups
and downs, the advances and the setbacks—you need to pay attention to how
you're growing on the inside. Are you becoming a better person in the process
of getting what you want? Are the trials and tribulations making you stronger?
Are you learning more about yourself? Are you more sensitive to others? Do
you see the world through other people's eyes just a little better?

Finding a job is a practical, valuable thing to do. Ironically, every job is
temporary—after all, life itself is temporary. And I guess you could go through
the job-finding process simply focusing on the tactical, practical value of
finding a job, which is to make a living. But the process will be tremendously

284

more gratifying if you also focus on the kind of person that you become in the process. You'll not only get a better job but you'll also become a better person.

Key point: *What you become in the process of getting what you want is more important than what you actually get!*

· · · Index